"*Backyard Brawl* i ⟨...⟩ d history as it is about football; Stratton draws out the details and emotions of each in a style that is more like talking with friends than reading a book. Even as he includes some of the dirt about each school, his overall tone is one of respect and admiration. For anyone who likes football—and for many who don't—this book will be a winner." —*Daily Oklahoman*

"Money, power, and football dominate Texas culture, and nowhere is that truth revealed more than in the rivalry between Texas and Texas A&M. In *Backyard Brawl*, W. K. Stratton takes you inside the crazed intensity of the conflict between the 'hippie freaks' (Texas) and the 'sheep-loving rednecks' (A&M) and produces a compelling portrait of both college football at the highest levels and the contemporary state of affairs in Texas." —Peter Gent, author of *North Dallas Forty* and *The Franchise*

"W. K. Stratton's *Backyard Brawl* runs to daylight and takes its place with the all-time best literature on college football. You don't have to be a maroon-underweared Aggie or a burnt-orange jockstrap Longhorn to love it, but it'll help." —Dan Jenkins, author of *Semi-Tough*

"Texas versus Texas A&M ranks among the great college football rivalries, right up there with Army–Navy and Harvard–Yale. Stratton presents the rivalry as though it were a Texas tall tale, passed along over a couple of longneck Lone Stars at a Lubbock roadhouse. Funny, intelligent, insightful, and just a little Texas crazy—great reading." —*Booklist*

"Stratton weaves a story that is informative and entertaining as he takes readers inside both universities and mines the lode of football lore therein." —*Bryan-College Station Eagle*

BACKYARD BRAWL

INSIDE THE BLOOD FEUD

BETWEEN TEXAS AND TEXAS A&M

W.K. STRATTON

THREE RIVERS PRESS

NEW YORK

Grateful acknowledgment is made to the following for permission
to reprint previously published and unpublished material.

Salon.com: Excerpt from "Memories of an Aggie Bonfire Boy" by Dave Morris
(December 8, 1999). Copyright © 1999 by Dave Morris.
Reprinted by permission Salon.com.

Southern Music Company: Excerpt from the song lyric "The Aggie War Hymn."
Copyright © 1921 J.M. Reynolds. Copyright transferred 1938 to J.V. "Pinky" Wilson.
Copyright assigned 1968, to The Association of Former Students, Texas A&M University.
Southern Music Company, San Antonio, Texas, 78292, publisher and distributor.
All rights reserved, including public performance for profit.
Reprinted by permission of Southern Music Company.

Published by Three Rivers Press, New York, New York.
Member of the Crown Publishing Group, a division of Random House, Inc.
www.randomhouse.com

THREE RIVERS PRESS and the Tugboat design are registered trademarks of
Random House, Inc.

Originally published in hardcover by Crown Publishers, a division of Random House, Inc.,
New York, in 2002.

Printed in the United States of America

Design by Leonard Henderson

Library of Congress Cataloging-in-Publication Data
Stratton, W. K.
Backyard brawl : inside the blood feud between Texas and Texas A & M / W. K. Stratton.
1. University of Texas—Football. 2. Texas Longhorns (Football team) 3. Texas A & M—
Football. 4. Texas A & M Aggies (Football team). I. Title.
GV958.T44 S87 2002
796.332'63'0976431—dc21 2002006888
ISBN: 1-4000-5111-8

10 9 8 7 6 5 4 3 2 1

First Paperback Edition

For my parents;
for Luscaine and Kimberly;
and for Jan Reid

You just can't live in Texas if you don't have a lot of soul . . .
— DOUG SAHM

Prologue

Lutcher Stark set the mold for the wealthy and powerful who served as regents for the University of Texas and used their considerable sway to direct the football program to their liking. Make no mistake about it, Stark was rich, Texas rich. His family lorded over one of America's great timber empires, with holdings that stretched from the Piney Woods of East Texas into southern Louisiana. Stark also harvested money from his dealings in real estate, banking, insurance, manufacturing, and oil and gas. Not surprisingly, he was well connected politically. And he lived and breathed University of Texas football. In 1910, his senior year at UT, he managed the team. Just nine years later, Governor W. P. Hobby named Stark a regent, and the thirty-two-year-old alumnus quickly became the most influential man on the Texas campus. Now, on Thanksgiving Day 1922, Stark was part of the overflow crowd that crammed the wooden bleachers of Clark Field to watch Texas play its cross-state archrivals, the Texas A&M Aggies.

What Stark saw from the stands didn't please him.

Coach Berry M. Whitaker had elevated football at UT to a status it had never before enjoyed. His first year as coach, 1920, saw Texas go 9–0. The next year, the team was 6-1-1. On this day, Texas was 6–1, coming off a big win over Oklahoma. The Longhorns came into the game full of confidence. Wins against A&M were tough to come by in College Station, but claiming victory against the Fightin' Farmers when they visited the Longhorns in Austin almost seemed a birthright. But not today. A&M coach Dana X. Bible's team played well all game, but they were especially tough after Bible delivered a rousing halftime speech that challenged his players to make a stand along the lines of what the the defenders of the Alamo had done nearly a hundred years earlier.

It worked.

When the final gun sounded, A&M was on top, 14–7. The at-home loss was unbearable for the Texas fans. And especially for Lutcher Stark. He stepped down from the stands, confronted Whitaker as he walked down the field toward the athletic offices (housed in those days in some World War I vintage shacks), and fired him on the spot— never mind that Whitaker was one of the most successful coaches in Texas history.

Or maybe it didn't happen quite that way. "That's a lot of baloney," Whitaker said years later about the legendary confrontation with Stark. "He never once opened his trap to me." Nevertheless, the highly successful Whitaker was gone from the football coach's spot within two days of the A&M loss, although he stayed on with the university for many years, running its intramural sports program. More important, the message was clear for future UT coaches. You don't lose to A&M in Austin and come back to coach again the next year. For the next sixty years, that maxim held true.

Such is the nature of the UT-A&M rivalry. . . .

Preface:

The Nature of the Thing

One afternoon in the fall of 2001, Texas A&M University President Ray Bowen sat in his office discussing with a visitor one of the 125-year-old school's most recent accomplishments, its induction into the Association of American Universities (AAU). The prestigious organization represents the sixty-three best research universities in the United States, private and public. A&M's name appears alongside Harvard, Yale, Stanford, Cornell, Columbia, Michigan, Cal Berkeley, Emory, Johns Hopkins, MIT, and other educational stars in the organization's roster, and that signifies A&M's arrival as one of America's outstanding universities. Bowen pointed out that A&M had been selected for membership thanks in part to help from the University of Texas in Austin, itself a member since 1929. (The only other Texas school in the AAU is Rice University.) Bowen said A&M's AAU membership was an example of the friendship and cooperation between Texas's two largest universities, and he smiled while saying it.

An hour or so later, the same visitor listened to the commandant of A&M's Corps of Cadets complain about the vandalism to his car occurring when the Aggie football team visited Austin to play the UT Longhorns in 1996. "Every car with an A&M bumper sticker in the parking lot of the Hilton there in north Austin had its tires slashed," the commandant said, bewilderment and anger still in his voice five

years later. Still later in the day, three senior cadets told of their experience in Austin in 2000: "There was some drunk UT fan who spray-painted my Fish [freshmen cadets] orange while we were in formation," one said. "This guy must have been forty years old. So I'm wondering. Why did you just do that? And I'm thinking, Man, you're old enough to be my dad."

There you have it. The yin and the yang of the relationship between UT and A&M. On the one hand, cooperative friends working toward the common goal of providing outstanding public higher education in Texas. On the other, bitter rivals who scarcely can stomach each other.

The schools and their partisans are not unlike brothers who squabble at just about every opportunity that avails itself to squabbling. UT can be seen as the son Mom always liked best, the one who got the new bike, the better clothes, and a larger allowance—and who gloated about it. A&M can be seen as the son with the chip on his shoulder who got the hand-me-downs and leftovers—and who stewed about it. For generations, disparity did exist between UT and A&M in size, quality of education, and funding as well as football prowess. Now the two are much closer, both among the ten largest universities in the United States, both with huge alumni bases, both with excellent academic reputations: UT and A&M tied for fifteenth in *U.S. News & World Report*'s 2002 ranking of the best public universities in the nation, just behind Penn State. Yet while both schools should revel in receiving such a high grade, the appearance of the the *U.S. News* rankings stuck in the craw of both Longhorns and Aggies. How could *they* be ranked as an equal with *us?*

Each year, the rivalry between the two schools peaks on the Friday after Thanksgiving, when the Longhorns and Aggies battle it out in a home-and-away football series that currently is the third-most-played rivalry among major college football teams (Lafayette-Lehigh, Yale-

Princeton, and Harvard-Yale having been relegated to the minor leagues). It also is the oldest intrastate rivalry among major college football teams. Typically the game winds up on television, either on one of the networks or on cable. Though years passed without the game playing a significant role in determining the national champion, UT-A&M resonates in special ways. The football on the field is spirited and hard-assed, make no mistake about it. The surrounding spectacle, especially when the game occurs at Kyle Field in College Station, is unlike anything else encountered in college football. The expectations placed on the players are incredible. And the whole world seems to be watching. "It's a big stage," said one All-America Longhorn. "People who go to Texas or A&M and don't understand the stage are going to be disappointed. It's not easy. It's a crazy environment to be in."

And of course UT-A&M goes beyond good football and astonishing exhibition. Despite the similarities between the two universities, the differences prevail. The game is a time when two competing cultures come face-to-face in combat for three hours. On one level, it can be viewed as a kind of morality play, with a lot of snot-loosening hits thrown in for good measure: *hippie liberals vs. cattle-loving hicks.* Aggies look at themselves as representing the values of small towns and rural areas—God, home, and country. Longhorns, on the other hand, see themselves as the epitome of sophistication—progressive, open-minded, worldly. Like it or not, the players on the field are imbued with political and ethical values as much as they are burnt orange or maroon. If the Longhorns win, the Orangebloods can lean back smugly, take a sip of single-malt scotch (or of beer), wink at God, and think, yes, everything is all right in the universe, just as it should be. If the Aggies win, partisans of the maroon Fightin' Farmers are whoop-whooping and chugging beer (or single-malt scotch) in every corner of the globe, celebrating not just a victory on the playing field but also the advances their university has made over the past three decades (advances that are impressive as hell) to lay claim to being *the* state university. It's a hell of a burden for a noseguard from, say, Boerne (pronounced *birney*) to take on, but so be it. The players, the overwhelming majority of whom played high school football in Texas, know what they're getting into when they sign their letters of intent. "In this part of the country," says A&M Coach R. C. Slocum, "this is the biggest game of the year. There are a lot of families in this state tied to one or both of these universities. That makes for a great rivalry."

★   ★   ★

A blood feud. A kind of civil war. Brother against brother. Cousin against cousin. Wife against husband. Friend against friend.

Take the betting that might go on at the office. Aggies vs. Longhorns in one-upmanship as the game approaches. Hitting a peak during that two-week period before the Thanksgiving weekend kickoff, when the bets are made. If the Aggies win, the Longhorn contingent at the office might have to wear Aggie T-shirts to work for a week. Vice versa if the Longhorns win. At home, a Longhorn wife might see her Aggie husband doing trash detail for a year if A&M comes up short. And a lot of money will change hands at the country club.

These are some of the more innocent aspects of the dispute. Officials at both schools like to call it a special rivalry, a friendly rivalry, with a lot of good-natured ribbing to go along with it. Texas Coach Mack Brown says that UT-A&M is blessedly free of some of the ugliness of other rivalries he's been associated with during his football career, Texas and Oklahoma among them. But UT-A&M has had its nastier components as well. Once, nastiness on and off the field grew so fierce that Texas refused to schedule A&M for several years. As recently as 1995 a near riot broke out when the Longhorns beat A&M at Kyle Field in College Station and jubilant Texas fans rushed the field while members of the A&M Corps of Cadets stood up to defend their turf. Yet, as members of feuding families usually do, the two factions proved that they could come together in an impressive showing of compassion and support in a time of adversity—as they did following 1999's deadly Bonfire collapse on the A&M campus.

★　　★　　★

It is easy to make generalizations about the two schools. The standard thinking goes that UT is one of the most liberal universities in the South and Southwest. A&M is one of the most conservative schools anywhere in America. One day not long ago a young woman with spiked and brightly dyed hair stood topless on the sidewalk along Austin's "Drag"—several blocks of businesses along Guadalupe Street adjacent to the UT campus. The woman had a packet of felt-tipped pens in different colors and she invited passersby to sign her torso, in the name of an artistic statement. People walking along the sidewalk or driving along Guadalupe took it in stride. It is Austin, after all. If the same woman had tried to do the same thing at North Gate, a similar business community adjacent to the A&M campus in College Station, she surely would have been arrested.

UT is an urban university, its primary campus surrounded on all sides by congestion. It is a noisy place, a frenetic place, a place swarming with people. These days it's often hard to gain the right perspective to fully appreciate some of the grandness of some its buildings. It's just too crowded around campus. It also has a cosmopolitan feel to it. Sure, you can see clean-cut frat men and honey-eyed sorority women. But to walk down 24th Street between

Guadalupe and Speedway when classes are changing is to glimpse the faces of the world, not just Texas. UT has one of the largest enrollments of international students of any American college or university. When the legendary football coach Darrell K. Royal came to Texas in the late 1950s, UT was a very large university (even then the largest in the South), but it was still very much a regional school. Not so today.

To be sure, A&M is an international school as well. The current president of Bolivia is an Aggie. But you don't get quite the same sense of the world coming together in College Station that you have on the UT campus. It has the feel of Texas small towns and suburbs. Things are spread out, laid back—a little old-fashioned, maybe. A bicycle in a rack on the UT campus might be held in place by two or three chains. At A&M, you can see bicycles lying on the grass or leaning against trees, their owners unafraid of theft. The Memorial Student Center has a sign at the door asking students to be respectful and remove their hats when entering. And they do. You see students in overalls. You see cadets in handsome uniforms that haven't changed much since the days before World War II.

★   ★   ★

On the UT campus, you find the presidential library of Lyndon B. Johnson, the architect of the Great Society (liberal). On the A&M campus, you find the presidential library of George Bush, the architect of the Gulf War (conservative). A visit by former Secretary of State Henry Kissinger to the UT campus was canceled recently after a group of self-styled radicals, led by a UT professor, threatened disruptions if the "war criminal" was allowed to speak. Had Kissinger gone to A&M instead, he would have received a hero's welcome.

Yet the political lines can get blurred pretty quickly.

Former Texas Land Commissioner Garry Mauro is considered by many left-leaning Texans to be the "last real Democrat" to hold state office. Mauro is a longtime friend of former President Bill Clinton, a friendship that dates back to their working together on the McGovern campaign of 1972. Yet Mauro is a true maroon-blooded Aggie, the "conservative" school.

Former UT Regent Tom Hicks, a Dallas-based investor and owner of the Dallas Stars and the Texas Rangers, remains a powerful man on the Texas campus, especially around the athletic department; he personally interviewed Mack Brown for the head coach's job after John Mackovic was fired. He was appointed to the board of regents by Democrat Ann Richards. Yet Hicks has close associations with conservative President George W. Bush, the man who unseated Richards as governor. When Hicks and other investors purchased the Rangers from Bush and the other owners of the Rangers, it made Bush his personal fortune—prior to his venture with the Rangers, Bush had been largely unsuccessful in business. Hicks also raised money for Bush's presidential race. He is one of a number of examples of people associated with the "liberal" school who have ties to conservative politics.

A&M is the school with the military heritage, and with the exception of the service academies, no school has provided more officers to lead the armed services. Probably no A&M officer has had a more stellar record that James Earl Rudder. During World War II, Rudder led a battalion of rangers who scaled the hundred-foot cliffs at Pointe du Hoc during the D-Day invasion. His troops suffered a casualty rate of 50 percent, and Rudder himself was twice wounded, but in true Aggie spirit, they persevered and established an important Allied beachhead. Soon thereafter, he led troops in the Battle of the Bulge, and he left the war as one of its most decorated soldiers. (Later, he was named president of A&M and oversaw its transition from an all-male military school to a coed university.) But Texas, too, has provided the nation with outstanding military men and women. One-time UT football coach Jack Chevigny died in the Battle of Iwo Jima. Austin attorney Frank Denius, for whom UT's practice fields are named, served heroically at Omaha Beach on D-Day and in the Battle of the Bulge. So A&M, despite its rich history of supplying outstanding leadership to the armed services, cannot claim a complete monopoly on military heroism.

Texas has its first Aggie governor in Republican Rick Perry, a former A&M Yell Leader. His Democratic opponent in 2002 is UT Regent Tony Sanchez. Yet Perry hardly could be described as being more conservative than Sanchez. Both men had deep associations with Texas's business-dominated power structure. Both are political allies of George W. Bush. While Bush's father's presidential library is on the A&M campus, the conservative president's daughter, Jenna, attends UT. So while UT definitely is more liberal than A&M, both schools are large enough for factions from all walks of society. Even an institution like A&M's excellent student newspaper, *The Battalion* (most frequently called *The Batt*), can come under fire from Aggies who think it's too liberal: "It might as well be put out by those hippies over in Austin."

★   ★   ★

There is a cultural difference between Longhorns and Aggies. For many decades, it was a class difference. The professional class (doctors, lawyers, politicians) was associated with UT. The technical class (municipal engineers, county agents) along with the agricultural class was associated with A&M. Nowadays, it's not so much about class distinction as it is attitude. The UT attitude is that of the self-assured offspring of years of social privilege. *I'm on top because I belong on top.*

The A&M attitude is that of the can-do social climber. *I'm going to get on top because I have the moxie to pull myself up there.* Or something like that.

In fact, *Texas Monthly*, which often has the same outlook these days as the power structure in Texas, proclaimed in a cover story in the 1990s that A&M had surplanted UT as *the* state university. Just as Longhorns with boiling blood were canceling their subscriptions, Aggies were grabbing up copies in droves to send to friends and relatives. Today, when you visit the A&M campus, you can still see that issue of *Texas Monthly* on prominent display on office coffee tables.

A&M's rise to academic prominence has made the football rivalry all the more itchy.

★   ★   ★

Nowhere among American colleges and universities is football taken more seriously than at Texas and A&M. Both schools can call upon the aid of rich boosters to help them build a new facility or to buy out the contract of a coach suddenly turned unpopular. Texas ranks with Ohio State and Michigan among the richest of college athletic programs. A&M has maybe 60 percent of the budget of Texas, yet it is still among the elite when it comes to financing. Both schools are proud that their athletic programs are self-funded and that they are able to fund a plethora of men's and women's varsity sports. Texas may send its basketball teams (both men's and women's) to the NCAA championship tournament with regularity, but there's no mistaking the reality in Austin: Football is king. Football is king too in College Station, maybe even more so than at UT.

No one has better football facilities than Texas. UT Athletics Director DeLoss Dodds has said that Texas does not have to keep up with the Joneses because "we are the Joneses." True enough. There may be stadiums that have more seats than Darrell K. Royal-Texas Memorial Stadium, which has an official capacity of 80,082, although as many as 84,082 people squeezed through the gates for the 1999 Nebraska game. But otherwise it is first-class. The Moncrief-Neuhaus Athletics Center at the south end of the stadium is a wonder to behold. When you walk in the main entrance, the first thing you see are the Heisman Trophies claimed by Earl Campbell and Ricky Williams when they played at Texas. There are a host of other trophies won by Texas players plus many team trophies. The rest of the center is enough to leave any recruit bug-eyed. The strength and conditioning area alone occupies 20,000 square feet.

Kyle Field at College Station is likewise first-class. Officially seating 82,600 fans, it is the largest stadium in football-mad Texas—and the stadium can accommodate several thousand more people when UT or another big opponent comes to town. While the other facilities are enough to be the envy of all but a very few major college football powers, they are one step behind Texas. Before each football season, Aggie alumni in Austin gather for the annual Fish Fry. Tradition calls for the A&M head coach to speak to the Austin Aggies, who line up for the program by the hundreds. A couple of years ago, Slocum spoke of the need for improving facilities to help him recruit effectively against Mack Brown's splendid amenities at UT. "He talked about this couch Mack has in his office," one Aggie said. "Mack's able to bring in four or five recruits at a time and have them sit comfortably on the couch as he talks to them. R.C. said his office was so small the best they could do was line up a couple of chairs along the wall and cram them in." The Aggies ponied up cash in a hurry for their answer to the Moncrief-Neuhaus Athletics Center. When the Aggies' facility beyond the south end zone of Kyle Field is completed in 2003, it will have about 20,000 more square feet than the Texas facility has. That should give Slocum plenty of room for a couch.

★   ★   ★

For years, Texas regularly beat up on A&M in football, with the record standing at 68-34-5 in the Longhorn's favor at the beginning of the 2001 season. The Austin school had more students, more boosters, more money, and that advantage showed in a lot of ways, especially on the football field. But beginning in the 1970s, A&M's football fortunes began to turn around under semilegendary football coach Emory Bellard. In the 1980s and early '90s, A&M superceded Texas as the dominant college football power in Texas. During the last quarter of the the twentieth century, A&M led the series, 15-10, including winning ten of eleven games in one stretch during the '80s and early '90s.

But by 2001, the pendulum appeared to have swung back in the Longhorns' direction. UT stood to have one of its best football years ever, fielding a crop of players representing three years' worth of top recruiting classes brought to Austin by Coach Mack Brown. That, combined with what appeared in the preseason to be a weak schedule, put the Longhorns in a position to win the national championship. The national championship was to be decided following the 2001 season in the most hallowed of collegiate postseason playing grounds, the Rose Bowl. "One, two, three, Pasadena!" the Horns shouted from huddles before and after summer practices. Roy Williams, who was viewed by many as the best wide receiver in the college ranks before the season began, programmed his wireless phone to display ROSE BOWL whenever he turned it on. The preseason hubris was enhanced when *The Sporting News* named Texas as its favorite to claim the crown in the Rose Bowl. It also hailed quarterback Chris Simms as its choice for god of college football (most likely to win the Heisman Trophy)—never mind that a controversy raged among UT fans as to who was the better quarterback, Simms or senior Major Applewhite, who was once named Big 12 offensive player of the year and ended up holding more than three dozen UT records, and who was a living, breathing hero to many Longhorn faithful. The prospect of UT's first national title in more than thirty years combined with a possible Heisman Trophy winner made for unbearable hype in the state capital in the days leading up to the kickoff against New Mexico State, UT's first opponent in 2001. Imagine being locked in a room with twenty people trying to out-blow each other on trombones. The blast of hype around Austin was about like that.

In College Station, the trombones were muted by comparison. Yet 2001 promised to be a brink-tilted season in its own way. The Aggies' schedule was somewhat more difficult than the Longhorns'. They were scheduled to host the most storied of all college teams, Notre Dame, though this year the Irish looked questionable. The Aggies also had tough Colorado and Kansas State on their schedule. Most of the experts were looking at the Aggies to have a 7-4 or 6-5 season. A finish of 6-5 no doubt would increase the volume of the muttered campaign already under way among some of the A&M faithful: Slocum's time had come and gone. He was a living legend at A&M, the most successful football coach the university has ever had, bringing the Aggies conference championships and appearances in prestigious bowl games. But many Aggie alumni, especially younger ones, thought that Slocum had not recruited well in recent years at A&M. Or at least not as well as he had earlier in his tenure at the head spot. Certainly Mack Brown in his first three years had captured more top-ranked recruits out of high school than his College Station rival. Without top recruits, A&M could not hope to compete with an improving UT and a reinvigorated University of Oklahoma, which had shocked the college football world in 2000 by winning the national championship, for dominance of the Big 12 South. "It's the quality of the players that matters," Barry Switzer once told me during an interview at a Dallas Cowboys training camp. "It's not the coaching staff, it's not the kind of offense you run, it's the players." It seemed Slocum didn't have them to a degree to make the Aggies competitive with the best of the Big 12. So the two big themes for the 2001 season were: Would Mack Brown live up to his billing and compete for the crown at the Rose Bowl? And would R. C. Slocum win enough games to restore the faith of all the A&M loyalists and remain at the Aggie helm?

That's why 2001 seemed like a good time to get inside the rivalry. I decided to follow the Longhorns and the Aggies through the season and up to their big Thanksgiving weekend shootout—not as a sports reporter ensconced high above the mob in the comfort of a press box, but down among the crowd, ass-to-elbow with the folks who live and die with the fortunes of these two teams. It turned out to be a hell of a season.

Introduction:

Texas, My Texas

Ifirst became aware of Texas A&M University when I was a boy, maybe ten years old, thanks to an old television that took up an entire corner of my bedroom. From the perch of my wagon-wheel bunk bed, I watched the TV's huge screen incessantly, sampling in black-and-white whatever the three commercial channels and one educational channel broadcasting out of Oklahoma City had to offer. The news. Cartoons. Sports. Westerns. Sitcoms. But mostly I watched movies. One night I saw a movie about A&M. And it stirred me like no other film ever had.

In retrospect, the film is ludicrous—ludicrous *and* racist. But at age ten, I found *We've Never Been Licked* to be inspiring. Released during the middle of America's involvement in World War II, *We've Never Been Licked* is the story of a young man with a chip on his shoulder who enters Texas A&M when it was still "Old Army"—an all-male military school—and gets it knocked off in short order by older members of the Corps of Cadets, one of whom is played by a young Robert Mitchum. *We've Never Been Licked* was filmed on the A&M campus, with actual cadets in supporting roles. There is more to the story, of course. The bigger part of the plot centers around the hero's near corruption by devious Japanese spies led by William Frawley. That's right, William Frawley, Fred Mertz from *I Love Lucy*. But the spirit of A&M prevails in the young Aggie, and at the end, he resists seduction by the Japanese. And America is saved.

When the final credits rolled, I wanted to leap from under my cowboy-and-Indian bedspread and get on the ball. But somehow I managed to stay in bed through the night. The next day, though, I was a wonder to behold. I did my best to transform myself into a ten-year-old Aggie. For the next few days, I kept my room as clean as it ever was, dressed as neatly as possible, ran as far as I could, performed the President's Council on Physical Fitness calisthenics I learned at my grade school, and did my best to climb the bedeviling rope that hung from an elm tree behind my house. No more would I be the soft, slothful kid I had been.

But I lost the battle before I made much more progress. My childhood nemesis, tonsillitis, hit me one afternoon as I battled the rope. It was horrible stuff: vomiting, high fever, throat too sore to swallow. Through the worst of it, I lay sweating, in and out of sleep, drifting into and away from weird fever dreams involving Japanese spies and valiant Aggies. By the time I'd recovered sufficiently to keep Campell's chicken noodle soup on my stomach, I didn't want to think about Japanese spies or Aggies for a good long while. And I didn't. Not for years.

★　　★　　★

As for the University of Texas, I'd known about it all my life. I'd never heard a good word uttered about it. Mind you, this had more to do with my being raised in Oklahoma than it did with the school's academic reputation. The disdain was based on one thing: football. But then again, in that time and place, football *was* just about everything, wasn't it?

I came kicking and screaming into the world just a couple of years before UT Athletic Director Dana X. Bible, in one of the final acts of his distinguished (and relatively unapplauded) career as a coach and athletic director, hired Darrell K. Royal as head coach of the Long-horns. Royal immediately righted a ship that had been drifting afoul, proving himself the best young coach of in the nation. For the decade before Royal took over, Texas had been the University of Oklahoma's crash-test dummy, with OU Coach Bud Wilkinson losing to UT only once during that time. One of the best weapons he had early in his career leading the Sooners was a versatile player from Hollis, Oklahoma, who knew how to run the split-T, punt, return kicks, and play defensive back about as well as anyone ever had. That player was none other than Darrell K. Royal. After Royal left OU, he coached at Mississippi State and Washington before moving on to Texas. And suddenly, OU could no longer beat Texas. Year after year, Royal was beating the Sooners, and in those early years, he was using OU's own weapon of destruction, the split-T formation, to do it.

No one in my family had ever gone to college; most did well to get a high school education. (My grandfather, for instance, said he had finished eight grades, but my grandmother told me it was really closer to four.) No one felt any particular athletic allegiance to OU—if any-thing, they rooted more for the Cowboys of Oklahoma State University than for the Sooners. Yet when October came around and the Texas State Fair got under way and it was time for the Sooners to meet the Longhorns in the Cotton Bowl located in Fair Park in Dallas, the University of Texas was our Darth Vader, our Snidely Whiplash, our Liberty Valance, for crying out loud. I think the whole state pretty well felt that way, except for those Texas exes in our midst (and there were plenty of those in Oklahoma's oil business).

The week before OU-UT, business-as-usual in the state of Oklahoma became transfixed by the drama about to unfold in Dallas. Crimson-and-cream could be seen everywhere. "Beat Texas" was a mantra. On WKY radio out of Oklahoma City, Danny Williams wouldn't just announce the time of day, he delivered it as "Beat Texas time," as in, "We're coming up on eight-fifteen Beat Texas time." Some OU students would get out their paintbrushes and touch up the Tuck Fexas graffiti on an Interstate 35 overpass south of Norman. You could hear Boomer Sooner car horns sounding off regularly through the day. It was an event only a notch or two below Christmas Day in importance.

I'd get caught up in it all, as any kid would, but I always secretly believed the hoopla would come to naught. I was convinced Texas would always win, somehow, some way, and that traitorous Darrell Royal would be grinning on the sidelines. After all, I was just two years old the last time OU left Dallas victorious.

But the fall after my infatuation with *We've Never Been Licked*, the astounding occurred. OU actually beat Texas, 18–9, in October 1966.

If I was thrilled by that victory, my exhilaration was couched in irony. For it was about this time that I stopped regarding the University of Texas as a kingdom inhabited by demons with Satan (Darrell Royal) seated in its throne. I found myself getting interested in UT as the next few years went by. And I started to like Darrell Royal. I can't explain it, although I'm sure the Longhorn band had something to do with it. I never uttered a word of this to any of my Okie friends or family, but I thought the Showband of the Southwest under the direction of Vincent DiNino was as cool as any band could get, with its cowbells and white Stetsons and its members free to wear sunglasses. I had youthful fantasies of playing drums in that band someday.

Moreover, during the next few years, I'd start hearing about Austin and the surrounding Texas Hill Country. Austin was a place I had to check out.

I never ended up playing drums in the Showband of the Southwest, however. Not even close. I accomplished my higher education at a commuter college on the Interstate. Thinking back on it, I'm not sure it even had a marching band. For me, college was a burden to be unloaded. My whole goal was to get through college and grad school pronto. I received a bachelor's degree in English, then followed it a few years later with a master's degree. On that final graduation day, I was not filled with regret or sorrow to see my higher ed days come to an end. Instead it was relief. For all I cared, the campus could have been bulldozed as soon as I walked away with my diploma and I wouldn't have shed any tears.

★   ★   ★

It was while I was in college that I at last traveled to Austin with some friends—the summer of 1975, to be exact. I had been to North Texas a number of times before that. My stepbrothers' mother lived in Fort Worth, and family business of different kinds would from time to time send my family southward. When that happened, I reveled in being on the other side of the Red River. I couldn't describe then, and can't describe now, what it was that made me love being in Texas so much. But the tug was there.

Vivid in my memory is Austin itself as it was in the mid 1970s. It lay on the cusp of the Texas Hill Country: limestone-lined, spring-fed creeks; huge live oaks; stone outcroppings; dramatic rises and declines. The landscape had the look of being the place where the South ends and the West begins. Austin was a lovely small city then, with a skyline dominated by Memorial Stadium, the state Capitol, and the University of Texas Library tower, where a rifle-toting former Eagle Scout named Charles Whitman introduced mass murder into the American psyche nine years earlier. Billie Lee Brammer described Austin in his classic novel about politics in the time of Lyndon Baines Johnson, *The Gay Place*: "From the hills, it is possible to view the city overall and draw therefrom an impression of sweet curving streets and graceful sweeping lawns . . . wide rambling walks and elaborate public gardens and elegant old homes . . . and always from a point of higher ground, one can the see the college tower and the Capitol building . . . joined for an instant, all pink and cream, catching the first light." Visually, Austin had not changed much by 1975 from the days when Brammer wrote those words.

There were plenty of leftover hippies strolling the streets in the mid '70s. I remember passing a long-haired guy smoking a joint as he walked up Congress Avenue near the old Stephen F. Austin Hotel. He was as carefree as if he were smoking a Marlboro Light. My friends and I visited Zilker Park and saw women nonchalantly sunbathing topless on the grassy slope on the east side of the spring-fed Barton Springs swimming pool. We might as well have been in Nice. I'm sure we ogled the tanning breasts like the rubes we were. Dope smoking on the main street of town, topless sunbathing at its best-known swimming pool—it was a far cry from any place I had lived. Didn't Austin have any fire-and-brimstone-laced Southern Baptist preachers to stir up the fundamentalist throngs to bring such behavior to an end? Apparently not.

Austin in those days was not entirely a peaceable kingdom, however. It was wild and woolly if you wanted it to be, a good place to get your ass kicked if you looked at the wrong person the wrong way. If it was home to a sizeable number of aging hippies whose lives spun around a commitment to the herb, it also was home to members of the Bandidos motorcycle gang, who would as soon stomp you as speak to you. It was the heyday of redneck rock (Jerry Jeff Walker, Willie Nelson, Waylon Jennings, Ray Wylie Hubbard, Townes Van Zandt, B. W. Stevenson, Willis Alan Ramsey), the prevalent Austin sound, and we stumbled into two of the genre's fabled palaces, the Armadillo World Headquarters and the Soap Creek Saloon. In each place, we encountered mean-eyed guys whose stares betrayed a volatile mix of Quaaludes and whiskey. I never doubted they had pistols stuck in their belts or down their boots. Or both.

Our last night in Austin, I broke away from my friends, who were drinking at Scholz Garden. I hiked to the university campus, "The Forty Acres," just a few blocks north of the Capitol. Sweating from the humid heat of an August evening in Central Texas, I walked to the library tower and stared up at its observation deck, 307 feet above me. The deck of death. Whitman's sniper perch. Later the diving platform for depressed students intent on suicide. It was haunting standing there. And frightening. In a famous essay about the tower, Harry Crews wrote, "All of us have our towers to climb. Some worse than others, but to deny that you have your tower to climb and that you must resist it or succumb to the temptation to do it, to deny that is done at the peril of your heart and mind." I must have been feeling something like that. I stayed at the tower longer than I planned.

When I left the tower, I walked to Memorial Stadium. The Texas football team would have a successful season that year, but you couldn't help but think that the program was in decline. It had been years since Darrell K. Royal had been able to beat Oklahoma in October; with Barry Switzer leading the Sooners, the UT-OU rivalry had become downright nasty. Texas partisans believed that OU was illegally recruiting players (the NCAA concurred) and engaging in espionage to control the series. Within two years, a new coach would be leading the Longhorns, Royal having tired of the job, some powers at the university having tired of him.

I sat on a curb across the street from the stadium, listening to traffic from the nearby Interstate, and reflected on all I'd taken in in the past few days. I sensed that my future lay in this city and the surrounding countryside. A few years later, I did indeed move to Texas.

★   ★   ★

I used to spend a lot of time in my early years of living in Texas just driving around the countryside in an old Mazda pickup, taking in the lay of the land. I liked to follow the old roads, the ones running along ridge tops or adjacent to streams. I'd visit small towns, ones whose existence depended on cattle ranchers, cotton or grain farmers, maybe the railroad. I liked to eat at the chicken-fried steak cafés or the barbecue joints or Mexican places. My rally point became Taylor, a town northeast of Austin where Dennis Hopper filmed *The Hot Spot*, and Taylor's legendary barbecue establishment, Louis Mueller's.

I recall one day in particular: After a Saturday morning of driving more or less aimlessly and listening to *conjunto* music on the AM band of the radio, I stopped in at Mueller's for a late lunch. I ordered brisket and sausage and Shiner beer, sat down at a table, and watched TCU and A&M play football on black-and-white TV. It was a heady moment. Great barbecue and Texas college football and more. Everything seemed to be in place for me at that moment, a rare enough experience for anybody. I felt like I *belonged* where I was. Granted, Texas had its flaws, but I'd discovered a kind of cultural richness, a richness of land and people, that I'd never known before.

I felt like I was home for the first time in my life.

Home was a lot of things. The Thanksgiving weekend matchup between the Aggies and the Longhorns was a huge part of it. I came to understand the game as a ritual that struck deep in the souls of Texans. It marked the end of the football season in a region where football is something akin to religion. It also marked the end of autumn; the dim days of winter lay ahead. The end of the football season was also the conclusion of a cultural rite, a rite in which the whole state was engaged in some way. It began three months earlier in the blast-furnace heat of a Texas summer and continued with weekly celebrations on the gridiron until the days grew short and the breezes blew chilly. To go through it and take in all the nuances was the quintessential Texas experience.

I looked forward to UT-A&M every year.

CHAPTER ONE

A Midnight Yell

THE CHANGES ARE SUBTLE against the blast furnace of Texas summer. Maybe the shadows seem a little longer. Maybe the heat breaks a little earlier in the day. Maybe the string of hundred-degree days is broken; it only gets to ninety-eight or so. And there are more clouds in the sky.

Maybe you notice the booming of shotguns in the distance at dusk. Practice for dove season, shards of clay pigeons in the uncut sunflower meadow. Maybe things are changing . . . maybe.

You sense those changes, the turning toward something new, and yet the fiery days continue to overwhelm.

I was running a lot before the football season began: four miles in the heat of the afternoon, mostly to get a feel for what the football players were going through during two-a-days in August. I was also making my regular training sessions at the boxing gym, and at six in the evening, I might as well have been stepping into the heater coil of a '77 Cadillac that's just made the fast run from San Antonio to Austin—that's how hot it was in that metal building behind the Goodwill. The heat sucked the air from your lungs. I'd be sweating before I unwound the jump rope in my gym bag. It was always two hours of hell.

Newcomers to Texas from such gentle climes as Northern California are dying for home. I'd hear it everywhere I went: They can't take any more. Yet I ran. I hit the boxing gym. I endured. I always kept thinking, How do those guys survive practices in this heat?

In fact, some didn't. Some high school kids collapsed and died in Texas. The newspapers and TV reports were full of it. Around the country, college players collapsed and died. Even a pro football player collapsed and died. Then I got a little taste of it myself. One afternoon, my feet seared, the sun scorching my forehead as I ran, a chill shot through my body, and my legs abruptly stopped running without my consciously deciding to do so. I scooted off the street to the sidewalk and the shade of trees. Pulled off my T-shirt, fearing, My God, is this what IT is like? I made it home, got a sport drink from the refrigerator, stepped into the shower with my jogging shorts and sneakers still on, and turned on the water. I survived. And the next day I was running again—this time in the relative cool of the morning.

Finally the remnants of a tropical depression stalled in the Gulf, and the long siege of heat broke. Waves of rain swept across the parched land. Everything seemed to be in recovery. Thank God.

★   ★   ★

The rain is about to give up as I stroll the campus of A&M in College Station, deep in the East Texas woods, late on the last Friday night of August. Just two or three hours ago, it was pouring, so I went to the Target store on Texas Avenue in search of some sort of weather gear. In the camping section, the rain gear display had been stripped, except for a lone Eddie Bauer jacket. A white-haired man and I arrived at the same time, eyed the jacket in friendly competition, joked with each other. Then he said, "I believe I'll let you have it, young feller. It's a little rich for my blood."

"You're sure?" I said, but it was only a feigned protest. I pictured myself being drenched at midnight, and imagined myself fighting off the codger to get the jacket.

"It's all yours," he said, smiling. He gave me a wave and pushed his red plastic Target shopping cart down the aisle. Aggie partisans might say this is the kind of hospitality you come to expect to find in College Station. Maybe so.

But now that I have the jacket, I don't need it. The rain comes to a complete stop. The clouds are parting. The moon appears, although it looks as if it is behind a scrim. And as it does, whatever breeze might have been cooling the evening disappears. The night swelters. Sweat begins to trickle down my temples. I take off the jacket, but my shirt is soon soaked with sweat anyway.

Still, walking around the campus tonight is not unpleasant. The walkways are softly lit. The air smells clean. The trees ebb into the night sky. I've always liked taking walks or running in the dark, and this is a good place to do it. In many ways, the A&M campus is more appealing in darkness than it is in the light of day.

The campus is not ugly, but you can't say it's lovely either. The two structures that dominate it are Kyle Field, the colossal football sta- dium illuminated by grayish-blue lights tonight, and a water tower that looks like a tan golf tee grown gargantuan on steroids. Between stand some graceful structures but also many boxy, uninspired build- ings—typical public building architecture of the '70s and '80s. All of them crammed onto the grounds to accommodate the school's enor- mous growth during the last three and half decades: the period dur- ing which A&M went from an all-male military college cut along the lines of the Citadel or Virginai Military Institute to one of the largest coed universities in the United States. It's short on hoary bell towers and ivy-cloaked libraries. There's not a flying buttress to be seen. But in the dark, the campus is agreeable, peaceful even, never mind the thousands of scurrying students or the occasional Aggie whoop or the pickup horn blasts from University Avenue.

Near the stadium, on the steps of the Memorial Student Center (MSC), I meet up with Ruth Coleman and Tommy Connell, two young friends of mine from Austin who are both recent grads of A&M—Aggies for life. We walk through the wet night to the Academic Building. It is an exception to most of the buildings you see on campus. Built in 1912, it is a handsome domed structure with columns out front, and in the sunlight it has a soft sand-yellow glow to it. At night, it has the look of a fortress.

A statue of Sul Ross—called Sully by A&M students—stands in front of the Academic Building. At his feet are a scattering of quarters and dimes and nickels.

"So what's the money about?" I said.

"It's one of the traditions," Tommy said.

Ruth said, "When you're getting ready for a test that you're nervous about, you can put money at Sully's feet for good luck."

"Yeah, when it's time for finals, you can see rolls of quarters stacked up here," Tommy said.

"I see," I said. The first week of classes and already there's money around Sully's shoes.

Texas A&M is a tradition-enriched (or a tradition-laden, depending on your perspective) institution. Paying a tribute to Sully in exchange for his help with a test is only one of scores of traditions the Aggies have managed to keep alive in spite of the university's enormous changes over the years. A couple of days ago, I told an Aggie joke to an Aggie friend of mine: How many Aggies does it take to change a lightbulb? Answer: Three. One to change the lightbulb. One to write a yell about it. And one to make it a tradition. My Aggie friend grinned and said, "That's about right." It's fitting that the statue of Sully graces the grounds in front of the Academic Building in this most tradition-conscious of all major American universities. Had it not been for Sul Ross, there might not have been any traditions at all.

Lawrence Sullivan Ross was born to Shapley Prince Ross and his wife, Catherine, in the Iowa Territory a couple of years after Sam Houston's army bested the Mexican troops of Antonio López de Santa Anna on the San Jacinto. But by the time Sul was a year old, his father had moved the family to Milam County, Texas. Sul became a bona fide Indian fighter while still a boy, and thus his legend took root. As an adult he fought Comanches both as a member of the U.S. Army and as the captain of a Texas Ranger company.

It was as a Ranger that he established his statewide fame, becoming a hero to the Anglo-Texans on the frontier. In the late fall of 1860, he lead a band of Rangers, civilian volunteers, Tonkawa scouts, and troopers from the 2nd Cavalry in pursuit of Comanche marauders who had struck East Texas. After several days, Ross's group located a Comanche encampment. Following the ensuing melee, Ross took credit for recovering a blue-eyed blonde woman once known as Cynthia Ann Parker. She was Texas's most famous Indian captive; her story more or less became the basis of the John Ford film *The Searchers*, starring John Wayne. Cynthia Ann had been taken from her father's "fort," located only seventy-five miles from the present A&M campus, twenty-five years earlier by raiding Comanches. For years Texans had attempted to "rescue" her. Like John Wayne's Ethan Edwards, Sul Ross always claimed to be the man who pulled it off—never mind that Cynthia Ann didn't want to return to "civilization," preferring instead to live with her children among the Comanches. No happy ending occurred for Cynthia Ann, in spite of Sully's efforts. Forced to remain among the Anglos, she died a few years later, legend has it of a broken heart.

During the Civil War, Sul Ross resigned from the Rangers to fight with the Confederates, fighting in the battles of Corinth, Pea Ridge, and Vicksburg, and getting promoted to brigadier general along the way. In the years after the war, he served as a county sheriff, helped write Texas's state constitution, was elected to the state senate, and finally, held the governor's office for two terms. As soon as he left office as governor, he became president of the fledgling Texas Agricultural and Mechanical College. The college was in bad straits when Sully took over, but he repulsed attempts to put it out of business, got more money from the legislature, increased enrollment, and oversaw an extensive building program. TAMC was on firm footing when Sully died unexpectedly in 1898. Comanche fighter, Texas Ranger, Old West sheriff, military commander, legislator, governor— Sul Ross was many things, but as Ruth and Tommy are explaining to me tonight, he is forever hallowed by Aggies as one of the men who saved A&M.

We leave Sully.

We pass a dorm that is not air conditioned. Unimaginable these days, living in a dorm in this part of Texas without air-conditioning. Brutal, even. But it is in part another tradition, Ruth and Tommy tell me. A way for students to experience dorm life the way it once was. And those dorm rooms are cheaper than air-conditioned rooms. Before the rain arrived, Texas had just come off a heat spell that in Austin, ninety miles to the west, included some twenty days of hundred-degree temperatures. Maybe some concessions to tradition definitely should be examined, I'm thinking—a dorm without air-conditioning in Texas might just constitute cruel and unusual punishment.

Before A&M officials halted the annual bonfire tradition—known by the proper name "Bonfire" in Aggie lingo—following the 1999 collapse that injured dozens and claimed twelve lives, students from this dorm were among those taking part in the early morning firewood cuts, arriving back in clothes caked with sweat and mud and leaning toward the fetid side: "grodes" (rhymes with "roads"). Tradition calls for grodes never to be washed. A common practice was to hang the filthy jeans and T-shirts from dorm windows following a cut—better that, I suppose, than have them smelling up the room. But true Aggies preserve their grodes long after they become Former Students (a proudly held formal title), sticking them away in a trunk like a talisman that might bring them luck someday. Tonight, nearly two years have passed since Bonfire last occurred, nearly two years since grodes flapped in the moisture-rich breezes blowing up from the Gulf of Mexico. But in the darkness we see people wearing them proudly.

Ruth, Tommy, and I continue walking, heading in a roundabout way to the stadium. Soon we're in the flow of thousands of people approaching Kyle Field. It is nearing twelve A.M., the magic hour for Aggies to engage in a hallowed tradition, Midnight Yell. Throughout football season, home and away, Aggies congregate at the cusp of game day for what I was going to call a cheerleading session, but that's not exactly accurate. It's more than that. And it's not *cheer*leading that goes on; it's *yell*-leading. The distinction means as much to the Aggie mind as the difference to a beer drinker between sipping from a chilled mug and chugalugging from a pitcher until you're ready to puke.

Yell Practice in general began in 1913 when different Corps companies gathered after dinner to "learn heartily the old-time pep." A practice at midnight took form in 1931 when members of the Corps, hanging around the Puryear Hall dorm room of a cadet called Peanut Owen, determined it would be an entertaining notion to have that year's Fish fall out on the steps of the campus YMCA building to practice yells. Two senior Yell Leaders, Horsefly Berryhill and Two Gun Herman, arrived shortly and, in the radiance of railroad flares and torpedoes stuck in flower plots around the building, directed the freshmen in practicing yells for the upcoming game against Texas. And just like that, a tradition was born.

As we pass through the Quad—the cluster of buildings housing the Corps of Cadets, A&M's connection to its "Old Army" days—we get caught up in an ever-growing stream of people moving toward Kyle Field.

★　　★　　★

For years the Corps *was* A&M. The land grant system of colleges that gave rise to A&M required military training be part of the curriculum, so there were no students who were not cadets. So when the first six students enrolled when the campus opened its doors, they became the first Corps of Cadets. The Corps currently is the largest body of uniformed students outside the service academies. While about a third of its members do go on to careers in the armed services, the Corps is not exactly an ROTC program, although all members must take basic ROTC classes during the first two years. Many cadets go straight into civilian life after graduating. The Corps is composed of around 2,000 cadets. The other students on the campus dwarf it in terms of sheer numbers, yet the Corps continues to be the most distinctive institution on the A&M campus. In a way, the Quad is sort of an enclave. Here the cadets hold daily formations, march to meals, go through drills, and undergo physical training as if it were its own little Army post. Though there about twenty students on campus for every one who is a member of the Corps, you nevertheless sense that when you enter the Quad, you are at the heart of the university. The things that are the most recognizable about A&M all spring from here: the Fightin' Texas Aggie Band; the Ross Volunteer Company, the oldest student organization in Texas and the official honor guard of the governor; the Parsons Mounted Cavalry; and so forth. The Corps holds much greater sway over campus life than you'd think, given its relatively small size.

★   ★   ★

Earlier that day, I'd driven over from Austin to witness a "new tradition" linked to this relatively ancient one—First Yell. For the past couple of years, the Aggies have scheduled a celebration to precede the first Midnight Yell of the season; it involves a barbecue cookoff and a celebrity performance, among other things. The first year of First Yell, the celebrity was Bill Cosby; for tonight's show, it was Jeff "You Know You're a Redneck If" Foxworthy. Wouldn't you know it? *Jeff Foxworthy.* I could envision Longhorn friends of mine nodding smugly at the news Foxworthy was playing A&M. *What else would you expect from a cow college?*

Some partisans of A&M say one great advantage of sending kids to College Station for an education is that the environment is more innocent, more wholesome than society at large. America as it used to be. America as it should be. What I saw at the First Yell did nothing to dissuade from that notion. The faces of the students in the FREE FOOD line seemed well scrubbed and wholesome—like they might have just fallen out of a commercial for Old Navy. It was a look of small towns and suburbs. A band set up outside the MSC played none of the angst-laced tunes a lot of people might associate with college students but, instead, "Radar Love," that staple of "classic rock" FM stations recorded by Golden Earring way back when Richard Nixon was president. The band went from Golden Earring into more classic rock, a song by Pat Benatar. I remember thinking rap or rave or house music or anything along those lines would have been as out of place here as pierced nipples.

A few of the students wore Carhartt overalls, most crisp and dark blue, as if they'd just come off the retail shelf a few hours earlier. But some obviously had been around for a while. These bore sayings embroidered into their tough denim. "Farmers Fight!" and "Howdy,

Dammit!" were the most common. But there were others: "West Point Is a Good Prep School for A&M." "Gig 'em." "t.u., t.u.— Where the Girls Are Girls and the Boys Are Too."

t.u.—always in lowercase—is the most common barb you find hurled at the University of Texas by Aggies. Longhorns, of course, call their school UT, but no diehard Aggie, which may be a redundancy, would ever do so. It's always t.u. That, in turn, is short for *texas university*—again, always in lowercase. (However, I've read that the t.u. barb actually began as a sarcastic reference to *the university* back in the long-ago days when A&M existed as a subordinate of the University of Texas.) Even though the next day's game was with McNeese State, the overriding focus of the Aggies' entire football season is the Thanksgiving weekend game with Texas. So I wasn't surprised to see anti-UT slogans already appearing on the last day of August.

I strolled through the covered walkway linking the MSC with Rudder Tower. I encountered three members of the Corps in T-shirts and gym shorts, hair shaved on the sides and back and very short on top—high and tight, the style sometimes referred to as the STRAC (Strategic Air Command) look, the style that a Marine buddy of mine said led to the Marine nickname "jarhead." The haircuts might have been hard-core military, but their faces were as virtuous as any of the kids on *The Brady Bunch*. Next I came across two overall-wearing boys sharing a bicycle, one on the seat pedaling while the other maintained a precarious balance on the handlebars. Wally might as well have been giving Beaver a ride around the streets of Mayfield. The guys on the bike both said "Howdy" to me, and I immediately failed the Howdy, Dammit test. "Hey," I said to them as I walked past. Dammit, I thought, I was supposed to say Howdy.

I walked back to the heart of the First Yell activities and I did start to pick out a few pierced eyebrows, a few tattoos, a few guys with hair

to their shoulders. But only a few. Pretty damned wholesome. And maybe not such a bad thing, I thought as I left campus.

From my room at the Hilton Hotel, I heard a squawk from a police car coming from the street. I looked out the window and saw two cars driven by Louisiana state troopers guiding the buses carrying the McNeese State team into the parking lot. A handful of McNeese State fans, having driven up from Lake Charles with the team, gathered around to encourage the players as they climbed off the buses. An NCAA Division I-AA school, the Cowboys looked as if they'd be pitifully outmanned when they met the Aggies the next day. But their fans were still enthusiastic, one woman wearing a blue and gold T-shirt that said "Geaux Boys"—a nod toward Louisiana's Cajun heritage. I had a hard time believing the Boys would *geaux* very far in tomorrow's game, however.

★　　★　　★

"I never heard of the State of McNeese," an Aggie Yell Leader is shouting as he engages in a well-choreographed pacing exercise in front of the east sideline of Kyle Field. Like the other four Yell Leaders, he is wearing overalls instead the white attire they don for game day. He steps in one direction, stops, cocks the toe of one foot behind the Achilles tendon of the other, delivers a line, paces in the opposite direction and performs the toe-behind-the-Achilles-tendon maneuver again, delivers a line, and so on. "So, Ags, I got out my map to try to find this State of McNeese. I looked but I couldn't find it." He continues with his description of the search for the State of McNeese until ending his monologue with the inevitable discovery that you can find it, Ags, by bending over and spreading the cheeks of your ass.

Welcome to Midnight Yell. Nothing subtle here.

Ruth, Tommy, and I are standing on the bleachers deep in the student section, first deck, east side of the stadium. The student section is packed. Earlier a torchlight procession entered the stadium. The Fightin' Aggie Band, not in its crisp Corps uniforms but in informal dress, many members in overalls, one sousaphone player with a straw cowboy hat beat up enough to look like it had been around for the last of the cattle drives. The Yell Leaders. Cadets. The A&M mascot, a female collie named Reveille VII, who was barking excitedly as the entourage entered the stadium.

No totem is more revered on the A&M campus than Reveille. Back in 1931, a group of cadets on their way back from a trip to Navasota struck a small black and white dog with their car. They brought the injured dog back to campus to care for her. The next morning, as a bugler blew reveille, the dog started barking and thus received a name. She became the official mascot of the football team during the fall 1931 season. The first Reveille lived for thirteen more years. Upon her death, the Corps gave her a full military funeral on Kyle Field, and she was buried in the north entrance of the field facing the scoreboard beyond the south end zone. Subsequent Reveilles were buried in the same fashion in same location, with the same kind of high honors.

Reveille has a curious relationship with the Corps that seems to baffle most non-Aggies. Certainly she is the most venerated canine on campus, but there's more, much more. She's also considered to be the highest ranking member of the Corps, the equivalent of five-star general. Under the care of Company E-2, she has the run of wherever she goes. If she curls up on a cadet's bed and falls asleep, the cadet sleeps on the floor. If she is in a classroom and barks during the lecture, the instructor is expected to dismiss class. Cadets snap to attention when she passes by. In Reveille, Aggies see a living, breathing embodiment of all their myriad traditions.

And that's why Aggies everywhere got so riled when some Texas students, calling themselves the Rustlers, kidnapped the previous Reveille.

During the heyday of the old Southwest Conference, the Aggies prided themselves for having kidnapped, at one time or other, all the mascots of the other schools in the league—the Baylor bear, the Rice owl, and so on. They even managed to nab big, snorting Bevo, the longhorn steer that functions as UT's mascot, three times: in 1917, 1962, and 1972. Meanwhile, the Aggies' precious Reveille never once fell into enemy hands—another source of Aggie pride.

But that pride got punctured in late 1993 when the Rustlers stole Reveille VI from a yard in Dallas while the Aggies were in town to play in the Cotton Bowl. Reveille was staying at the home of the parents of the Corps corporal in charge of her. The Rustlers had been keeping the house under surveillance, and when the opportunity availed itself, they struck. They held Reveille for the better part of a week under a demand that A&M officials proclaim that UT was better than them.

At first the Aggies tried to deny that their mascot had been dognapped. The corporal in charge of her steadfastly asserted that the Rustlers had captured the wrong dog. But after that embarrassment, the Aggies fessed up: Reveille was in enemy hands. University spokesperson Rene Henry said A&M would refuse the demand. "That's absolutely absurd and ridiculous," he said. A&M and UT issued a joint announcement saying the schools found it appalling that "anyone would steal a young puppy during the Christmas holidays." (Reveille was then just four months old.) A hot line was established for tips on the collie's whereabouts. And A&M officials called on the attorney general to begin felony criminal proceedings against the Rustlers. Henry said you couldn't really put a price on Reveille, "but in terms of marketing and tradition, she could be worth $1 million.

You're talking about a superstar on the order of Lassie and Benji." The AG's office never saw it in quite those terms and never prosecuted anyone. Reveille was discovered tied to a sign near a boat ramp on Lake Travis, northwest of Austin, a can of Alpo sitting nearby. The Ags had their honor sullied, but Reveille made it back to Dallas in time for A&M's game with Notre Dame.

★　　★　　★

So Reveille VII barks her fool head off as Midnight Yell proceeds. The band takes its place on the bleachers and begins to run through some of its numbers, marches that are familiar and substantial as any monument in Washington, marches John Philip Sousa himself would have approved of. First up, Jerry Goldsmith's stirring theme from the 1970 film *Patton*, and the whooping begins. *Whoop! Whoop! Whoop!* For the Aggies, the distinctive high-pitched whoop is an exclamation of triumph, of joy, of happiness. But more than anything else, it is a cry of solidarity, a one-syllable condensation of the song the Ags sing at the start of football games: "We are the Aggies, the Aggies are we / True to each other as Aggies can be." Any gathering of Aggies is guaranteed to produce whoops—football games and weddings and, for all I know, funerals too. And certainly anything pertaining to General George S. Patton, Jr., is bound to prompt whoops. As an A&M icon, he doesn't rate up there with Sully and Reveille, but he did say, "Give me an army of West Point graduates, I'll win a battle. Give me a handful of Texas Aggies, and I'll win a war!" For that, he will forever merit a position in the roster of A&M saints.

As the band brassily thunders through "Patton," the Yell Leaders gather at the center of the field. The three senior Yell Leaders kneel on the grass, arms around each other's shoulders, to watch the two junior Yell Leaders bang out push-up after push-up, dozens of them, as the band segues from march to march. I'm imagining what kind of fire must be burning in those young men's pecs by the time they finish all these push-ups. As if that isn't bad enough, they have to endure a tackle drill from the senior Yell Leaders before they can exit the field once the band completes its numbers.

Now the actual practicing of yells begins in earnest. Tradition demands that students stand throughout the football game. When it comes time to deliver the yells, they assume a position called "humping it," which involves leaning forward and placing your hands on your knees and shouting directly toward the field. A way of making the yells louder, as if they wouldn't be loud enough with 28,000 students showing up for every home game. The Yell Leaders direct the crowd using hand signs:

Gig 'em

> *[Hand Sign: Closed fist with thumb pointed straight up]*
> Aaaaaaaa
> Gig 'em, Aggies!

Aggies

> *[Hand Sign: Hands flat, with index fingers and thumbs touching to form an "A"]*
> A-G-G-I-E-S
> A-G-G-I-E-S
> Aaaaaaaa
> Fight 'em, Aggies!

Farmers Fight

*[Hand Sign: Closed fists rotating around each other in alternating
directions]*
Farmers fight!
Farmers fight!
Fight! Fight!
Farmers, farmers fight!

And so on. I do my best to try to keep up with the yells. But I
feel like an interloper. I'm wearing what will become my nonparti-
san uniform for the fall: a black T-shirt from the Cleto Reyes boxing equipment company in Mexico, a pair of Levi 501s, a cap
from the Hill Country Outfitters in Fredericksburg, Texas, and well-
broken-in Stan Smith tennis sneakers. Everyone around me, on the
other hand, is wearing some sort of A&M gear. I fear that I stand
out, to say the least. I also feel sort of like the sole Southern Baptist
participating in a Roman Catholic High Mass. I have no idea what
the hell the game plan is, no idea about when to genuflect or when
to whoop.

So when people in the crowd cry, "Off the wood!" my mind draws
a blank. What the hell does that mean? Then I see Ruth and Tommy
step off the bleachers and I do the same. The bleachers are metal, not
wooden anymore, but tradition is tradition, so it's "Off the wood!"
The band strikes up "The Aggie War Hymn," one of the best fight
songs in all of college football. It is a rousing tune. And protocol dic-
tates that you not stand on the bleacher while singing it.

(Chorus)
Hullabaloo, Caneck! Caneck!
Hullabaloo, Caneck! Caneck!

Goodbye to texas university
So long to the Orange and the White
Good luck to the dear old Texas Aggies
They are the ones that show the real old fight
"The eyes of Texas are upon you . . ."
That is the song they sing so well
So good-bye to texas university
We're going to beat you all to . . .
Chig-gar-roo-gar-rem
Chig-gar-roo-gar-rem
Rough! Tough! Real Stuff! Texas A&M

Immediately after singing the war hymn, we cross legs with our neighbors and link arms and begin swaying side-to-side as the band strikes up "Saw Varsity's Horns Off," which almost always follows the war hymn:

Saw Varsity's horns off!
Saw Varsity's horns off!
Saw Varsity's horns off!
Short!
Varsity's horns are sawed off!
Varsity's horns are sawed off!
Varsity's horns are sawed off!
Short!

Goodbye to texas university and sawing off a longhorn's horns. Hard to gather from the songs that tomorrow's opponent is McNeese State, but so be it. The Aggies will play ten games before November 23 arrives, but the obsession of the A&M season is clear from the beginning. Beat Texas.

The Yell Leaders tell other stories, including a couple about a mythical Aggie—an Aggie Everyman—called Rock T. Aggie. One went something like this:

Rock has a job as a bartender, and a McNeese State Cowboy comes in with an ostrich at his side and orders a beer. Rock says that will be three dollars, and the McNeese State Cowboy reaches into his pocket and produces exact change. The next day, the McNeese State Cowboy comes in with the ostrich and orders a beer. Again he pays with exact change. This goes on precisely like this—including the ostrich and the exact change—for some time. Then one day Rock encourages the McNeese State Cowboy to try some fine sipping whiskey instead of beer, and the McNeese State Cowboy is agreeable. Rock pours the drink and says that will be four dollars and fifty cents. The McNeese State Cowboy pulls out exact change. Amazed, Rock says he has two questions for the McNeese State Cowboy. First he wants to know how he manages to always have correct change for his drink. The McNeese State Cowboy says he found an old lamp and rubbed it. A genie appeared and said he would grant the McNeese State Cowboy two wishes for setting him free. So, the McNeese State Cowboy wished that he would always have money in his pocket to buy a drink—so that's why he always has exact change in his pocket when the bar tab arrives. Rock understands that. Now Rock's other question is, Why does the McNeese State Cowboy always have that ostrich with him? The McNeese State Cowboy shrugs and says he used his second wish to request a chick with long legs.

No rimshot needed.

Every time McNeese State is mentioned, the crowd lets loose a loud hiss. A horse laugh, in Aggie parlance.

And then the stadium lights go off and in the darkness, the Aggies kiss their dates. If they have dates. If not, they ignite Bic lighters and hold them in the air to demonstrate their availability. A guy to my right holds two lighters together, creating a flame that's maybe eight inches high. But I don't see any women running his direction.

Midnight Yell comes to a close.

★   ★   ★

Ruth, Tommy, and I are inching our way through the jam of people exiting the stadium. It's nearly one o'clock in the morning.

"So what did you think?" Ruth says.

I nod. "That was pretty impressive," I say, but I'm not sure what exactly to make of it. I can't really say anything else. I'm a little overwhelmed by it. The reverence for tradition is amazing. A&M now has around 45,000 students on its College Station campus, ranking it among the ten largest universities in the United States. Relatively few of them have any connection with agriculture except for consuming steaks and bowls of cornflakes. Yet the future CPAs and electrical engineers crank themselves up to shout out yells that harken back to the day when virtually every student here had agriculture in his future. Or the military. No more than one in twenty of the students are members of the Corps, yet the Old Army yells endure as well. Given my higher ed background at the commuter college on the Interstate, it's all somewhat perplexing.

But impressive, yes.

Ruth waits for me to say more, but all I can do is nod again.

I part with Ruth and Tommy outside the stadium and cross the street to the MSC. On the steps are some postmidnight proselytizers, pamphlets in hands. "You know it!" one shouts, sounding most impassioned. "You know it in your hearts! You know your sins! You know you've been to a sinful display! You know your sins!" No one seems to be accepting the pamphlets. "You know what you have done! You know your sins!"

Up front someone yells, "Ah, he's just an Aggie!"

Laughter rises into the damp night.

CHAPTER TWO

The Wild Bunch

COLLEGE STATION AND ITS SISTER TOWN, Bryan (often the community is referred to as Bryan-College Station), occupy an area carved out of the thick forest that dominates the area where Central Texas gives way to East Texas. Not exactly the landscape conjured up by many outsiders when they hear the word Texas. The stereotype of Texas is something out of Edna Ferber's *Giant*, big skies and spread-out plains punctuated by the occasional oil well or Cadillac Ranch. But Texas is in fact a huge place, oozing out across several regions, and no stereotype can come close to capturing it. At 3,700 feet elevation, El Paso marks the lowest all-weather pass in the Rockies, and it sits in high-country desert and tumbleweed country. Beaumont, 804 miles to the east, is just over twenty feet above sea level, and it is marked by haunting forests and stagnant bayous—backwater country. Up on the Cap Rock, Lubbock and Amarillo are plains cities, associated with big wheat and big cattle and big oil. Dallas and Fort Worth are separated by a mere thirty miles, but each has a distinctive feel to it, Dallas marking the end of East Texas; Fort Worth, the gateway to West Texas. Galveston and Corpus Christi are port cities, with laughing gulls and palm trees. Alpine is a mountain town—more or less. And from San Antonio south, Texas looks a lot like parts of northern Mexico. To the west and north, however, is the fabled Texas Hill Country, which isn't exactly like any other place on the continent with its live oaks and mountain cedars and limestone studding and gushing "mountain streams," as the old-timers sometimes used to describe them.

The ninety-mile drive from College Station to Austin is a short one, by Texas standards. But it involves moving from one distinctive place to another, from the South to the edge of the West, from small town to urban area. And the psychic distance between them is vast. The Bryan-College Station area prides itself on bedrock conservatism, small-town values: God, home, and the Republican Party. Austin, on the other hand, is, well, Austin. That rare place in the Lone Star State where Democrats still dominate. A city that has, for a decade sent an openly gay state representative to the Capitol. A city dusted with the glitter of Hollywood and the music industry. A city of high accomplishments and a city of a lot of horseshit. A high-tech center, a place that boasts about how many of its citizens are wired, but when it comes to automobiles, it's a place of damnable traffic knots and far too many deadly accidents. To the Aggie mind, College Station is a place to be revered: "Mecca" is how I've seen it described on different Internet discussion boards. Inevitably, those same boards refer to Austin as "Sodom."

Around noon of the day following the Midnight Yell at A&M, I drove from College Station to Austin in my SUV for the Longhorns' first game of the season. Down out of the woods and into the flat, rich Brazos River Valley, punctuated with oil well pump jacks and tank batteries. Back up into the woods. Through the small towns, past hay meadows, grazing pastures, cotton and corn fields. Then into suburban Austin. Soon enough, I was in the city. On the far east side, much of Austin looks like most other Sunbelt cities. Urban sprawl. Unimaginative tract houses. Strip malls. Traffic congestion. Brammer's sweet curving streets and graceful sweeping lawns and wide rambling walks are on the other side of town, west of the Capitol, in an older, more genteel part of Austin; in neighborhoods where relatively small houses can cost a million dollars or more.

I exited U.S. 290 onto Interstate 35 and headed southward, then got off on MLK, passing the dozen or so ticket scalpers working along the access road, a sure sign game day had come to Austin. I prowled the streets, which were already jammed with traffic though the kick-off for UT's first game of the season—a night game with New Mexico State—was still hours away, looking for a parking place.

I was stuck for a while at an intersection and lowered the two front windows to let in some fresh air. Suddenly I heard a "Hi there" come from the open passenger window of my SUV. A blonde in a low-cut black Spandex top leaned in the window, giving me a grand view of tanned, nearly perfect cleavage. "Can I give you one of these?" she asked. Before I could say anything, she tossed what I assumed was a UT spirit towel onto the seat. "Here, take two or three of them." I didn't argue. "Have a great time at the game!" she said. Then she was gone. One thing about UT home games: There is no shortage of stunningly beautiful women in the crowd. And here I was, presenting such an attractive picture of masculinity in the seat of my SUV that one of them felt compelled to walk over and share her stock of spirit towels with me. My ego soared.

I unfolded one of the towels and my opinion of myself abruptly returned to lower altitudes. It turned out the towel was nothing more than advertising. The print on it approximated burnt orange, but nowhere did it mention either UT or the Longhorns. Instead, it pro-claimed itself to be a "Tailgater's Towel" and carried the logos of a bank, a taco chain, a fried chicken chain, a travel agency, a car dealer, a jewelry store, and so on. By avoiding the university and team names, whoever distributed the towel was able to duck paying licensing fees to UT for use of its carefully guarded trademarks. Someone turned a nice bit of cash selling ads for the towel promotion. That's what big-time college football is about these days, turning cash. And everyone seems to want to get into the act, from the university athletic departments to the ticket scalpers on the access roads. At the top level of college football, the fan on game day is barraged with a constant volley of marketing. Even the replays shown on the stadium JumboTron are sponsored by somebody. And why not? The fans appear more than willing to hand over money at every turn. So all the people associated with staging the game day spectacle walk away like buccaneers with baggy pockets bulging with booty.

Everyone, that is, except the young men who make it all possible. The players.

*   *   *

Before the season began, Texas found itself listed by *USA Today* as one of the culprits responsible for the increasing costs incurred by big-time college football programs because of what it was willing to pay the man it wanted to head its program.

"A number of athletic directors point fingers at Florida and Texas as leaders in salary escalation. Neither is apologizing," wrote the newspaper's Steve Weisberg. "Texas will pay football coach Mack Brown $1.45 million. . . . But the football program has sold out all of Memorial Stadium's sixty-seven luxury suites at $65,000 a pop—and the waiting list is fifty deep. Season-ticket sales are up some ten thousand since Brown took over in 1998, and athletic donations have gone up by half to $15 million a year. Coming off a 4-7 record and the firing of John Mackovic in 1997, 'we could have hired a $250,000 coach. Money was tight,' Texas athletic director DeLoss Dodds says. 'But we hired somebody who could turn our business around, and he [Brown] has. If you ask me or you ask anybody, "Is he worth what we're paying?", absolutely he is. Now would we like to pay him less? Yes. But we're in a market that won't let that happen.' "

Salaries of the sort that Texas paid Brown, that Florida paid Steve Spurrier, and that Florida State paid Bobby Bowden spurred many of the critics of big-time college sports to call for placing a cap on big paychecks for coaches. The Knight Commission on Intercollegiate Athletics, a group trying to reform abuses in college sports, went as far as suggesting that the NCAA seek relief from federal antitrust laws so that the organization could enact salary caps. Faculty senates at eight of the Pac-10 Conference schools chimed in, passing resolutions calling for their presidents to find ways to curb the college sports "arms race." Even in the football-crazed Big 12 some people were wondering when enough was enough. In Iowa, members of the state legislature began to ponder whether state laws should be enacted to control the escalation. This came after Iowa State was forced to cancel its men's baseball and swimming programs in large part because of the cost of floating its football program.

There weren't many critics sounding off in Texas, however. As long as winning was part of the formula of the football programs of both Texas and A&M (which paid R. C. Slocum about a million a year), not many people had a problem with the money it cost. UT President Larry Faulkner told me that while he had concerns that collegiate sports could become too big, he also understood when he took his job that football was a huge part of the university—it came with the turf and had for years.

Yet there was one consistent gadfly in Austin—and a most unlikely one.

Jeff Ward was the product of big-time football, starting with his prep career at Westlake High School (one of Texas's prime football factories) in suburban Austin. He became an All-America kicker for the Longhorns in the 1980s, then spent a brief time in the NFL, playing for the Dallas Cowboys and the Atlanta Falcons. His post-football career centered around teaching (he was a lecturer at UT, where one of the courses he taught concerned management of sports franchises) and talk radio. His afternoon drive-time program on Austin's KLBJ-AM had the highest ratings of any local talk show. He told me his football days at UT were "great, outstanding—it was fabulous. The academic environment was competitive as heck and the social environment was competitive as heck. College football can teach you these outstanding lessons that come in very brutal ways. You start to learn what it's all about. And that is, the same people who would buy you beer on Friday are the same people who will call a call-in show on Monday and complain about what a bum you are. So you learn this beautiful lesson. I got my nose bloodied enough to know that you don't take people *that* seriously."

Just as Ward manages to stir the rage of KLBJ's largely conservative listening base with his Libertarian political views, he also can crank up the indignation of UT fans when his commentary about college football turns critical, and frequently his criticism is about the way college football functions as a business. "Texas is great at what it does. Texas is one of ten to twelve—and A&M is probably in there, too—football programs that are huge entertainment enterprises. Unless they really really screw it up, they'll always be different from everyone else. They have an alumni base that few others can touch. They have a revenue stream that few others can touch. They could turn out the lights over there for a month and a half and the cash would still keep coming in. Texas went to the Fiesta Bowl a few years ago, but you read in the paper that they lost money. They had a $3.5 million payout and yet they lost money. That tells me two things. First, they don't manage their money well at all. And, two, money is easy for them."

None of that makes sense to Ward from a business standpoint. But he does give credit to DeLoss Dodds and others at Texas for admitting what they're involved with is just that—a business. But it is a business that takes a toll on the ones who do the legwork: the players.

"When you cut through it all," Ward said, "you're talking about pretty average nineteen-year-old guys who are stuck in the middle of this giant publicity machine. And everybody is having a good time around them. I'm all for people making a buck at it, but in the end, that nineteen-year-old is going to be chewed up and spit out and have no idea what in the hell has happened."

★   ★   ★

It took a while, but I finally found a place to park near Symphony Square, not far from the Capitol. I had a half-mile or so to walk before I caught up with Scott Wilson, an Austin attorney who had attended upwards of 300 consecutive Longhorn football games, home and away, including bowl games—every UT football game since the 1977 matchup with Arkansas in Fayetteville. His travels had taken him to games in Hawaii, Pittsburgh, the Meadowlands in New Jersey, Auburn, Stanford, and the Rose Bowl, among other sites. For all anyone knew, he might have held the record for a living fan attending consecutive Texas football games. I did meet a man who would have had a longer attendance streak than Wilson's had it not been interrupted by the Dallas policeman who arrested him in a Friday night melee on Commerce Street prior to the annual OU-UT game. The man listened to the game on the radio while cooling his heels in jail, then resumed his own streak the next weekend.

"I do it to support Texas," Wilson told me when I asked him why he had attended so many games in a row. "Also, when you hit about eighty or so games, it's kind of hard to stop. You know, you want to keep it going."

Wilson was just shy of fifty, born in Austin on September 29, 1951. That day the Longhorns were in West Lafayette to play Purdue. Texas won, 14–0. He grew up in the middle-class Allendale neighborhood of Austin, graduated from McCallum High School, graduated from UT, then got his law degree from Baylor. Wilson was one of those increasingly rare Austinites: He sounded like a Texan, slowly drawing out his words when he spoke. He had never married, although he had a couple of relationships that made it into the late innings of the game before they fizzled. Bespectacled and a little thick with middle age, he was a familiar figure in his Longhorns cap and burnt orange T-shirt among the thousands of Texas fans who gathered in the vicinity of Scholz Garden to tailgate prior to the game. He was a hail-fellow-well-met, about three-quarters crazy, and not the least bit boring. I liked him from the minute I met him.

Wilson lived in a working-class neighborhood off Braker Lane in northeastern Austin. Driving down the street, a visitor might not think there was anything unusual about Wilson's house, except, perhaps, for an uncommon, shall we say, vehicle parked in the drive. But step inside the door and you were in a virtual museum of UT memorabilia. Want to see a ticket stub from the legendary 1969 game with Arkansas in Fayetteville? Wilson can show you his. Interested in a book about UT sports? Most likely it's in Wilson's library. Curious about what kind of promotional posters UT has put out over the past quarter century? Drop in and take a look at Wilson's walls. And ceilings. And doors. Miss an important televised UT game from recent years? Not a problem. There's probably a video of it in one of the closets. The UT *stuff* dominates every room of his dwelling, except for one, which houses Wilson's extensive collection of caps. Hundreds of them line the walls and hang from the ceiling. In fact, there is no room left for any more to be hung, so now they're stacking up in the corners. Hats from every college and pro team imaginable, hats from oil well drilling companies and car dealers, hats from everywhere. The garage, too, is a shrine of sorts. Standing in lines along narrow shelves attached to the walls are hundreds of different beer cans and bottles. Beer is an essential part of the casa de Wilson experience. In fact, I was sipping a Milwaukee's Best as he showed me around. "We've had some parties out here for the baseball crowd," Wilson drawled. "One night, thirteen kegs met their end in the backyard. That's the record." No wonder, then, that Wilson's house is revered in some UT sports circles. Almost as much as his car.

Members of the Longhorn Foundation are able to park in the state parking garages that have sprouted around Scholz Garden over the years—nonmembers are sent packing by Texas Department of Transportation troopers. If by no other way, you can tell it's game day by the portable satellite dishes hanging out of the upper floors of the garages and the clusters of Suburbans squeezed into the parking spaces. No one among the fans parked there had a more recognizable car than Wilson's: a 1975 burnt orange Cadillac with a set of horns mounted above the grill. A tow truck operator had picked up the car as an abandoned vehicle and let Wilson know about it. Wilson was able to buy it for less than some bottles of Scotch cost. Since then, he has driven it around a lot of America as he's followed the fortunes of the Longhorn football and baseball teams. Once, while Wilson was in a state adjacent to Montana—Wyoming, maybe—he and his traveling buddies decided the Caddy needed to cross the state line into Montana so it could be added to the tally of states the car had been in. They headed off on a highway in the direction of Montana. Eventually the highway became a dirt road. They drove and drove through unpopulated country until they passed a farm where a kid was standing in front of the house. While the kid stood there with his mouth wide open, Wilson blew the Caddy's klaxon, sounding the opening strains of "The Eyes of Texas." The kid ran inside the house.

"I bet he gets spanked for lying," Wilson speculated to his companions. The big Caddy headed on to South Dakota.

The Cadillac with the horns on front might have made it to Montana. But it had never been to College Station for the A&M game or to Fair Park in Dallas for the OU game. Too much of a chance for vandalism.

Wilson, who always arrived hours before the start of a home game, had backed the Caddy into his regular place in the parking garage at 16th and Trinity and was relaxing in a lawn chair when I arrived.

"You want a beer?" he asked. "I thought you'd be here earlier."

I explained about getting away from College Station late and the heavy traffic in Austin and the hard time I had finding a parking place and all of that. Wilson nodded, took a drag off his Swisher Sweet cigar, and fished a Milwaukee's Best from the ice chest. I don't think he bought any excuse for showing up late for UT tailgating. He gave the beer to me and walked to the back of the car and opened the trunk to freshen his own drink. The trunk of the Cadillac was an amazing thing. You could find just about everything in there, from the makings of a White Russian to a spare tire. Dig far enough and you might have found an original copy of the constitution of the Republic of Texas.

Wilson introduced me to Frank Donaldson, his postgame designated driver ("This is Frank. I like to say he has a handicap. He went to OU."), and a few others snacking on queso and drinking beer in the garage. Outside, on 16th, a stream of orange-shirted fans made their way northward to the stadium. Everybody seemed to know him. Spotting him, people shouted, "Wilson! Hey, Wilson!" And Scott replied to them by name. He could recall an astonishing number of names. A standard part of UT home games is the Texas Fight cheer. TEXAS!!! the fans on the east side shout. FIGHT!!! respond the fans on the west side. A variation sometimes occurred at the parking garage as the fans filed past. SCOTT!!! someone on the street would shout. WILSON!!! would be the response from the inside.

"Let's go," Wilson said to me. "I want you to meet some people."

For the next hour, Wilson led me from tailgate party to tailgate party, working the crowd like a politician. Handshakes, inquiries about health and well-being. At one stop, he introduced me to a portly short woman in a burnt orange T-shirt and explained to her that I was writing about the UT-A&M rivalry.

"Well, honey," she said, "all you have to do is say we hate them."

"No, we don't hate them," another woman at the party said. "We just feel sorry for them."

Along the way, people offered me beers and I was able to upgrade my Milwaukee's Best to Shiner Bock and then to Negra Modelo. At one party, a guy had a stock of his home-brewed Czech pivo. At yet another party, the fans sipped single-malt Scotch and smoked illegal Cuban cigars. Everywhere was barbecue—traditional Texas brisket and sweet Elgin sausage rolled up in tortillas—and the air was thick with mesquite smoke. The drinking was heavy in the increasing heat of the day. I found myself downing a six-pack in an hour. But the crowd seemed orderly. People scampered under the Waller Creek Bridge to relieve themselves.

At gatherings of UT fans, one mantra involving the time of day can be heard over and over. I heard it now, for maybe the tenth time since I arrived, as I followed Wilson. "It's four-fifteen!" someone shouted. "And OU STILL sucks!" came the shouted reply of everyone who heard the call. Not a word about this evening's mighty opponent, New Mexico State. And certainly nothing about A&M. That's one difference between Aggie culture and Longhorn culture. The Ags have one rival. The Horns have two. For Texas, OU is a burr that's always under the saddle. Even on the day of the A&M game, you can hear Horns doing the "And OU STILL sucks!" mantra.

★   ★   ★

My notebook was filling with names and phone numbers. I knew I'd never be able to remember all these faces. But the gregarious Wilson kept on leading me from party to party. He told one group of tail-gaters that I had been to A&M to watch Midnight Yell.

"Damn," said a woman, grimacing. "For the life of me, I don't know why anyone would have to practice yelling."

Everyone in the group laughed.

"So you've been over there, huh? Did they have their jackboots on and their little swords out?" a gray-haired man asked, winking.

"Well, no," I began. "It was actually—"

He didn't let me finish. "Just like that Leni Riefenstahl movie," he said. "Hitler and his boys having fun in Munich." He winked again.

Nazis frequently come up when you talk to UT fans about the Aggies. One Longhorn told me that he watched the Corps parade up the Drag back in the 1960s when the Aggies were in town to play Texas. "It was like Hitler marching into Paris," he said. Still, the mention of the Nazis was a little ironic, given our location. We were standing no more than a block from Scholz Garden, the cog of UT tailgating activities and one of the few functioning connections to nineteenth-century Austin still flourishing in the city. Austin, like much of Central Texas, had a substantial population of German immigrants in its early years, and for a time numerous beer gardens graced the city. If you wanted to get falling down drunk and pick up a whore, you hit one of the city's saloons. But if you wanted to enjoy a pitcher or two of beer that met the high standards of the German immigrants, and do so in genteel company beneath the shade of a live oak, you sought out a beer garden like Scholz. August Scholz owned the property where the beer garden that bears his name stands as early as 1866; the current buildings on the site date back to 1871. Scholz became involved with the Democratic Party and the University of Texas soon after his business began to flourish. Political meetings began being held there in the 1870s, and in 1883, Scholz was named an official fundraiser for the university. Ever since, his beer garden has held a key place in both politics and UT football. O. Henry (William Henry Porter) enjoyed gulping his fishbowls of beer at Scholz Garden during his time in Austin, so it has also had a place in Austin's literary affairs ever since; years later, Brammer would use it as the setting of some of the more memorable scenes of *The Gay Place*. In 1893, the undefeated Longhorn football team not surprisingly chose Scholz Garden as the place to celebrate its victories. Of the famed photo of that team that hung at Scholz Garden for decades, O. Henry once wrote, "Newcomers to Texas are warned to beware of the long-haired citizen. He may be only a desperado, but it might be discovered, when too late, that he is a football player." A half century later, O. Henry might have seen a more frightening sight at Scholz Garden: goose-stepping Central Texas farmers with German roots. It's long been rumored that local meetings of the pro-Nazi Bund took place there in the 1940s. Not that many of the tailgaters who now scurried over to Scholz Garden to use the rest rooms knew about that.

"Didn't you think that was all a little strange?" the winking gray-haired man asked me.

"Well—"

"I tell you, just like Hitler's boys." He shook his head in mock disgust and went off to find another beer.

★　　★　　★

Tailgating may not have been invented at UT, but it's hard to imagine anybody doing a better job of it than the Texas fans. The tailgaters begin to circle parking lots in the vicinity of Royal-Texas Memorial

Stadium the day before game day, like so many land-rushers attempting to stake the perfect claim. The most sought-after spots, of course, are those closest to Scholz Garden. Once the prime spots are staked, the different tailgating group members start to filter in, some driving hundreds of miles just to take part in the activities. As Mark Vann wrote in the *Austin Chronicle*, they appear much like werewolves on the night of a full moon.

Some of the groups are very well organized. Vann ran into a group of officers from Fort Hood, the huge army post about sixty miles northwest of Austin, who described themselves as being "just your average drunken federal employees." They pooled their funds to rent a Ryder truck to haul down couches, overstuffed chairs, lamps, and an Astoturf carpet painted with yard markers along with the requisite ice chests and beer kegs and generator to power the big-screen TV and sound system. Another group, The Guys with the Sectional Couch, is made up of the flag football team from Lucy's Retired Surfers Bar, located in Austin's famous 6th Street entertainment district. Yet another group builds its rituals around "shotgunning" beer from cans (which involves punching a hole in the can near the bottom, placing your mouth over the hole, then popping open the top so that all the beer in the can almost instantly drains through the hole and into your mouth: the fastest way in the world to guzzle down a whole can of beer)—a practice no mama would ever approve for her son or daughter. Over at the Hornfans.com party (which you can find by the orange blimp hovering above it), a hundred pounds or more of ribs, sausage, and pork tenderloin might be sizzling away.

So the tailgating becomes an event unto itself. Among the best-known tailgaters is an aging hippie nicknamed Hunnert, as in "hunnert-year-old hippie" (Austin has no shortage of aging hippies), who arrives early, partakes of the merriment, then relaxes in a lawn chair as the rest of the tailgaters migrate to the games. As the crowd roars each time the Longhorns score in the distant Darrell K. Royal-Texas Memorial Stadium, Hunnert can be seen sitting alone, the breeze ruffling his shoulder-length hair, avoiding the stadium because he believes football is a violent sport. But he's not about to back away from the revelry before and after the game.

Hunnert does, however, go to the UT baseball games at Disch-Falk field, across Interstate 35 from DKR-Texas Memorial. In baseball season, he along with Scott Wilson and others I met this afternoon are part of a loose coterie of robust fans dubbed the Wild Bunch some twenty-five years ago by *Austin American-Statesman* sports columnist Kirk Bohls. Among teams that regularly visit "the Disch" to play the Longhorns, this Wild Bunch is as notorious in its own way as the gang in Sam Peckinpah's film. The annals of Wild Bunch pranks are legion. When UT regent and ultimate Texas political power broker Frank Erwin was alive, he attended Longhorn baseball games regularly. At the bottom of the fifth inning, the Wild Bunch would stand en masse, raise their cups, and say, "Hey, Frank, it's the bottom of the fifth." Erwin, a championship drinker who most likely was nearing the bottom of his own fifth, would rise and tip his cup back to them.

In the Wild Bunch you'll find a lot of walks of life. You might meet a retired high-tech guy with a full beard and long hair tied back in a ponytail wearing a Hawaiian shirt. Or you might be introduced to another guy with no visible means of support who still manages to get tickets for the games. The social connections between the individual members get complex in a hurry. Longtime friends suddenly start carrying grudges toward each other. Then after a few weeks, they're best of buddies again.

I knew two old friends who weren't speaking because of a dispute over "Let Me Call You Sweetheart." They were driving along the lonely highways in Oklahoma on their way to a baseball game. One of them wanted to sing barbershop quartet songs to fill the time as the asphalt hummed under the rubber; the other guy wanted to go the more traditional route—find a country-western radio station to listen to. The disagreement grew uglier as the trip went on, carrying over to the motel room they shared and lasting until they got back to Austin. The dispute went on for a while, but now they're sharing handshakes and beers again.

★　　★　　★

No name was more closely associated with the Wild Bunch than that of José Peña, who died in early July 2001 in Dallas of a respiratory ailment, a couple of months shy of his fifty-first birthday. His passing had certainly dampened today's tailgating, as the dozens of his friends wearing memorial pins on their shirts or hats attested. In a parking garage adjacent to the one where Wilson parked his Caddy, a small cenotaph of sorts for Peña had been erected. I walked over there with Wilson and his good friend, John Kelso, the *Austin American-Statesman*'s humor columnist, barbecue expert, defender of South Austin hippies and rednecks, and ultimate survivor of shifts in management at the paper.

Kelso actually had been born in Oklahoma while his father did a stint with the Army at Fort Sill, but he came of age on the East Coast, graduating from the University of Missouri. He then became a writer on a paper in South Florida. When his boss took a job as the editor of the *Statesman*, Kelso left Florida for a gig as the outdoor editor of a paper in the tundra of Wisconsin, where he seemed destined to spend his days composing analytical pieces on the nuances of ice fishing. He lasted something like three days, maybe long enough to buy a set of snow chains for his tires, before he called his old editor in Austin and said he couldn't stand it anymore, *help!* His old boss offered him a job as a columnist and Kelso drove south in a hurry.

That was twenty-five years ago. In the meantime, he'd become a fixture at the paper, one of the primary voices of those who've tried to "Keep Austin Weird" in the face of overwhelming forces that have made it a high-tech center, home to movie stars, one of America's most expensive cities in which to live, and, heaven help us, a trendy place to say you're from. A typical Kelso column might be about a musician who made hats from roadkill. Or a family feud disrupting business at a legendary Central Texas barbecue joint. Or his disapproval of a proposed city ordinance that would prohibit Austin residents from parking cars on their front lawns. All written with tongue riveted to cheek.

Kelso has become a fixture at UT games. His photo has run with his column for years, and with his trademark full beard—now well on its way to becoming white—he is one of the most recognizable figures in Austin. Today people were stepping up to him to compliment him on a moving yet unsentimental farewell to Peña he'd written.

"After an Oklahoma game the Longhorns lost," Kelso wrote, "I saw José openly sobbing. A grown man, weeping over a football game. That was José Peña. If they'd won, he'd have been jumping around like he just hit the lottery. . . . He just wanted UT to win the football game. That's all José seemed to care about: UT winning the game, and him being there to see it."

Like Wilson, Peña grew up in Austin, although Peña came of age on the south side of town in a more hardscrabble neighborhood. After graduating from Travis High School as valedictorian, he attended UT at the same time Wilson did. Wilson played french horn and carried a flag in the Showband of the Southwest. Peña was a cheerleader, becoming head cheerleader in the early '70s. They seemed destined to become longtime friends.

Following college, Peña went to grad school at Stanford before settling in at a job with Southwestern Bell in Dallas. Like Wilson, he never married. Well, maybe that's not quite right. Maybe he wed himself to the same bride Wilson had: UT sports, particularly football and baseball. Peña in the stands waving a huge Lone Star flag was for a lot of years as much a part of Texas home games as Bevo, UT's familiar longhorn steer mascot, pawing the patch of Astroturf he stands on during the games. Peña burned up a lot of miles on Interstate 35 between Dallas and Austin to make sure he was in place for the kickoff or opening pitch.

Stories about Peña are as legion as the stories about the Wild Bunch itself. For instance, Peña was on the sidelines in 1969 during the famed Texas-Arkansas game ("The Big Shootout"—with President Nixon in attendance and the focus of the college football world on Fayetteville, the game ranks up there with the 1971 OU-Nebraska matchup as the best college football contests of the twentieth century) that more or less decided the national championship that year, although he spent part of the game on the turf, flattened and knocked cold by an errant Hook 'Em, Horns flashed by a fellow cheerleader.

Tell that story at most gatherings of diehard middle-aged UT fans, and you'll hear a dozen more to match it. That's how well Peña was known.

Not surprisingly, the high point of each football season for Peña came when the Longhorns traveled to Dallas to play OU. The door was open for Peña's friends to sleep over while they were in town for the game. His house was small, with a single bathroom, and it saw the business end of a broom about as often as the sun rises in the west, but it would be bedecked with burnt orange streamers for the weekend, and staying there was an experience you could carry for a lifetime. Take that solitary bathroom, for instance: For some reason a wall in the shower had a hole that opened to the bright sunlight outside. Peña addressed the problem by covering the hole with a shower curtain.

And so his shower had two curtains: One to keep the water off the floor, one to keep the water off the grass outside. "There might be thirty or thirty-five guys staying there for the game," Kelso told me. "And one bathroom. With this one little radio in there, always tuned to some country station."

On the Saturday night following the duel in the Cotton Bowl, hundreds of Longhorn faithful would make a pilgrimage to Peña's house and cram themselves into his postage-stamp backyard for chips and dip and beer and the inevitable, "It's ten-thirty!" "And OU STILL sucks!"

Wilson told about going to see Peña as he lay dying in the ICU of a Dallas hospital. Wilson and other Wild Bunchers gathered around his bed and quietly sang, "The Eyes of Texas." When the heart monitor flat-lined, someone whispered, "It's eleven-twenty." "And OU STILL sucks." The call and response went out again a few days later following Peña's rosary. The next day, a couple of hundred people gathered at St. Ignatius in South Austin for the funeral mass, all of them wearing either Hawaiian shirts or burnt orange Longhorn gear—at Peña's family's request. At least once a year, Peña would show up for a UT home game wearing his three-decades-old head cheerleader's uniform. His family buried him in it.

"José wanted to make us smile," Kelso wrote. "I never heard anyone say anything ugly about him."

I was sorry José Peña tripped on to whatever awaits us before I had a chance to meet him.

CHAPTER THREE

Tomato Cans

LIKE A LOT OF FOOTBALL FANS, I find the days approaching September to be a heady time. I catch myself thumbing through the preseason magazines in the newsrack at the 7-Eleven down the highway from my house, even though I know they don't have a history for turning out to be very accurate. I'm no big fan of talk radio, yet I'll start tuning in to the sports talk shows along about mid August. My time in front of the tube watching ESPN goes up. I'll pull over and watch a high school team going through practice.

It's a guilty pleasure. I've bemoaned the excesses of big-time football as much as anyone. And yet I've remained a fan.

So September is special to me.

It's also a letdown for me. At least as far as college football goes.

You can find good pro matchups on the opening weekend; you can find great high school games, if you look, on those early-season Friday nights; but for the most part, the first games of the college season are a yawn. More and more, major college programs like UT and A&M schedule tomato cans for their September games. Nothing on paper looked more like snore city than A&M-McNeese State and UT-New Mexico State. In Austin, that was more or less the case. In College Station, things took a little different turn.

Before the game, McNeese State officials gave R. C. Slocum its

Distinguished Alumni Award. Slocum played tight end at McNeese State, located in Lake Charles, Louisiana, in the mid 1960s and left with five school records. After graduating with a master's degree in 1968, he began coaching at Lake Charles High School, thus beginning the career that would make him one of the best-known college coaches of his time. As a Distinguished Alumnus of McNeese State, he joined ranks with luminaries ranging from the esteemed author Andre Dubus (the late father of the contemporary novelist with the same name) to the founder of a wastewater treatment company.

After bestowing the award, the Division I-AA McNeese State Cowboys turned out not to be nearly as hapless as I'd thought they would be on the Friday before. They managed to *geaux* indeed, at least during the first half of the game. By early in the second quarter, the Cowboys led 16–0, thanks largely to two turnovers by Aggie quarterback Mark Farris, who suffered a hip-pointer injury in the game. In the third quarter, the Cowboys had moved out to a 24–10 lead. Farris, who interrupted his college football career for a few years to play AA baseball as a shortstop in the Pittsburgh Pirates organization, proved himself to be something like Hack Wilson, the old heavy-hitting, weak-fielding Chicago Cub about whom the Wrigley Field fans used to say, "Hack Wilson giveth and Hack Wilson taketh away." If he gaveth to McNeese State in the first half, Farris tooketh away from them in the second, accounting for three touchdowns, including scoring on runs of 11 and 8 yards and on a 16-yard pass to freshman Terrence Murphy. When the game ended, A&M was on top, 38–24. But the scare was enough to diminish the celebration at the Dixie Chicken and other North Gate bars. If the Ags could fall behind 16–0 to a Division 1-AA school, what did that portend for upcoming meetings with the likes of Notre Dame, Kansas State, Colorado, and Texas? *Dallas Morning News* beat writer Al Carter called the game "the most disquieting scare of [Slocum's] A&M career." And that seemed to sum it up about as well as anything. As for Slocum, he said, "I think we learned more from this than if we had had a blowout victory. This can be a positive thing for us."

Well, a win is a win.

What everyone who watched the game learned is that the A&M offense would be suspect this season—just as it had been in recent seasons. The victory went to A&M's defense, which clamped down in the second half and choked McNeese State's comeback attempts.

The McNeese State Cowboys climbed back on their chartered buses and, behind their Louisiana state trooper escorts, returned to Lake Charles with a fat paycheck, exposure to the largest crowd to have ever seen the Cowboys play (70,656), and a lot of stories about what might have been if there had been a way to keep A&M's Wrecking Crew defense from wearing them down in the second half.

★   ★   ★

I heard Mack Brown on the radio prior to the New Mexico State game engaging in the age-old coaching practice of "godding-up" the opponent. By the time he and his radio host had finished discussing the dangers posed by New Mexico's version of the Aggies, you might have believed Eric Crouch and the rest of the Nebraska Cornhuskers had been uprooted from Lincoln and relocated to Las Cruces. I suppose it's part of a cover-your-ass philosophy just in case things go terribly wrong. *You see, I told you we needed to worry about these guys!* (Coaches will always have that day come along, even the best of them, when everything turns to shit. It happened in 2001 to OU *wunderkind* Coach Bob Stoops against an Oklahoma State team that had been just one step above fetid all season long.) And it might be to help keep interest in the game from swirling away like whiskers down a bathroom sink drain.

The New Mexico State Aggies had no game that day at all, with Texas winning 41–7. Mack Brown's ass didn't need covering. What the 82,856 fans in a sold-out Royal-Texas Memorial Stadium stuck around to see primarily was two things. First, would Chris Simms have an outing fitting for a quarterback on his way to winning the Heisman Trophy? Second, how well would Cedric Benson perform as a true freshman in his first Longhorn game?

★ ★ ★

Everything about Simms seemed golden. Literally and figuratively. Members of the Longhorn team had voted him Mr. GQ. His hair was blond and shined. His smile, perfect. His eyes, bright. He was a handsome young man whose face at once reflected the insouciant bearing of a stud athlete and the innocence of a back-country Opie.

In fact, he was no innocent bumpkin but an East Coast boy of some sophistication, growing up in the New Jersey suburb of New York City called Franklin Lakes, the son of a football legend, Super Bowl MVP Phil Simms of the New York Giants. Simms played football under Mike Miello at Ramapo High School, where he was the only player in school history to play in every game for four consecutive seasons. He was 381-640 for an astonishing prep mark of 7,055 yards passing. He scored sixty-three touchdowns against only thirteen interceptions. He led Ramapo to a New Jersey state championship during his junior year and to a 9-2 season his senior year. And as if all that weren't enough, he also started on the Ramapo basketball team.

Surely they had to use trucks to bring him the awards he received after graduation. New Jersey Player of the Year by Associated Press and *USA Today*. *USA Today*'s National Offensive Player of the Year and first-team All-USA selection. Top quarterback on the 1998 *Parade* All-American team. And so forth. So it sent hearts fluttering when he appeared on

ESPN, placed a cap on his head bearing a T on it, and announced that he planned to wear UT orange during his college career.

The problem was, those fluttering hearts were in Tennessee.

Simms told the national audience his intention was to follow another great NFL quarterback's son, Peyton Manning, to the other UT, the one in Knoxville, where he hoped to win a lot of games for the Volunteers. What happened between that TV appearance and signing day is anyone's guess, but Mack Brown apparently put some major recruiting mojo into motion and soon enough Simms was extolling Austin and the UT in Texas to his Jersey homeboys. When it came time to sign his national letter of intent, Simms chose to become a Longhorn.

Signing Simms was an important coup for Brown early in his Texas career. It proved to the Orangebloods that he would be able to romance the best football talent in America. Yet the circumstances surrounding Simms's signing—the verbal commitment to Tennessee, then the decision to attend Texas—left some fans a little cold. It sort of flew in the face of age-old Texas values: *A man stands by his word, by God!* Yet, for the majority of the UT faithful, the signing of Simms merited celebration.

When freshman football players report to UT, it's a family affair. Moms and dads and little brothers and sisters will drive with the recruit to Austin in the family car and spend some time looking at Royal-Texas Memorial Stadium and the Capitol and other sights before saying their tearful goodbyes. A lot of the players come from families in pretty humble circumstances. Even players from more affluent backgrounds aren't likely to make the kind of appearance that Simms did when he reported as a freshman. He and his mother stayed at Austin's toniest hotel, the Four Seasons, downtown on the shores of Town Lake. The story goes that Chris's mom asked the hotel staff if the Four Seasons could provide transportation to the university. No problem. The next day Chris Simms showed up to report as a freshman in the back of a stretch limousine. From that point onward, he became known by the sobriquet "Limo" to at least some of his detractors.

Never mind *The Sporting News*'s prediction that Simms would win the Heisman in 2001. In Austin, he had had his critics ever since Mack Brown alternated him as starter during 2000. That he even came into the 2001 season as the announced starting quarterback didn't set well in the craws of many an Orangeblood, who felt that their beloved Major Applewhite had been relieved of the starter's job unfairly. Simms trailed Applewhite in eligibility by a year, and frankly, it was hard to understand why Mack Brown and UT offensive coordinator Greg Davis had made the decision they did. Applewhite had come off knee surgery in the off-season and the official word from UT was that Simms had a better spring and a better summer on the practice field. Still, the feeling among most fans I talked to was that Applewhite should have been given a chance to prove himself. Brown announced Simms would be his starter early, perhaps hoping to ease the uncomfortable situation of the year before in which he'd alternated the two.

★　　★　　★

Against New Mexico State, it took Simms until late in the second quarter before he located his game. In the early going, Simms found himself dropped behind the line of scrimmage several times, and his passes were tipped by the New Mexico State defenders—not an auspicious start for a would-be Heisman winner—although the numbers he put up by the end of the game—17 of 33 passing for 182 yards, no interceptions, and two touchdowns—were good. They wouldn't hurt his Heisman chances, but they weren't exactly the kind of numbers to set off enough fireworks to put him at the front of the Heisman pack.

The highlight of the day came with the debut of Cedric Benson in the backfield. For the Orangebloods, Benson's first snap from scrimmage had been awaited with only slightly less anticipation than the second coming of Earl Campbell. Or Jesus. Take your pick. A clasp of heavenly thunder (or maybe it was just applause from the stands) resounded when he first touched the ball. And as time was just about to run out, Benson smashed into the end zone on a three-yard carry for his first Longhorn touchdown. The gates of burnt orange salvation had opened.

Benson was a true freshman, but already he had achieved a level of immortality in Texas football. He had led Midland Lee High School out in the Permian Basin country of West Texas—where the priorities in life just might be high school football, oil, and God, in that order—to three straight state 5A championships. Not to mention a *Parade* magazine national high school championship. All three of those years, he was Texas's 5A offensive player of the year. He had rushed for 8,423 yards during his career, scoring 127 touchdowns—averaging 183 yards and three touchdowns per game. Moreover, he wore his hair in dreadlocks, just like Ricky Williams, the Horns' Heisman Trophy winner in 1998. The Orangebloods saw nothing but good things coming from Cedric Benson.

★　　★　　★

The second week of the season featured another set of apparent tomato cans, the University of Wyoming for A&M, the University of North Carolina for Texas. But the games turned out to be more interesting than expected. A&M drifted off the high plains into Laramie for a Thursday night game televised by ESPN. In the thin air at 7,220 feet, before a crowd of fewer than 19,000 spread out over Wyoming's War Memorial Stadium, and with only four days of rest since rebounding against McNeese State, the Aggies faced a Cowboy team that had gone 1-10 in 2000. By the time the game was finished, the Ags watching on TV back home in College Station must have been thanking their lucky burritos from Freebird's (a beloved North Gate eatery) that their team avoided a Rocky Mountain disaster. It was a good thing for them that Mark Farris posted offensive numbers as high as the Wyoming altitude, completing 30 of 42 passes for 341 yards. Even with that kind of night from their starting quarterback, the Aggies were able to defeat lowly Wyoming only by a score of 28–20.

Farris was the great hope of the Aggie offense. He'd come from Angleton, Texas, a small town hard by the Gulf Coast. The Aggies signed Farris in 1994, but he left school after he received the contract to play baseball with the Pirates organization. He then returned to A&M in 1999 and saw some football action, including an appearance in the Alamo Bowl. In 2000 he claimed the starting QB position, and he went about posting the second-best season passing numbers ever put up by an Aggie quarterback, completing 208 of 347. He threw for more than 200 yards in seven games. His performance in 2000 was good enough to prompt ESPN's Chris Fowler to say, "All in all, A&M has its best passing attack in, well, a long time."

There was little doubt of that. The problem was A&M historically was not a passing school of the likes of a Miami or a Texas (at least the Texas teams of the 1990s). Not even close. You sensed that in his heart of hearts, R. C. Slocum still loved the grind-it-out, three-yards-and-a-cloud-of-dust offense that dominated college football for years. Besides, gritty offense combined with a knock-their-heads-off defense appealed to the traditional Aggie mind-set. But it became apparent with the emergence of Miami in the 1980s that teams would have to be able to light it up offensively if they were to be in the running for the national championship. For a lot of younger Ags, who had grown up sitting in front of the TV and watching pass-happy football played at other colleges, the A&M offense under Slocum was an anachronism. And that was the cause of A&M's increasingly difficult time in beating top-ranked schools. Eking out victories against McNeese State and Wyoming did little to silence the criticism, never mind the numbers that Farris posted.

After the Wyoming game, wide receiver Bethel Johnson was admitted to St. Joseph's Hospital in Bryan for treatment of a bruised spleen. Not your most common football injury. Yet it was indicative of what would be a recurring theme for the Aggies in 2001. It would be a season of banged-up players.

★   ★   ★

The next Saturday, Wilson, Kelso, and I sat in Royal-Texas Memorial Stadium watching the Longhorns struggling offensively in the early part of the game with North Carolina. Simms had zero yards passing in the first quarter. And the boos rained down from the stands on Number 1—Simms—while people shouted for Number 11—Major Applewhite—to put on his helmet and enter the game.

On the bleachers behind me, a dad sat with his grade-school-aged son and patiently explained what was happening on the field. When the boos grew the loudest, the dad said, "Now, that's something that happens at Texas games that Daddy doesn't like. You should never boo your own team." It was the kind of thing I'd heard from my own parents. But the grandstand clangor against Simms indicated that the age of *Leave It to Beaver* values, at least as they pertain to always root-root-rooting for the home team, were long gone. If they were ever *really* around at all.

It was an emotionally charged day anyway. Mack Brown was leading his Longhorns againt the team he'd forsaken when Texas came wooing. Moreover, it was the day when Texas held a memorial cere-

57

mony for Cole Pittman prior to the kickoff. Pittman, a defensive line-man, died in a one-car accident on U.S. 79 outside Easterly, Texas, the previous February. Brown was visibly shaken and shedding tears as he embraced Pittman's parents before the more than 80,000 fans in the stadium. Before the game, burnt orange stickers with Pittman's ini-tials and number (44) circulated by the hundreds through the tail-gaters and were worn on their hats and T-shirts. I even saw a woman in a Tar Heels T-shirt wearing one of the stickers.

As it turned out, Texas shook off its early problems and won the game handily, 44–14, thanks mostly to its defense and special teams play. Nathan Vasher shined as punt returner, scoring on a 44-yard return in the fourth quarter and setting a UT record for punt return yards with 153. "When they said it was a record," Vasher said after the game, "I had to ask someone to make sure they were talking about me. I couldn't believe *I* did that."

Major Applewhite took a knee to end the game with Texas holding a number of points to match Pittman's old jersey number. Inevitably, Texas fans thought some sort of mystical mojo was at work for the score to turn out like that. And maybe it was.

Both Texas and A&M had the next two weeks off. The good news for both teams was that they stood at 2-0. Still, both needed the time to address shortcomings that had appeared in their initial outtings—particularly the Aggies.

Of course, no one suspected the world would turn upside down while they prepared for their next opponents.

CHAPTER FOUR

Good Bull, Bad Bull

A S THE WORLD RECOILED IN SHOCK and horror from the terrorist attacks of September 11, the decision makers in college football found themselves facing a tough conundrum. Should the games go on as planned the next weekend? In the face of a catastrophic series of events that claimed thousands of lives, injured thousands more, caused hundreds of millions of dollars of damage, and sent the nation to war, it almost seemed like an inane question to ask. Yet college football had a difficult time with it—an embarrassingly difficult time with it.

I found myself wondering what would happen at A&M. I knew the school would have a response of some sort, as all colleges would. But I also knew A&M's response would be different. It would have to be. With its enrollment of around 45,000, A&M has all kinds of people representing all stripes of life. But on the whole, it is a conservative university in one of the most conservative regions of America. Certainly no major public university has a greater or more visible connection with the military than A&M. Most of the school's students project the values of George W. Bush Republicanism—and why not? His father's presidential library is located on their campus. God, home, country. They still count on the A&M campus in as big a way as you'll find anywhere this side of Bob Jones University. Just as sure there would be antiwar demonstrations in left-leaning Austin (and there were) when the U.S. began military action in response to the attacks, A&M would come up with a patriotic rejoinder. But no one dreamed it would be on quite the scale that it was.

★　　★　　★

Both UT and A&M now had an especially good reason to be thankful for their off week. Because they weren't scheduled to play on the Saturday after the attacks, they were able to lay low while college football stumbled over the issue of whether it should play its games during what would be a weekend of mourning. Everyone seemed to turn to the weekend following President Kennedy's assassination for the protocol of what was appropriate and what was not. The NFL's decision to play a full schedule (although CBS, which had the NFL television contract at the time, declined to air the games) on the Sunday after the assassination had long been seen as a mistake. The late Pete Rozelle, then the young NFL commissioner, called the decision to play the worst error he made during his long tenure leading the league. At the time, Rozelle had just three years behind him as commissioner and may not have fully consolidated his power; it's long been speculated that some greedy owners who didn't want to be out the expense of refunds bullied him into making the decision.

Major League Baseball, perhaps keeping Rozelle in mind, decided not to play in the days following the September 11 terrorist attacks. The NFL was weighing its decision. But big-time college football— bound up by ticket sales (and its own unpleasant prospect of refunds), television contracts, and a host of other financial commitments, plus, frankly, its own myopia—decided to move ahead with the schedule, leaving it up to the conferences to determine if they wanted to cancel games. The Big East, Atlantic Coast Conference, and the Pac-10 immediately postponed their games. "This will allow for an appropriate period of reflection and respect," said ACC commissioner John Swofford. But football powerhouse conferences like the Big 12, the Southeastern Conference, and the Big Ten, as well as several smaller conferences, apparently had different opinions about the need for reflection and respect and planned to play.

Big 12 commissioner Kevin Weiberg said, "We feel that it is important that we demonstrate that we can move forward with our events. President Bush has encouraged a return to normal activities as an important part of our response to this tragedy, and we want to do our part in the effort."

Frankly it sounded hollow, and the sports columnists had a field day with the kind of sentiment Weiberg expressed. One writer in Kentucky got it about right: The colleges would observe a moment of silence; would chalk red, white, and blue ribbons onto their end zones; and would have some sort of decal on the helmets—all gestures that have been done so many times in so many circumstances that they have become meaningless. With this 10-ccs of civic responsibility out of the way, the games would be played, the commercials on TV would air, the cash would roll in—"a return to normal activities."

A day later, public sentiment forced the colleges to pull the plug. Essentially, the colleges were shamed into acting by pro football commissioner Paul Tagliabue, who announced that the NFL would postpone its upcoming games out of respect for the victims. Tagliabue evoked the memory of Pete Rozelle and basically said the NFL didn't want to make the same mistake twice. So the college leagues that had planned to play reversed themselves. Perhaps not surprisingly, you didn't hear much in the way of mea culpa from the colleges. Instead, Weiberg said, "It became obvious as the day proceeded that the practical and logistical challenges of making this work were going to be impossible to overcome. . . . The basic sentiment of wanting to return to normal competition remains."

So the grandstands and TVs were devoid of college football that weekend. But, perhaps not too surprisingly, the national sport of Texas, high school football, went on as planned. Apparently it would take out-and-out world war to darken those Thursday and Friday night lights. I heard one official involved with making that decision say on the radio that he was proud that financial considerations never entered into the decision.

Meanwhile, students in College Station were busy writing a new chapter for the book of Aggie legends.

★　　★　　★

To understand what happened at the Aggie's next home game, you have to get a handle on that which Aggies will tell you cannot be understood. It's this *thing* they have, for lack of a better term. This *thing* is the outcome of the myriad rituals and legends and traditions that thrive in College Station. It often seems as hard to nail down as quicksilver. It is what prompts A&M detractors to label it a cult stuck off in the East Texas woods. It often seems as complicated and secretive as the rites of the Masons. It is a kind of mojo that Ags feel no need to try to interpret to non-Ags. As I said, they believe it is unexplainable: "From the outside looking in, you can't understand it, and from the inside looking out, you can't explain it." That is the line you get when you start poking around and asking questions. This *thing* is most often called the Spirit of Aggieland. Or just Aggie Spirit. Aggieland is, of course, the campus at College Station, but in a way it also extends to wherever a Former Student might go in life. In this sense, Aggieland now covers virtually the entire globe. And the

Spirit—well, it's practiced with as much fervor by some as any religion. People who have seen it at work are astonished by it—it's what Patton was talking about when he said he could win a war with Aggies. Even Longhorn fans with the most burnt of burnt orange coursing through their veins will grudging admire what it will accomplish.

It may not really be so hard to understand after all. A huge part of it has to do with A&M's military history. All military schools of note (the service academies, the Citadel, VMI) have a lot going in the way of tradition and ritual, all of it designed to encourage future fighters to shed their egos and become part of a unified effort. Single-mindedness toward achieving a goal is essential in any military endeavor. It also has a lot to do with A&M's being relegated for so many decades to an existence as a small, isolated school made up of only male students. The sons and daughters of Texas's best and brightest were heading to Austin to the prestige university in those days, so what did that leave for A&M? The also-rans? The hicks from the sticks? I was talking about the Aggies to a friend who lives on the Gulf Coast, and she, a diehard Longhorn, said, "They want to be like us so bad they can taste it. But they aren't and they never will be." Maybe that was so for a lot of years. It was apparent to everyone who looked at the situation that the smaller, poorly funded A&M wasn't in a league with UT. So how were the Ags supposed to compete on the football field and elsewhere? The Spirit of Aggieland was the answer. Behind it is a belief that the whole is always greater than the sum of the parts—and that whole can achieve phenomenal things. Whenever you start looking at Aggie Spirit, you always see that it emphasizes solidarity in some form or another.

As much as anything, it is e pluribus unum taken to the fullest—one out of many. Observe Kyle Field on game day. The well-choreographed and *loud* yells give the Ags perhaps more of a home-field advantage than anywhere else in college football. Longhorn fans are sedate by comparison.

★　　★　　★

For many students, orientation into the Spirit of Aggieland begins the summer before their first semester at A&M. By the hundreds, they ride A&M buses—some of them unair-conditioned—through the steamy East Texas countryside to a church campground outside Palestine (pronounced *palace-teen*), Texas, to take part in Fish Camp. Actual fishing is not big on the agenda. "Fish" are incoming members of the Corps—and by extension, Fish can mean any freshman at A&M. So it's freshman camp. It began in 1954 when the director of the campus YMCA, Gordon Gay, took a few of the incoming freshmen camping and explained to them the facts of life on a college campus as well as the traditions at A&M.

In the half century since then, Fish Camp has grown to a complicated, student-run affair in which about 4,700 new students (roughly half of an incoming freshman class) take part. Something like 900 upperclassmen serve as Fish Camp counselors. Once in Palestine, the students are divided into six camps, each designated by a color. The camps are then broken down into ten- or twelve-person discussion groups, and the imparting of tradition begins. Other than that, Fish Camp is like a lot of summer camps. There's hokey entertainment provided by the campers. A dance or two. Two-step lessons for those whose backgrounds haven't availed them to the finer points of Western swing. Romance can grow out of Fish Camp, too. My friend Billy Moran was hooked up with the woman he eventually married by Fish Camp organizers who thought they would work well as a team. Sure enough, they did. They're still a team.

When they leave, the Fish take with them the fundamentals of the Spirit. Ask them about "bad bull," and they'll tell you it's anything that doesn't promote the Aggie Spirit. "Good bull" is something that does promote Aggie Spirit. A "Dead Elephant" is any senior during his or her last semester. A "Hole" is a cadet's dorm room. A "Frog" is a cadet who joins the Corps after he or she has started school. A "B.Q." is a member of the Fightin' Aggie Band. And so on. The sign at Fish Camp carries that slogan the Ags like to spout: "From the outside looking in, you can't understand it, and from the inside looking out, you can't explain it." When the freshmen hit the two-lane and roll away from Palestine, they've stepped inside.

★   ★   ★

In mid September, the Aggie chatrooms and message boards on the Internet were busy places. And it didn't take long for the Spirit to get cranked up. By the evening of that dark Tuesday, someone had posted a suggestion: Wouldn't it be great if a "red-white-and-blue-out" of the stadium could be enacted for the upcoming Oklahoma State game on September 22 to make a massive pro-America statement? It was a variation on the "maroon-outs" that had been occurring at Kyle Field in recent years. In these games, the idea was to sell enough Aggie-colored T-shirts to give all of the stadium, except the visitors' section, a look of solid maroon. Solidarity. E pluribus unum.

The Internet suggestion was to show a different kind of unity. Unity expanding beyond Aggieland. Sell enough T-shirts to give the whole of Kyle Field an Old Glory effect. One tier of seats red, one tier of seats white, and one tier of seats blue. At least on the student (east) side.

A group of students belonging to a two-year-old Aggie men's leadership organization called One Army met at a member's house. "We were just sitting around discussing about why we were in the organization," said Josh Rosinski. "And then we started talking about the red-white-and-blue-out suggestion. You know, a kind of *did you hear about that?* conversation. And everyone was saying *yeah, that's awesome, that's awesome.* So we just sat down and said *let's do something.*"

The organizers had their work cut out for them. They met very early the next morning to begin what they said was the hardest part—cutting through the red tape to get approval. There was concern that they might not be able to pull it off, that they might not be able to get the numbers of people to buy T-shirts to create the visual effect they were after. But people on campus loved the idea. "If you can do this, it would be incredible," they heard over and over. And eventually they won the various student leaders over and the organizers won the blessing they needed.

They hooked up with a local merchant, C.C. Creations, which, among other things, was a supplier of T-shirts, caps, polo shirts, and silk screening services to A&M. The students, of course, had no money to purchase the T-shirts for resale to the fans, so C.C. Creations went out on a limb to help cover the costs of the shirts. On the Monday before the game, the shirts went on sale. And as the week progressed, the numbers mounted and mounted until it became evident they were going to do much more than red-white-and-blue-out the student section, that they might well just pull it off for the whole stadium. More businesses kicked in to help, including T-shirt suppliers Creative Illustrations and Screened Images; other area companies helped in other ways. By the time kickoff arrived, the students had sold 68,200 shirts—"we sold everything we could get our hands on." (T-shirt sales continued even after the game, and by the end of the year, around 80,000 had been purchased.) Word of the red-white-and-blue-out reached Stillwater, and the student body president of Oklahoma State called the A&M student body president and asked if they could get involved.

The organizers dedicated the money from the T-shirt sales to relief funds helping the survivors of the September 11 attacks. The Aggie Club in Baytown, Texas (just east of Houston), flew five of the organizers to New York, where they presented a check for $180,000. And where they were staggered by what they saw. And smelled. Maybe the smell—something like the stench of an electrical fire—that hung over the city stuck in their minds the most, a smell so strong they could taste it. As much as meeting Barbara Walters or Dan Rather. Or maybe it was the Lone Star flag they saw flying from a crane, just below an American flag—the Lone Star had been hoisted by Texas Task Force One, in the city to help with the recovery efforts.

Thinking back on how the stadium looked decked out in red, white, and blue, I can't help but think no other college in America could have accomplished this so quickly. It was a testament to the Aggie Spirit. And outstanding bull.

★   ★   ★

Only 14,000 people of the 82,600 who crowded into Kyle Field weren't wearing red, white, and blue. Even the coaches on the side-lines were wearing it. The Ags on the playing field rose to the occasion, downing the Cowboys from Oklahoma State, 21–7, behind an outstanding defensive performance. "That's the best I've seen them play," Mark Farris said about the defenders once the game had concluded. "It seemed like someone was in the backfield every play. They won the game." Farris himself had less than a stellar day, throwing for fewer than a hundred yards. And the Aggies had more injuries.

The Longhorns, ranked fifth in the country, returned to play after the two-week layoff against the University of Houston before only 37,000 fans in rickety Robertson Stadium. In the end, the Longhorns won handily, 53–26, but only after trailing late in the second quarter. After the game, Mack Brown expressed concerns about his lackluster defense. And with good reason. The next week, the Longhorns faced Texas Tech, which featured a pass-oriented offense full of tricks that could cause the Longhorns a lot of havoc if the defense didn't shut it down early.

But both teams were now playing again after the horror followed by the mourning. And that was good bull, too.

CHAPTER FIVE

Bible and God

TEXAS HAS NO SHORTAGE of legendary college football coaches. Some are well known throughout the football world. Others have their reputations limited to within the borders of the Lone Star State.

Take, for instance, one of my favorites, Joe Kerbel.

Joe Kerbel?

Joe Kerbel, a former Marine and one-time assistant for Bud Wilkinson at OU who also had been a successful high school coach in Texas, led the West Texas State Buffaloes in the easily overlooked Panhandle town of Canyon. During the 1960s, Kerbel managed to upset a national football power or two and send some extraordinary talent to the NFL. Kerbel was more than 300 pounds of excitement on the sidelines, and his program—well, let former Buffalo Tom Krempasky describe it: "West Texas was known throughout the land for a bellicose coach and a bunch of guys who may not have been the greatest athletes in the world and whose dipstick didn't touch the oil but who played the game from the inside out and left it on the field after the game."

Exactly. I guess.

As a coach, Kerbel was a hard-ass yet a straight shooter. He had a knack for inspiring less than gifted players to overachieving. And he had a knack for signing extraordinarily gifted players that other schools

didn't want. Moreover, when it came to football talent, Kerbel was color-blind at a time when race still mattered big-time in Texas sports—both UT and A&M were lily-white on the football field, for instance. Not everyone at West Texas was enthused about Kerbel's color blindness. One racist dean, in particular, irked Kerbel. "I told that son of a bitch," Kerbel explained to running back Duane Thomas, who, along with Mercury Morris, was one of his more spectacular players, "I want to win and you can't win with this shit around here." Kerbel was up front about the opposition he was receiving. He told a team meeting once, "If black players will win for us, we're gonna keep recruiting 'em, and no damn dean is gonna tell me what to do. I run this show."

And run it he did.

But he couldn't control the rest of the college. For a while, it continued to hold its annual Old South Day, run by the Kappa Alpha fraternity, which celebrated the days of the Confederacy. One year, the Kappa Alphas hanged an African American man in effigy as part of the "celebration." Finally, as the number of black students grew, West Texas got rid of Old South Day, and Kerbel was glad to see it go.

On the sidelines, Kerbel got so emotionally wrapped up in the game that he sometimes seemed to lose his sense of reason. He fired assistants during the game, only to hire them back at halftime or when the final gun sounded. He once had his own wife escorted by security from the stadium for being a distraction. No one could better motivate a team on game day than he could. One Saturday, the Buffaloes were playing San Diego State when it was coached by offensive genius Don Coryell. After the pregame warm-ups, Kerbel slipped and fell on the ramp. Kerbel was too fat to get up unassisted. At that moment, Coryell walked past and muttered, "You fat son of a bitch. That's what we're going to do to you in the game."

"When Kerbel brought us into the locker room," Duane Thomas wrote in his memoir, "he was practically in tears. 'I was coming down

the ramp,' he said, 'and Coryell saw me fall down and called me a big fat son of a bitch. Men, I want to kill those guys!' Then he turned around and hit the blackboard—Wham! It cracked. Guys were screaming and pounding on their lockers. 'Yeah!' 'Yeah!' " And West Texas went out and stomped San Diego State.

★   ★   ★

Or take Gil Steinke, who led the Texas A&I Javelinas to six small-college national titles. Steinke had a way of finding overlooked talented athletes like Eugene Upshaw in obscure places like Robbstown in South Texas and transforming them into prospects the NFL clamored for. He also took personal responsibility for the sanitation of the rest rooms at the stadium. When Edwin "Bud" Shrake showed up in Kingsville to profile Steinke for *Sports Illustrated*, he found the coach with a jug of Clorox and a brush scrubbing out the toilets. Once, after he'd retired from A&I, Steinke took current University of Washington Coach Rick Neuheisel to see a UT game. Neuheisel later related the story that Steinke couldn't make the traditional Hook 'Em, Horns hand sign because he'd lost a finger in a lawn-mower accident. So he did a one-finger variation. "God bless Gil," Neuheisel said, "but it was more like Hook 'Em, *Horn.*"

Or take Spike Dykes, every sportswriter's dream, who used to say things like, "Oh, we played about like three tons of buzzard puke this afternoon," following a particularly tough outing for his Texas Tech Red Raiders.

★   ★   ★

It always seemed curious to me that the improbably named Dana Xenophon Bible hasn't been more exalted in Texas than he has been.

I asked sportswriter and novelist Dan Jenkins about that once, and he said that Bible came off a little bit on the stuffy side. I'm guessing he didn't talk much about buzzard puke.

Stuffiness aside, Bible was a great coach and, remarkably enough, had a course-changing impact on both the A&M and UT programs. And Nebraska's too, for what it's worth. Born in Jefferson City, Tennessee, in 1891, he was a three-sport athlete at Carson Newman College and the University of North Carolina before he became the football coach at Mississippi College. After brief stints as freshman coach at A&M and temporary head coach at LSU, he returned to A&M as head football coach and athletic director in 1917—he was all of twenty-six years old. Youth aside, he was a coaching fool. His first Aggie squad won all eight of its games and claimed the school's first Southwest Conference title. He took 1918 off to help America and the Allies win what was then optimistically called the War to End All Wars, during which he piloted one of those newfangled flying machines, then came back to A&M in 1919 to lead the Ags to a 10-0 record and another Southwest Conference title. He had another undefeated team in 1927. He compiled a record of 72-19-9, with six Southwest Conference championships, before he departed to coach the Cornhuskers following the 1928 season.

His coaching style was cut right out of Knute Rockne. Build up your players, make them think they could achieve the impossible. He didn't have a Gipper, but in November 1922, playing the Longhorns in Austin, with the score tied 7–7 at the half, he dragged his foot across the visitors' locker room and said, "Men, those who want to go out and be known as members of an A&M team that defeated Texas in Austin, step over the line." With their record at 4-4, the outcome of the Texas game would determine if they had a winning season. The Fightin' Farmers tripped all over themselves to step over the line, then went out and scored seven more points while holding Texas scoreless. A&M went back to College Station with a 14–7 victory and a 5-4 season.

Nothing Bible did at A&M was nearly as significant as a decision he made in January 1922, when he started the tradition of the 12th Man. The Aggies were in Dallas for their first ever bowl game, the Dixie Classic (a precursor to the Cotton Bowl). They faced Centre College of Danville, Kentucky, a Presbyterian college that had upended the flapper-era football world that fall by defeating Harvard, mighty Harvard, which had not lost a game in five years and was the number one team in the country. The defeat of the Crimson by the Praying Colonels often is cited as the biggest sports upset of the twentieth century. The Fightin' Presbyterians and the Fightin' Farmers played a tough game that day. So much so that Aggie E. King Gill received a summons that was totally unexpected. King recalled what happened:

"I had played on the football team but was on the basketball team at that time, and those in charge felt I was more valuable to the basketball team. I was in Dallas, however, and even rode to the stadium in the same taxi with Coach Bible. I was in civilian clothes and was not to be in uniform. Coach Bible asked me to assist in spotting players for the late Jinx Tucker [sports editor of the *Waco News-Tribune*] in the press box. So I was up in the press box helping Jinx when, near the end of the first half, I was called down to the Texas A&M bench. There had been a number of injuries, but it was not until I arrived on the field that I learned that Coach Bible wanted me to put on a football uniform and be ready to play if he needed me. There were no dressing rooms at the stadium in those days. The team had dressed downtown at the hotel and traveled to the stadium in taxicabs. Anyway, I put on the uniform of one of the injured players. We got under the stands and he put on my clothes and I put on his uniform. I was ready to play but never was sent into the game."

A&M downed Centre 22–14.

As far as tradition and the Spirit of Aggieland and a few steel guitar idylls are concerned, it's a good thing Dr. Gill swapped clothes with the injured player underneath the stands and was ready but not actually called onto the field. The e pluribus unum of the Aggies has been known ever since as the 12th Man. All Aggies are ready to go out onto whatever metaphoric playing field to which they are beckoned when the need arises. That's why the entire student section, not to mention a good many of the Former Students, stands throughout each game. Outside Kyle Field, there's a statue of Dr. Gill in his football uniform, ready to go. It gleams in the sunshine just like the statue of Sully up the way.

With a good won-loss record at A&M, the Ags' first bowl appearance, and the 12th Man legend to his credit, Bible notched out a place on the roll of Texas coaching greats. But he wasn't finished.

He left A&M and made Nebraska a football powerhouse. He was 50-15-7 in eight seasons at Nebraska and claimed half a dozen Big Six championships. But the fact is that you can't find a proper chicken-fried steak, bowl of chili, or barbecued brisket in the whole of Nebraska. Or something was missing for him in Nebraska. The story goes that he wanted to return to Texas. And the University of Texas was anxious to have him.

★　　★　　★

Just before midnight on November 29, 1893, an alleged football team of fewer than twenty players boarded a train in Austin for a trip to Fairgrounds Park in Dallas. About a hundred fans accompanied these upstarts on the train, according to Lou Maysel in his thorough accounting of the history of UT football through 1970, *Here Come the Longhorns*. This was so long ago that burnt orange hadn't been invented yet. The fans wore what were then the UT school colors, gold and white. The next day, Thanksgiving Day, the fans in Dallas engaged in an actual yell practice—imagine that, teasips (that all-purpose pejorative Aggies have for Longhorns) practicing yells. Maysel reports their favorite yell was:

> Hullabaloo, hullabaloo,
> 'Ray, 'Ray, 'Ray,
> Hoo-ray, hoo-ray,
> Varsity, varsity, U.T.A.

At Fairgrounds Park, the UT team went up against the Dallas Foot Ball Club, which had not lost a game since about the time the last of the Comanches were exiled to Oklahoma. The sports prognosticators of the day predicted a blowout for the Dallas club, and of course Texas won, 18–16. A lot of guys who bet against the line went out on a spree of sarsaparilla drinking that night, snapping their shirt garters at every woman they met and leaving large tips for every barbershop quartet they heard. And the University of Texas football tradition was born. UT finished the season 4-0, 'Ray, 'Ray, 'Ray.

For the next forty years, Texas was consistently good (you have to look all the way up to 1933 before you find the first losing season), although there seemed to be a steady churn around the program as coaches came and went. But by 1936, the Longhorns were bottom dwellers in the Southwest Conference. To bring stability to the program, Texas looked to Lincoln, Nebraska, and made Bible an earth-shaking offer: a twenty-year contract, the first ten as head coach and athletic director, the last ten solely as athletic director. For this, he would receive a starting salary of $15,000—double what UT President H. Y. Benedict made, triple what the highest paid university professor made. And at a time when most people in America walked around with holes in their shoes, singing "Buddy, Can You Spare a Dime?" Bible had been making $12,000 a year at Nebraska. By comparison, his Texas predecessor, Jack Chevigny, made only $5,000. But Bible always maintained the salary wasn't what brought him to Texas. No, no—it wasn't *that* much different from what he made heading the Cornhuskers' program. It was the opportunity, the challenge.

The Longhorns were terrible his first two seasons, but off the field, Bible had things working. He had divided the state into districts and put members of the Ex-Students Association in charge of recruiting the best players in their districts for Texas. The so-called Bible Plan was thus born.

By 1940, thanks to the recruits the plan brought in, the Horns were back. If you needed proof, you could have just looked at the Thanksgiving matchup with Bible's old team, the Aggies. A&M was at its peak as a football power. The year before, it had claimed its first and only national championship. The Aggies were the favorites to be invited to the Rose Bowl to take on the best of the West Coast, Stanford. All they had to do was beat Texas in Austin and wrap up the Southwest Conference title. It seemed they should be able to do just that. They'd humiliated the Longhorns in College Station the year before, 20–0, on their way to their national crown. But Texas managed to score on four plays in the first fifty-eight seconds of the game, including the "impossible catch" by Noble Doss, then protected the 7–0 lead for the next fifty-nine minutes and two seconds. Goodbye, Pasadena. Hello, Dallas and the Cotton Bowl for the Aggies. A&M Coach Homer Norton told his team, "This is perhaps the bitterest pill you will ever have to swallow, but there's one good thing about it. If you can take what happened to you today as a lesson when you go out into life and don't get cocky and overconfident at some other time, then this defeat might not be as bad as it seems." After saying this,

Dan Jenkins wrote in *I'll Tell You One Thing*, Norton found solitude in a corner and wept. As Norton cried, the Longhorns were dancing with joy.

Between 1940 and when Bible stepped down from the head coach's job, Texas was 53-13-3, with three Southwest Conference titles and three appearances in the Cotton Bowl. His overall coaching record ended up at 192-71-23, a .712 winning percentage, which was good enough to get him inducted into the College Football Hall of Fame and to get his name on several lists of the fifty best college football coaches of all time.

But his big contribution to Texas was bringing stability to a program grown rickety. That and he hired Darrell K. Royal.

★   ★   ★

Just a few years before Bible parted the mountains and the plains to bring St. Darrell to Austin from the University of Washington, George Blanda saw the face of God on the campus of the University of Kentucky. And though Adolph Rupp, Kentucky's head basketball coach, might have thought that he himself was God, the actual Almighty didn't give much of a flip for basketball. He was a football man. God spoke with a Fordyce, Arkansas, accent tempered by stays in Alabama and Maryland and too many Chesterfield cigarettes and a few too many sips of Scotch whiskey. He went by the name of Paul William "Bear" Bryant. Blanda was a sophomore on the Wildcat football team when he saw his new coach in a meeting room that first time and took in that face—a face that Mickey Herskowitz once observed was made for the side of Mount Rushmore. That had to be what God looked like.

After just one year as a head coach in Maryland, Bryant already was widely regarded as the best young college coach in the land when he arrived in Lexington in 1946. Over the next eight years, he would perform a miracle—making Kentucky, a basketball school, into a Southeast Conference football power. He ran up a record of 60-23-5 and took the Wildcats to the Orange, Sugar, and Cotton bowls. And yet an almost Miltonian drama was unfolding on the Kentucky campus as Bryant brought national prestige to the football program. A titanic war of egos broke out between him and Rupp. It was resolved only when Bryant cast himself out of the paradise of Lexington and into the Wilderness.

The Wilderness was College Station. When Mary Harmon, Bryant's wife, first saw the A&M campus, she turned pale and burst out crying. Bryant himself said, "At first glance, Texas A&M looked like a penitentiary. No girls. No glamour. A lifeless community. I was like Mary Harmon. I nearly died when I saw what I was getting into."

Bryant knew he had his work cut out for him from the get-go. Recruiting players to what Bryant said was called "Sing-Sing on the Brazos" would be difficult. Don Meredith, then a blue-chip stud quarterback at Mount Vernon High School in North Texas, wanted more than anything to suit up for Bear Bryant. Well, almost more than anything. "When it came down to the nut-cutting," Bryant said, "it was a matter of selling him on A&M, and I couldn't do it. I flew up to Mount Vernon and he drove me to his house, and the tears came to his eyes. When I saw those tears I knew I'd lost him. He said, 'Coach, if you were anywhere in the world except A&M—anywhere in the *world . . .* ' "

As the romance at Kentucky had worn thin, Bryant had been courted by a number of colleges that could have given him national prominence. But as things worked out, only the A&M job was available when he determined he could no longer stomach things at Kentucky. He arrived at College Station's Easterwood Airport on a small plane on February 8, 1954, still full of doubt. But some of the doubt started to bleed away as soon as he arrived. He'd never had an experience quite like this one:

"There must have been three thousand cadets there, and half of them escorted me to the Memorial Student Center, where they had hotel rooms. I was trying to register, and they were crowding around, and I made several false starts with the pen. The 'address' part threw me. Finally I put down, 'Paul W. Bryant, Texas A&M, College Station, Texas.' The Aggies loved it. They took me over to the Grove outdoor theater where they had their 12th Man yell sessions. Jones Ramsey, the publicity director, coached me on what to do when I faced those Aggies, five thousand of them, all suited up and screaming. I took off my coat and stomped on it. Then I took off my tie and stomped on it. Then as I was walking up to the mike I rolled up my sleeves. It was like voodoo. Those Aggies went crazy. I was awed, I'll tell you. Ten Aggies can yell louder than a hundred of anyone else."

Don Watson, an A&M player in the crowd that night, had the same reaction George Blanda had had in Lexington. "I just saw God!" he shouted.

Gene "Bebes" Stallings, later to become a coaching legend in his own right, was also on the A&M team. As he stood in the crowd, he heard one of his teammates shout, "Bebes, we've been saved!"

Indeed, it must have been something like a revival that night in the Grove. The only light came from the torches the uniformed cadets—no overalls tonight—carried. In the dancing illumination, Bryant performed as capably as any first-rate brush arbor evangelist would have. There always was a little ham in his makeup. He might as well have been Billy Sunday up there on the stage.

"Boys," the Bear growled, "it's time to win some football games." Horns blared. Someone fired a cannon. "I want to tell y'all one thing. We'll win again. We *must* win again."

Bryant knew he had the Ags by the heart. He said later he could have pissed onstage and they would have hollered and cheered.

The Bear cleaned house and kicked asses at A&M. He also ensured that the Old Ags who had courted him made good on the dowry. Jim Dent reports in his bestselling *The Junction Boys* that Bryant was still in his temporary digs at the MSC when he summoned the big money boys who had promised him the moon and three-quarters of the rest of the universe when they hired him at a Dallas hotel a few weeks earlier. Time to pay up. The funds to be used for recruiting came in wads of hundred-dollar bills held together by rubber bands. With the house clean and the asses kicked and the money in hand, Bryant started acquiring a team. He began the process of returning the Aggies to their winning tradition while instituting another legacy that would trouble Aggieland until the 1990s, that of bending and breaking NCAA recruiting rules to get the best players on the college market.

But first he had to deal with the 1954 season. He did not have many players who rated very high on the skills index, to say the least. Mickey Herskowitz, a nineteen-year-old Houston sportswriter at the time, covered that team and called them "the smallest and weakest team Bryant would ever have." So the Bear had to whip them into the best shape possible to get the most he could ratchet out of them. At a time when the coaching consensus was that harder and tougher was the best approach to molding athletes, Bryant was the biggest badass around. (He ran off the trainer at A&M when he arrived, basically for being too scientifically inclined in the way he handled his job. He preferred Smokey Harper, whose treatment for every ache and pain ranged from an aspirin to a hot shower and nowhere beyond. Well, okay, under *really* dire circumstances he might pull out his private pint of I. W. Harper and give a player a hit of that.) Plus Bryant was troubled by self-doubt, which made the badass even badder. He was in his early forties and he was not at all sure his career was ascending when he took the job at College Station; he had "the fear of plowing cheap bottomland in his soul," as one longtime friend put it. And he had that visage that no one had seen since the days when the earth was cooling and a voice that sounded something like a volcano erupting. All that combined to make him as intimidating as hell.

"Around Bryant," Herskowitz wrote years later in *Southern Living*, "even sportswriters dropped some of their sissy habits. One day we sat in his office, both nursing winter colds, both armed with bottles of cough syrup. The Bear twisted the cap off his and guzzled it like soda pop. He stared at me while I fumbled with a spoon and slipped it back into my pocket. I think of that as the day Bear Bryant taught me to drink cough medicine from the bottle."

The Former Students who had recruited him and supplied him with bucks both on and under the table expected results immediately. Bryant couldn't go to his customary six A.M. breakfast without having Old Ags hanging around, slapping him on the back, and bragging about how they were going to win the Southwest Conference and more. "Those doggone wonderful Aggies are unbelievable," Bryant would say. "They make the worst enemies there are. You get two of them together and you get big talking. Just the sweetest, most obnoxious guys."

That summer, with the start of the season closing in, Bryant felt he had to get his team out of College Station, away from all the sweetest, most obnoxious guys. A geology camp A&M had 236 miles to the west in Junction, Texas, seemed like the solution. Bryant decided to take his team there for ten days of summer drills—and more legend was added to the Aggie annals.

Junction, located in the Hill Country, was the kind of place that bragged when it got its streets graveled. The seat of Kimble County, it had a population of just under 1,500 when the Aggies arrived there in the summer of 1954. Then as now it was a community mostly known for being the site of the confluence of the North and South Llano Rivers (hence the name Junction) and for its livestock, wool, mohair, and pecan production. And for its deer hunting. You might say it was just a tad out of the way. And when Bryant took his charges there, Texas was locked in a terrible drought. Visit Junction today and you'll find a pleasant community with plenty of greenery along the rivers. In 1954, it was a desert-like hellhole with cactus and sandspurs as the dominant vegetation. If you don't count rocks as vegetation. The terrific coach Jack Pardee, who was on the Aggie squad then, says, "Junction got a bad rap when we were there in the 1950s. It's really a beautiful place." It's amazing that anyone who was there under Bryant ever came to any aesthetic appreciation of the place.

The Bear worked his players in ways that have become the stuff of legend. Scorched under the heat of a late-summer Texas sun at full blast, the Aggies literally bled on the gravel of the playing field for their new coach. Many fled Junction in the dark of night. It took two buses to haul the team to Junction when the summer practices began; it took only one to take the twenty-seven survivors back. Bryant said, "When you're teaching a boy to work for the first time in his life and teaching him to sacrifice and suck up his guts when he's behind, which are lessons he has to learn sooner or later, you are going to find boys not willing to pay the price. It's always sad, really, because if a kid quits, I've got to feel I've failed—not him or his daddy or anyone else but me."

Nevertheless, those feelings didn't stop him from running off players he determined were no more than soft fat-asses just taking up turf, including Fred Broussard, who had been an all–Southwest Conference center. Then putting the ones left over through such hell many of them invited themselves to leave. The twenty-seven players he had remaining were *his* players, by God, with no particular loyalties to the Old Ags, only loyalties to the Bear.

They started the '54 season against Texas Tech and prompted got their asses handed to them. The same thing happened week after week, except when the Aggies traveled to Athens to play the University of Georgia, where they picked up their sole victory of the year. One to nine—it was the only losing season of Bear Bryant's long career, yet it was the season that meant more to him than any other. He loved those Junction Boys who walked through hell with him.

His method worked, though, over the long run. The next year, the Ags were 7-2-1. And the year after that, they handed the Longhorns their first defeat (34–21) by an Aggie team in Austin since Memorial Stadium was opened in 1924 (before then, the Longhorns played at Clark Field); the last time A&M won in Austin was when D. X. Bible's team upended Texas in 1922. In the locker room celebration that followed, the team threw their coach into the shower, then retreated to Scholz Garden, which was overrun with cadets on that particular Thanksgiving evening. The Aggie band showed up and soon the Aggies were guzzling Lone Stars and swaying to "Saw Varsity's Horns Off." Bryant, meanwhile, missed his ride and had to walk from the stadium to the Driskill Hotel, where the team was staying, while soaking wet.

A&M finished 1956 at 9-0-1 and claimed the school's first Southwest Conference title in fifteen years, although the Aggies would not be eligible for the Cotton Bowl (or any other bowl) because of NCAA sanctions imposed on A&M for recruiting violations. In Bryant's last year at College Station, the Aggies were 8-3 and got a Gator Bowl berth—the first time they had gone bowling since 1950. Then he was gone . . . called back home to his alma mater, Alabama, where he never again had to fear that he was plowing the cheap bottomland in his soul.

CHAPTER SIX

Comeuppance

Aggies do not lie, cheat, or steal,
nor do they tolerate those who do.
—THE AGGIE CODE OF HONOR

THE BEAR WAS ON MY MIND when I drove to College Station the last Saturday in September to watch the Fightin' Farmers play the Fightin' Irish of Notre Dame. Not that I was making any connections between Touchdown Jesus and God. I wasn't. No, I was thinking about John David Crow, as much as anything. Of all the recruits Bryant brought to College Station, Crow was the most important. It seemed like half the big-time college programs in America camped out around his Louisiana home during his senior year in high school to nab him. Bryant was the victor. But in those loose days of recruiting, before the national letter of intent rule came into effect, Crow signed letters to several schools pledging his services. He was free to head off to another school at any time until he was actually enrolled in the college of his choice, which in those days took place sometime in early September. While the Bear had his boys in Junction, thrashing the ever-loving out of them, he left the still-unenrolled Crow behind in College Station. He also left behind a few watchdogs with instructions to do the Paul Revere thing if they witnessed anything resembling bag-packing going on in Crow's apartment.

But Crow stayed and Bryant turned him into a Heisman Trophy winner in 1957. Crow was Bryant's slug of Scotch as a player—a bruising, punishing runner. He gained only 562 yards from the line of scrimmage that season, which one sportswriter suggested to Bryant seemed a little shy for a Heisman winner. "That don't count all the people he knocked down," the Bear replied.

In my mind, Crow epitomized those everybody's all-American kind of players from the years following World War II. Crow and Doak Walker from SMU and Billy Vessels from Oklahoma and Paul Hornung of Notre Dame and Billy Cannon from LSU. Their names figured into some of my earliest sports hero worship, based entirely on my hearing them mentioned over and over as examples of what college football players should aspire to. Of course I was far too young to see any of them actually play, even on television. But their names were a kind of poetry to me.

At halftime during the Notre Dame game, Crow would have an official public retirement ceremony, marking his departure from employment with the A&M Athletic Department. Crow had a remarkable football career. After bringing glory to A&M as a player, he suited up for eleven seasons with the Cardinals and '49ers, setting several NFL records. Then he coached under the Bear at Alabama before returning to the pros to serve as an assistant for the San Diego Chargers and the Cleveland Browns. He spent five years as head coach and athletic director at Northeast Louisiana University before joining the A&M Athletic Department, where he served as athletic director, associate athletic director, and director of development. I'd heard he'd not worked much in the Koldus Building, which houses the Athletic

Department, during the past few years. The golf course was where he concentrated most of his labor these days. The ceremony this afternoon was to make official a goodbye that already had taken place. I didn't want to miss it.

The game itself had a compelling subplot too. Notre Dame's head coach, Bob Davie, once had been the bright, up-and-coming defensive coordinator at A&M. Davie hungered to be a head coach, but it didn't seem that R. C. Slocum would be going anywhere soon. Davie's coaching mentor, a weathered offensive line specialist named Joe Moore who coached with Davie at Pitt under Jackie Sherrill, had gone to Notre Dame to work with Lou Holtz. Moore had lobbied Holtz to consider hiring Davie to head the Irish defense. Holtz was hesitant, largely because of A&M's reputation at the time for NCAA compliance problems. But eventually Holtz came around. As for Davie, Moore counseled him to move to Notre Dame because there was no better way to step up into a head coach's job at a top program than to be a successful assistant in South Bend. So Davie became the defensive coordinator for the Irish. When Holtz stepped down at Notre Dame, Davie took his place as head coach.

I suppose leaving A&M for the same job at Notre Dame had a certain amount of bad bull to it. What Davie did to Moore certainly flew in the face of the fundamentals of Aggie Spirit. Shortly after taking the head coach's job, Davie fired Moore. "At your age," Davie said, "I can't count on you for five more years. I need somebody younger." Later, Davie met with the Notre Dame offensive linemen and told them Coach Moore had decided to retire, Richard Lieberman, Moore's attorney, reports in his account of the affair, *Personal Foul*.

"On Monday morning you fire me," Moore growled at Davie a couple of days later, as reported in *Personal Foul*. "Then on Monday afternoon you meet with my offensive linemen and tell them that I retired or resigned."

"I did it for your benefit," Davie replied.

"My benefit! You didn't do it for my benefit, you did it for your benefit! You were afraid to tell them you fired me. You were afraid you wouldn't look good."

"What do you want me to do?"

"All I want is the truth, no more. Just the truth. I am not retiring. I don't have any money. How am I going to retire? I have to work. And I promised those kids I wouldn't leave them, and then you go ahead and tell them that I retired. I want you to tell the truth! Just tell the truth!"

According to Lieberman, Davie stood up and calmly told his longtime friend and advocate, "Fuck you," then walked out of the room.

Moore then did the unthinkable. He sued Notre Dame—good ol' Notre Dame of Rockne, the Gipper, Hornung, and Joe Montana; Notre Dame, supposedly the epitome of all that was wholesome and ethical about college football—for age discrimination. And won. The embarrassing trial went on as Davie floundered as coach of the Irish; as his Irish failed to meet the number of victories expected by the win-crazy Notre Dame fans, his character came into question when it was revealed he'd actually had a criminal fraud indictment (later dropped) when he was part of the University of Arizona coaching staff. Davie might well have not even had the opportunity to be on the sidelines in 2001 had he not had a nearly miraculous season in 2000, turning things around for a 9-3 record. He received a new contract after that year, but the noose was already around his neck again as his team traveled to College Station: The Fighting Irish had yet to win this season, and Davie's floundering seemed to have turned to foundering.

None of this put Davie in very good stead in the hearts and minds of the Ags. They sure as hell didn't want to see any Irish eyes smiling at the end of the day.

★　　★　　★

I swung up to Taylor and stopped by Louie Mueller's on my way to College Station. The venerable barbecue paradise stayed pretty constant from year to year. About the only differences that had taken place over the last ten or twelve years were an expanded dining area and an upgrade of the old television to a color model. Several generations of business cards along with copies of magazine accolades for the place coat the walls and grow dingy with age and wood smoke. In fact, everything appears to be a little sooty at Louie Mueller's. It's a storefront building, yet Louie Mueller's seems pretty cavernous inside—and, in fact, the Taylor High School Ducks basketball team used to play its games here.

I got there about eleven-twenty in the morning, and Mueller's already was busy. I took my place in line and looked around at the other customers. I was the only person not wearing school colors. The loyalties were split right down the middle, half UT burnt orange (the Longhorns were preparing to play Texas Tech later in the day) and half Aggie maroon. I accepted my complimentary sample of brisket. After tasting it, who could say no to more? I ordered a half pound of brisket cut on the lean side with Mueller's remarkable sausage and beans and coleslaw and pickles and onions and jalapeños and several slices of white bread and a sweating bottle of Shiner Bock. And I do believe I heard the cardiologists moan in unison at the Scott & White Clinic up the highway.

I tarried a little too long at Louis Mueller's watching Oklahoma playing Kansas State on TV. In the early part of the game, OU seemed to have lost little of its championship season form, and that would mean trouble for Texas the next week in Dallas. The Texas fans around me seemed concerned as they put away their brisket. Finally I left and headed on to College Station.

Because I'd stayed in Taylor longer than I'd planned, my regular parking spots were all taken by the time I got to College Station. I ended up parking in a desolate, dusty lot that might have once been the city dump. I paid ten dollars for the privilege of doing so.

★   ★   ★

The A&M campus essentially closes down on game days. Wally Groff, the A&M athletic director, told me the school sold 30,000 student tickets for 2001, probably more student tickets than any other college or university. That means that close to 70 percent of A&M's 45,000 students crowd into the east side of the stadium for each home game. In turn, that means not many students are left to do much of anything on campus away from the stadium. At Texas, on the other hand, the proportion of tickets reserved for students had dwindled over the years. When Scott Wilson went to UT in the 1960s, football games were much more of a student event. But the demand for tickets grew and grew in Austin, and the demand was coming from people willing to shell out significant amounts of dollars to get season tickets. As a result, students became less and less a part of the makeup of the game day crowd. In fact, some Longhorn alumni complained during the 1990s that they were losing out on game seats to high-tech immigrants from out of state with deep pockets who wanted to be part of the UT football scene, never mind that they'd never set foot in a classroom on the Forty Acres, as the Texas campus is known.

★   ★   ★

Security was supposed to be tighter now at the games in the wake of the terrorist attacks, but I didn't really notice that it took much longer to get into the game. I always get a little confused by the system of ramps at Kyle Field, and after stopping to buy a bottle of water, I followed a passel of shirtless boys who looked as if they hadn't missed too many Quarter Pounder with Cheeses in their lives (with double orders of fries). I don't know if they were all related, but I'd never seen guys with so much hair on their backs. Onto their matted pelts had been painted the maroon A&M emblem, and not a great lot of artistic attention to detail had gone into the painting. They looked pretty damned primitive. If I'd been one of Bob Davie's Fighting Irish, I would have been frightened running into these painted Neanderthals. And they weren't even on the team. I trailed them up the system of ramps, it never occurring to me to make the logical assumption that they would be going to the student section until it was too late. Well, duh. When I got to the top, I realized I had to go all the way back down to the bottom, then back up *another* set of ramps to get to my seat. I felt like the brunt of my own Aggie joke.

That day, I was sitting in the Bernard C. Richardson Zone, most often simply called The Zone. The Zone was just two years old, and it was a peculiar place to watch a game. This addition to Kyle Field contained thousands of seats and shot steeply upward from just beyond the north end zone. A&M's architects had designed The Zone with the idea of keeping the fans sitting there as close to the action as possible. It also was widely believed that the engineers who planned it had a mandate to come up with a design that also would help increase the volume of crowd noise on the playing field, thus even further amplifying the already deafening noise made by all those Ags humping it. Whatever, The Zone was tall and narrow and I never could sit there without having the eerie feeling that at any instant I might pitch forward and plummet a hundred feet or so to my death on the turf behind the goalpost. That fear had been intensified that fall after I read about a Chiefs fan in Kansas City who bent over to pick up his drink and fell out of the third tier of Arrowhead Stadium, landing in the crowd two tiers below him, surviving with relatively minor injuries. The Zone was particularly frightening whenever the Fightin' Farmers linked arms and legs to saw off Varsity's horns after singing "The Aggie War Hymm." The Zone, like the rest of the stadium, literally swayed along with the Aggies. But elsewhere in Kyle Field, you at least felt attached to *something*. Up there in higher levels of The Zone, so far up that jet contrails sometimes blocked your view of the field, you sensed that you had nothing to hold on to during the swaying. It was almost as if you were dangling beneath a helicopter rather than standing on anything firm. I never had vertigo until I sat in The Zone.

The creation of The Zone made Kyle Field the largest football stadium in Texas. It gave the Aggies bragging rights, made their games a lot more profitable, and slapped their traditions upside the head. Tradition is an awesome and powerful thing, but it, like almost everything, always falters when challenged by money.

If you watch *We've Never Been Licked* on video, you get a good look at Kyle Field as it was intended to be. A single tier in a horseshoe formation, with the open end of the horseshoe at the south end zone. The scoreboard sat in the open end. And the opposite end of the stadium was an arch that ran under the north end zone seats and opened onto the grass beyond Kyle Field. It was here that the Aggies solemnly buried their Reveilles when they died. They were buried in such a way that they could "look" from their graves through the arch and see the scoreboard at the other end of the field. If The Zone were to be built, the dogs would have to be disturbed from their endless rest to make way for the project. I'm not sure how much deliberation went on about it, but disturbed they were. The arch disappeared as well with the construction of The Zone. When the dogs were buried in their new graves, there was no way they could see the south end zone scoreboard anymore. So a tiny scoreboard went up on the outside of The Zone for the benefit of the dogs in their eternal slumber.

By the time I wormed my way through the crowd (87,206 of us were wedged into Kyle Field, a record number to see a football game in Texas) to my assigned bleacher, I could see from the aisle that my seat had been taken. Well, not exactly taken. A woman had the seat next to mine on the left and she was sitting on her number all right, but she was a woman that my old high school buddy the Atomic Mole would have described as being "two ax handles wide." And her, uh, *spread* had completely encompassed my number as well. I stepped over people until I got to her and said, "Uh, I'm supposed to be there," timidly pointing in the direction of where I assumed my number to be.

"I don't care," she said with a tone that betrayed too many double shifts working the drive-thru at a Dairy Queen. "They didn't make these big enough for people."

"Well, I—"

"I'm not moving, no matter what you say. We paid to be here." She turned her attention away from me and to the double order of nachos on her lap.

"Okay," I said.

Fortunately, a young couple on the bleacher rearranged themselves to make a small gap for me to slip into. I guessed the couple was in their mid-twenties, and she wound up sitting on his lap for almost the entire game. People in love in their mid-twenties will do that sort of thing. Thank God.

As I settled in, I remembered reading a newspaper story about some researchers in the Aggie agriculture section who had come up with a maroon carrot. It was an occasion for celebration in some parts, because carrots in their normal state are the dreaded orange of UT. Now I noticed that the corn chips in the nachos were not your standard yellowish variety; they were Aggie maroon and white. The top-ping—a glop of cheese-flavored processed food product goop standard to all stadium nachos—was its normal yellow. I wondered if it too would be turned maroon at some point in the near future; maybe those same researchers who came up with the maroon carrot could find a way to work some hoodoo on the topping.

As the game progressed, I never once heard anyone from the crowd shout anything using the word Aggie. At least in my section, it was all, "Let's go, Army!" and "Tear 'em up, Farmers!" In fact, three farmers sat in front of me. No mistaking them. I knew these sorts of folks. Hell, they might have been relatives of mine. Each weighed enough to have been a professional wrestler. Huge shoulders, tree-stump-thick necks with deep creases burned into them by the sun. They somehow had stretched maroon T-shirts over their thick torsos. When the breeze was just right, I'd catch an odor lifting off them suggesting they'd spent the morning hauling hay before showing up at the stadium for kickoff.

Bob Davie had his Irish run the Wishbone offense—the formation designed by Emory Bellard when he was one of Darrell Royal's assistants at Texas—so nostalgia reigned supreme for me for about thirty seconds or so when I thought about the old run-oriented Southwest Conference and how they and Darrell claimed their last two national titles running the Wishbone. The Aggie Wrecking Crew broke it immediately, though, and suddenly I was back in century 21. *Dallas Morning News* beat writer Al Carter called the game the most complete performance by the Ags since they upset Nebraska in 1998. They completely stymied the Irish offense, and for the first time in the season, the offense looked lively. Derek Farmer, a 190-pound freshman running back from Tyler (the same town that produced Earl Campbell), had 100 yards on twenty carries, and the fans were as delighted by that as they were by his last name. Mark Farris was 14 of

26 passing for 155 yards. Meanwhile, the Wrecking Crew held the Irish to a total of 191 yards and racked up six sacks and three interceptions. When the carnage was over, the Ags were on top, 24–3.

Kyle Field is simply one of the most difficult home fields in America. When the opponents have the ball, the sound is something akin to what you'd hear sitting inside an accelerating jet engine. Plus there are all these wild Aggies going through complicated gesticulations in unison in the stands. It has to be as distracting as hell. In one lull in the sound as the woeful Irish offense slogged off the field, one of the famers in front of me boomed, "Hey, Notre Dame! You need a better coach!" Bob Davie was bent over studying something on the ground when the farmer said it, and of course he couldn't have heard it. But a lot of the fans in The Zone did and cheered the sentiment. I guess the Ags gave him the comeuppance a lot of them thought he deserved.

By the end of the season, he would have one thing in common with tens of thousands of high-tech workers over in Austin. He would be out on the street, floating his resume.

★　　★　　★

At most football stadiums in America, halftime is when you get up, stretch your legs, head to the snack bar for a Coke and a dog, and generally recover from the previous thirty minutes of football—or you rush madly to an exit, get a pass, hurry to a place where you can down a couple of cold ones, then sprint back to your seat. But at Kyle Field, the fans mostly stay put at the half so they can watch the Fightin' Aggie Band—in my opinion, one of the true treasures of Americana. So I stayed. How could I miss any band that *still*, after so many years have passed since Vietnam, performs "The Ballad of the Green Berets"? There's a beer joint in Austin that keeps the original recording of "The Ballad of the Green Berets" on its jukebox as a kind of ironic joke, but in Aggieland, it's still taken seriously. You have to admire the Aggie tradition of sticking by your guns even when your guns are seriously out of fashion.

With 425 members, the band is the largest collegiate band in America, with all of them belonging to the Corps of Cadets. It actually is composed of two smaller bands, the Infantry and Artillery Bands, and they are the two largest units in the Corps. Members live together in their own residence hall as well as dine together. For decades, it was a matter of pride at A&M that it offered no music major: Students who participated in the Aggie Band and other music programs did so purely out of love for music and love for the university. In the last year or so, A&M has started offering a degree in music—"We found an extra piano or two and decided we might as well offer a major," one Aggie told me—but few future band members will likely pursue that degree. Instead, they put in two hours of rehearsal five days a week, beginning at seven in the morning, to be part of a great tradition as much as anything, although they do receive a single academic credit each semester for their efforts. "It puts a pretty good learning curve on the kids," band director Colonel Ray Toler told me. "By the way, our grades in the band are the best in the Corps, and I'm very proud of that."

The band is extremely impressive as it takes the field, led by the twelve seniors who compose the bugle rank, their strides magnified by the distinctive Corps boots that they wear. The men march military style, of course, which means six strides for every five yards instead of what's become the standard eight-for-five practiced by most marching bands. The longer steps look like parts moving in a finely tuned machine from the distance. And the sound is jarring but great. There are forty-eight sousaphones (marching tubas) in the Aggie Band, and that puts a tremendous bass line under the music. The formations are geometric and precise. They are carefully devised by Toler and the drum majors on paper with diamond-shaped grids before being put into practice on the field adjacent to the band hall. And they aren't simple: "Some of the band's maneuvers are so complex that a computer says they can't be done because they require two people to be in the same place at the same time," is an adage the band likes to publicize, though that probably says more about the quality of the software running on the computer than about the band's maneuvers. Nevertheless, what the cadets in the band do is very difficult and they do it very well. I love to watch them.

★   ★   ★

The retirement ceremony for John David Crow was short and sweet. As he stood on the field, his white hair blowing in the breeze, clips of his glory days with A&M and in the NFL played on the JumboTron in the south end zone.

"Who's that?" asked the young woman sitting on the lap of the young man next to me.

"Oh, it's just some guy who used to work for the Athletic Department," the young man replied. Talk about feeling old.

CHAPTER SEVEN

Day of the Locust

SOMETIMES FOOTBALL AND LIFE AND DEATH get wrapped up with each other in ways that you never expect. As Texas prepared to travel to Dallas to play OU in one of the most storied rivalries of all college football, I found myself in Oklahoma for the funeral of my grandmother, with whom I'd been so close that she was almost like a second mother to me. I saw relatives I'd not seen in years and visited the haunts of my boyhood, and I flew home to Austin an emotionally wrung-out wreck. Then I immediately drove north to witness the big shootout between the Longhorns and Sooners in the Cotton Bowl at the State Fair of Texas.

The OU game had returned to marquee status. And that was a good thing. Texas simply was not "Texas" through much of the 1980s. And Oklahoma—well, in the years after Barry Switzer was forced to step down, it had almost slipped off the radar screen altogether, as far as national football prominence was concerned. The Sooners under Gary Gibbs were never really bad, but they were never really good, either. They ranged from mediocre to pretty good. Gibbs couldn't beat Texas or Nebraska the way OU fans expected and he was gone. Next came the disastrous hiring of one of Bear Bryant's proteges, Howard Schnellenberger, under whom the Sooners imploded. He was around for a season before being shown the door. Then there was

John Blake, whose teams struggled on the field even though, as it turned out, he was recruiting some very good if unheralded talent. After that, Oklahoma hired Bob Stoops from Steve Spurrier's Florida staff. Stoops, aided by an extraordinarily talented corps of assistant coaches he put together, proved to be the rainmaker. In just one season, the Sooners became competitive again. After two seasons, they were a dominant power once more. Unbelievable. I remember walking on Parrington Oval on the OU campus with President David Lyle Boren just after Stoops was hired. "We have the right man now," Boren said gleefully. Stoops proved him right.

No place in America has more demanding fans with greater (and sometimes entirely unrealistic) expectations than the University of Texas. It's been that case for years. Coach Dave Allerdice, with a 33-7 record, quit the Texas job because fan grumbling was too harsh. Ed Price, leading the Longhorns to a 1-9 season in 1956, had the opportunity to see himself hanged in effigy not once but three times; UT President Logan Wilson was also hanged in effigy that year, but only once. After viewing the three strung-up dummies of Price, Wilson remarked, "I guess the only job more demanding than the president is the football coach." Even Price's successor, the legendary Darrell Royal, heard calls for his firing by regent and powerbroker Frank Erwin just four years after Royal brought Texas its first-ever national championship. The reason for Erwin's discontent? Royal committed the crime of having three four-loss seasons in a row.

Stoops's immediate success at OU tended to make the more cantankerous members among an already vociferous UT fan base wonder why Mack Brown hadn't achieved what Stoops had—and sound off about it on the Internet and on sports talk radio. After all, Texas had not slipped nearly as far as Oklahoma had. Brown had some of the best recruiting classes in America to his credit. It strained the memory to recall Oklahoma's last time to claim a top class. And yet

the Sooners were last year's national champions; Texas finished out of
the top ten—again. Moreover, that year, in a chilly Cotton Bowl
under rainy skies, the Sooners handed Texas one of its most humiliat-
ing losses in years. By the time the gun sounded, Oklahoma had
scored 63 points to Texas's 14. The Sooner offense, led by Josh
Heupel (who should have won the Heisman Trophy that year), accumulated an incredible 534 yards while the Sooner defense held Texas
to a mere 157 yards—with a negative 7 yards rushing. More than a
few folks south of the Red River were inspired to compose thought-
ful, helpful e-mails to send to UT President Larry Faulkner and
Athletic Director DeLoss Dodds.

After losing the game in 2000 so badly, the Longhorns and their fans
hungered for revenge in 2001. OU seemed anxious to prove that 2000
was no fluke. Both teams came into Dallas undefeated and ranked at
the top of the polls. It promised to be a whale of a game. And it needed
to be. When both schools were good, it was *the* prestige college football matchup of October. It was a dangerous portal to pass through,
but if you won, good things lay on the horizon. Around a fifth of the
last fifty or so national championships had been claimed by the winner
of the OU-Texas game (or the Texas-OU game, as it is called in
Austin). For undefeated Texas, the road map of the season was clear.
Beat OU. Run the table against the decidedly lesser opponents it
would face before Thanksgiving weekend. Beat A&M in College
Station. Win the Big 12 championship game at Texas Stadium in
Dallas. Then go to Pasadena for the national championship.

★ ★ ★

Texas was ready.

Quarterback whiz Kliff Kingsbury and his Texas Tech teammates
had come into Austin the week before with one of the most potent

and confusing offenses in the nation. Kingsbury completed 40 of 57 passes for 260 yards, but Tech was only able to convert all that offense into one touchdown as Texas showed some impressive variations in its already impressive defense. It shifted from man coverage—its bread and butter so far in the season—to zone with scarcely a yawn. On short yardage, the Horns lined up in a 3-4-4 formation to stuff the Red Raiders. The gold in Chris Simms shined as he threw a school-record ten consecutive completions and he ended the day 21 of 26 for 224 yards, including a 40-yard scoring pass to Roy Williams. Simms also scored two touchdowns on one-yard runs. And when the onslaught was over, Texas was on top, 42–7.

With the running game getting into gear, the offense was beginning to have a national championship look to it. Darrell Royal used to say the OU game was a "knucks-down gut check." Never mind what happened in 2000. I really thought that this year Texas would have the advantage when it came time to turn the knucks down.

★   ★   ★

Fridays before the OU game are impossible as far as traffic on the highways is concerned, unless you get an early start. Long stretches of vehicles on Interstate 35 between Austin and Dallas might move at no faster than twenty-five or thirty miles per hour as more and more cars adorned with some sort of burnt orange markings cram the roadway, much to the chagrin of the eighteen-wheelers hauling NAFTA cargo and the unsuspecting family travelers in their minivans. I drove up Friday morning in order to miss it all.

The Friday night activities before the OU game are the stuff of legend. My old newspaper mentor Rendal Hamby used to tell me to skip the game on Saturday, just show up on Commerce Street in downtown Dallas on Friday night—Commerce Street was the real show. He advised wearing neutral colors—maybe blue and green. If you happened onto a party where people were decked out in burnt orange, flash the Hook 'Em, Horns sign and help yourself to drinks. If you went to one where crimson and cream were the colors, turn the Hook 'Em, Horns sign upside down and help yourself to drinks. He also described it as being a lot like Sodom and Gomorrah, only more fun. You judged how successful an OU weekend was by the number of Friday night arrests reported by the Dallas Police Department. For years, getting thrown in jail for rowdiness on Commerce Street was something of a rite of passage for young men from Texas and Oklahoma. If you hadn't seen the inside of a Dallas jail tank that you shared with a bunch of puking drunks, you just weren't a man.

In the heyday of Commerce Street mayhem, the Dallas police erected barricades to keep the revelers segregated from the innocent. Maybe 50,000 fans would stagger around the intersection of Commerce and Akard near the Baker and Adolphus Hotels. Nineteen sixty-seven seemed to be a peak year for downtown debauchery. Gary Cartwright was there and described it: "Bars were jammed. People stood four-deep at the Akard Liquor Store. Students dangled from hotel windows, lowering six-packs to thirsty bystanders. A naked man in a bathtub rode in on the bed of a pickup truck, and another hawked rolls of Boomer Sooner toilet paper. . . . Several hours before it started raining furniture, Indian Jim Frye and I ducked into the Baker hoping to find two cups of ice. This was before the open-saloon law passed in Texas. Two coeds wearing cutoffs and nothing else jiggled across our sight line, then vanished."

After decades of this, Dallas had enough and banished the Longhorns and the Sooners from Commerce Street. Nowadays, the Friday night celebration takes place within the yuppie-safe confines of the West End and Deep Ellum. I wasn't in much of a mood for revelry, but I headed downtown, parked a safe distance away, and walked to the West End. There was a huge rush of people in the area, but not many of them seemed very interested in tomorrow's football game. Instead they were hurrying to the American Airlines Center, the new arena that was home to the Dallas Stars. Hockey. In Texas. So it's come to this, I was thinking. But it's true. Hockey is a big sport in Dallas these days. Wonder what Bobby Layne would have thought about that. Where have you gone, Doak Walker?

Scott Wilson once borrowed a trumpet and played "Texas Fight" standing in the middle of Commerce on a whim, eliciting a mixture of delight and disdain from the crowd. Hell, everything on Commerce used to be on a whim. But nothing in the West End tonight seemed at all whimsical to me. Everything had the stamp of careful planning by corporate marketers. You'd hear someone call out, "It's ten o'clock." And the Texas fans would reply, "And OU STILL sucks." Just as they do every time they gather. But on this dreary night, it seemed melancholy, strained. But maybe it was just me. Wilson and some of the other Wild Bunch affiliates had gone to a party at a house in the suburbs that night. Now I wished I'd gone with them, even though the first OU game in years without José Peña was probably a drag for them. I wanted to be somewhere where I wouldn't have to look at corporate logos. Last year there was a woman running around the West End wearing nothing except a Lone Star flag, which managed to fall off pretty often. Maybe if I'd stayed around a little longer I would have witnessed some rowdy goings-on along those lines. But I left the West End pretty early.

Except for in the West End and Deep Ellum, the downtown streets were all but deserted. I walked and walked in the darkness, my hands tucked deep in the pockets of my jacket, until I got lost.

★　　★　　★

I ate breakfast at a Denny's, then came back to the hotel to hang around the lobby. Tillman Holloway's dad was there, pleasantly passing the time of day with a woman who had gotten married on the day of the 1964 OU game. Tillman Holloway was a 300-pound offensive guard for the Longhorns who played high school ball at Faith Christian Academy in Basalt, Colorado. Though raised in Colorado, he had to have burnt orange blood—there couldn't have been much question about where he would play his college ball. Both his parents and all four of his grandparents were Longhorns. One grandfather, Bud McFadin, was a two-time All-American and member of the College Football Hall of Fame who played guard at Texas in the late 1940s. I was always amazed at how deep the waters ran around Texas football.

I didn't want to deal with the parking nightmare at Fair Park, so I shared a limo from the hotel. There were three other people in the car, all Sooners. Bill Seay and his wife were from Sapulpa, Oklahoma. Their daughter, Terribeth, taught at a school outside Fort Worth. We started talking and I revealed my Oklahoma roots, and soon enough it was like old-home week.

I knew Sapulpa well. When I traveled with my grandparents, it seemed as if we almost always took Oklahoma 33 to wherever we were going. And that would take us through Sapulpa. God knows why, but I remember it was home to the largest glass factory in the state. I had a job with the Oklahoma state senate when I was fresh out of college, and one of my bosses was Sapulpa's senator, John Young. To hear Senator Young speak on the floor of the senate was an amazing thing. He screamed into his microphone, getting louder and louder until the sound system speakers registered nothing but static. Once, as the legislature battled over money, Young and his allies were accused of being "like Pancho Villa" for dipping into some fund or another. Young responded by pantomiming a horseback ride up his aisle in the senate chamber.

I smiled thinking about Senator Young. Politics had some verve in those days, and Commerce Street before the OU game was a wild and wicked place. I was feeling nostalgic.

★   ★   ★

Football aside, Texans and Oklahomans have repulsed each other for as long as anyone can remember. At least that's true for Texans and Oklahomans with any semblance of roots. About half the people in Texas today seem to have come from someplace like Michigan or California about five minutes ago, and to them Oklahoma is just a place the Interstate runs through. But for people who grew up in either place, it's a cat and dog sort of thing. One of the first jokes I can remember hearing as a kid went like this: *Why does the cold, cold north wind blow so hard in Oklahoma in the winter? Because Texas sucks.* The truth is, Texas and Oklahoma are a lot alike. Both were forged by the Myth of the West. The same economic forces were at work in both places: big oil, cattle, wheat, cotton. The fact is, people in Borger, Texas, probably have a lot more in common with people in Elk City, Oklahoma, than they do with people in Lufkin, Texas. But the old-timers in Borger would never admit it. Lufkin is in by-God Texas. Elk City is in that other place.

Texans are pretty certain that the source for most (if not all) of the guests on *The Jerry Springer Show* is Oklahoma. They see Oklahomans as inbred trailer trash who thump their Bibles, then steal your wallet. Who obsessively watch evangelists on TV when they're not busy doing their sister by the propane tank out back of the trailer. Who handle snakes and quote the Gospel of St. Mark when they're not occupied with using an Okie credit card—a length of rubber hose— to steal gasoline from cars with Texas plates.

Oklahomans are pretty certain that the source for most (if not all) of the guests on *The Jerry Springer Show* is Texas. They see Texans as self-deluded, greedy, arrogant, loud-mouthed bastards who act rich but who can't keep up their payments. Who are so obsessed with money that they consider guys who come up with successful schemes for swindling money from old ladies and orphans as "good bidnessmen." Who sit back in sterile, upscale Bible churches and quote the Gospel of St. Matthew when they're not occupied with using a Texas credit card—leveraged capital—to force mom-and-pop businesses into bankruptcy.

The variables change, but the sentiment has remained solid for a hundred years or more. In the 1930s, Oklahoma Governor Alfalfa Bill Murray, one of the great demagogues of his time, declared war on Texas and dispatched the state militia to seize a disputed bridge over the Red River. No one north of the Red River complained much when he did. Forty years later, Barry Switzer allegedly dispatched spies to Austin to get the lowdown on Darrell Royal's Longhorns. And no one north of the Red River complained much when he did.

Football fueled an already burning fire, turning it white hot every October. And fuel itself was at the heart of why football mattered. Oklahoma and Texas started playing each other when biplanes were the latest high-tech innovation. But the game didn't become exactly what it is now until after World War II, when both Texas and OU stepped up to become national powerhouses. In large part, oilmen provided the funding to allow this to happen. Before the collapse of the domestic oil industry in the 1980s, the most audacious stories came out of Dallas each October. You'd hear about producing oil wells put up as bets on the game. You'd hear about the president of an oil company betting the services of his best geologist.

Winning and losing mattered more than you can imagine. Blair Cherry was a good coach at UT. D. X. Bible's handpicked successor (when Bible ended his coaching responsibilities at the end of ten years to concentrate on being athletic director), Cherry was the first native-born Texan to coach the Longhorns. His teams, featuring players of the likes of Tom Landry and Bobby Layne, never lost to A&M. In his first season, he went 10-1 and bested Alabama in the Sugar Bowl to finish fifth in the nation. In his last season, he was 9-1, suffering a solitary loss to eventual national champs Oklahoma by a single point. The problem was, it was his third loss in a row to the Sooners. When the season was over, Oklahoma was ranked first; Texas third. To read the official version of things, you'd assume that the 32-10-1 Cherry willingly gave up the coach's position after that season, citing his ulcer and his insomnia and the hypercritical nature of the press. In truth, alumni pressure forced him out. "Cherry never forgot or forgave," the great Dallas sports columnist Blackie Sherrod wrote. That one-point difference in Dallas against Oklahoma pulled the plug on his life-support system in Austin. Even a saint can get yanked down if he loses enough times in a row to Oklahoma. Just ask Darrell Royal.

★   ★   ★

Bill Seay played for Bud Wilkinson back in the 1950s, and "he thinks Bud was the greatest man who ever lived," Terribeth Seay is telling me. "And the Texas game is the biggest day of the year for him." Bill is in the backseat and seems to be ignoring our conversation. He has Pick's disease, an ailment with symptoms very much like Alzheimer's. It strikes the frontal and temporal lobes of the brain with a resulting dementia. There is no cure. The Seays have had him treated at the Mayo Clinic, but the disease is progressing; scientists have yet to discover how to even slow it down. The prognosis is dire. Right now the disease is at a stage in which Bill has difficulty walking very far. He seems impatient. He interrupts conversations with comments unrelated to the topic. When we get out of the limo at Fair Park, Terribeth says quietly, "This is the last time we're bringing him to the game. We just can't handle him anymore."

"That's too bad," I say. But it doesn't seem like enough to say. It's a sad thing, Bill's last trip to the State Fair of Texas and the college game of games.

Terribeth has been telling her mother that there's no way Bill can walk all the way to the Cotton Bowl inside Fair Park, and her mother concurs. So Terribeth and I go off to find a place to rent a wheelchair. Fortunately, there are wheelchairs for rent just inside the gate of the fairgrounds. We go through security—it doesn't take very long to get waved down with a metal-detecting wand now, two hours before the game, but later I'll hear about long lines of people stuck at the Fair Park gates, waiting their turn to prove they are unarmed. Then we get Bill's wheelchair and we're set.

We head into one of the most absurd environments in the world. Nathanael West could never dream up anything quite like this. A fifty-two-foot mechanical cowboy—billed as the World's Tallest Cowboy—looms overhead. Moving with eerie, robotlike motions, Big Tex calls out, "Howdy, folks! Welcome to the State Fair of Texas," over and over and over and over, and if it has inspired delight among children at the fair, there's also no telling how many seeds of childhood nightmares have been instilled by the sight. Big Tex's been doing this for fifty years. (Prior to becoming Big Tex, he spent a year in Kerens, Texas, billed as the World's Tallest Santa Claus.) Today he's wearing a patriotic red, white, and blue shirt—size 100 180/181—made up for him by the Dickie work clothes company. He also has on an enormous red, white, and blue ribbon. His jeans have a 284-inch waist and a 185-inch inseam and weigh more than sixty-five pounds. His boots are a size seventy and stand seven feet tall. Big Tex may strike some people as being a little on the bizarre side now, but you should have seen him way back when. Jack Bridges, who created Big Tex's original papier-mâché head, said he took his own face, that of Will Rogers, and that of a rancher named Doc Simmons and abstracted the worst features of each and gave them to Big Tex. The result? A kind of bug-eyed horror that could have been in a bad 1950s monster film. *Frankenstein Meets Shane*. It must really have scared the kids.

In front of Big Tex's boots moves a phalanx of OU fans, all in crimson shirts that say TUCK FEXAS. Up the way, someone calls out the time. The Longhorn fans all shout, "And OU STILL sucks!", while at the same time the Sooner fans scream, "And TEXAS SUCKS!" Everyone trying to outshout everyone else. Meanwhile, Big Tex booms, "Howdy, folks!" This is going to be very weird, I tell myself.

Terribeth meets some OU fans on the way to the booth where you buy tickets to use at beer and food concession stands. As she passes them, she makes a really quick hand sign from her waist. They do the same. Like a gangsta hand sign. I never saw anything like it in all the time I'd lived in Oklahoma, so I assume it's a relatively new innovation. Other Sooners are walking around with their hands high in the air, making the inverted Hook 'Em, Horns sign. Longhorns are walking around with Hook 'Em, Horns right side up.

Hand signs are a fine old football tradition, especially for the colleges that belonged to the old Southwest Conference. Not surprisingly, it started with A&M. At a Yell Practice in 1930 in preparation for a game with TCU, Pinky Downs (Class of 1906) shouted, "What are we going to do to those Horned Frogs? Gig 'Em, Aggies!" Gigging, of course, is a way of hunting frogs in which you basically impale them on spikes attached to a long pole. My own childhood gigging was accomplished using a sort of barbed trident attached to a length of cane about fifteen feet long. To approximate gigging, Pinky threw his fist up in the air with his thumb extended. And the first Southwest Conference hand sign—not to mention A&M's best known slogan, "Gig 'Em, Aggies"—was born. Twenty-five years later, UT cheerleader Harley Clark (who later became a judge of distinction) first used the Hook 'Em, Horns hand sign at a pep rally that, coincidentally, also proceeded a TCU game. It's since gone on to become the most recognizable hand sign in all of college football. Students at SMU, home of the Mustangs, raised their fingers in something approximating pony ears. In the stands at Baylor, fans bent their fingers like bear claws. Out in Lubbock, the Red Raiders made forefinger and thumb pistols for Tech games. At Houston, the Cougars came up with a peculiar sort of claw by taking the Hook 'Em, Horns sign and adding the middle finger—although the addition of the middle finger *really* had a lot more to do with how the Cougars felt about Texas than accurately portraying an actual claw. Across town at Rice, Paul Burka reported in *Texas Monthly* with tongue-in-cheek alarm resounding, the students occasionally started extending a single middle finger that they would tell you with a perfectly straight face stood for "Peck 'Em, Owls"—Burka added that Rice officials never officially sanctioned that hand sign. Right. TCU, the original inspiration for all this, didn't come up with a hand sign of its own until 1980: a bent forefinger and index finger.

★   ★   ★

Terribeth and I get long snakes of drink and food tickets, then head to the Fletcher's Corny Dog stand closest to Big Tex. The corny dogs are as much a State Fair tradition as Big Tex. Fans of the corny dogs are legion. The late Dallas Cowboy Mark Tuinei would order five at a time. Other enthusiasts range from former Cowboys Coach Jimmy Johnson to former Soviet leader Mikhail Gorbachev. The one-time Cowboys unofficial mascot Whistlin' Ray or Crazy Ray (Wilford Ray Jones) perfected his stick-horse riding shtick outside a Fletcher's stand at the fair to drum up business before he took his gig to Texas Stadium. Somehow the OU game just isn't an OU game unless you have a Fletcher's corn dog. I smear mine with mustard and bite into it and instantly feel my cholesterol count jump by forty points.

We stop at a place that sells Shiner Bock, then head off to find where ESPN is broadcasting *GameDay*. We locate the set, but it is empty for the time being. However, a large contingent of OU fans stands by, waiting for one of the hosts, Lee Corso, to come back. The Sooners are irrate with Corso, who, as a player at Florida State, was Burt Reynolds's roommate. They believe he dissed their team all through their championship season and hasn't given OU enough credit this year either. They wait so they can heckle and boo when he returns to the set.

Terribeth and her mom leave to find a rest room. Bill and I are left staring at the empty *GameDay* set. Around us people are screaming about who sucks the worst. I ask Bill a couple of questions about his OU days, but he gets confused as he tries to remember. Then the music starts. It's classic oompah stuff, and the crowd parts to reveal some dancers who look as if they've just blown off the side of an Alp. The announcer tells us they're performing dances from northern Italy, and then someone shouts TEXAS SUCKS! The dancers begin their performance and in the distance I can hear Big Tex: "Howdy, folks!" The Fletcher's corny dog feels like a short length of two-by-four in my belly. How did Tuinei eat five of these things?

Bill wants to see the dancers up close, so I wheel him up front. The Longhorns and the Sooners seem to be about as interested in this per-formance as they would be in reading the collected speeches of George McGovern, so it's not hard for me to find a spot for Bill. After a while, Terribeth and her mom return, and I excuse myself to find a rest room. I enter a giant hall filled with new cars. Longhorns and Sooners are crawling over each other to get a look at the newest Chevy pickups. I get into one of the long lines coming out of the men's room. As I finally—thank God—approach a urinal, a guy in an adjacent line says, "None of you boys have tried the sinks yet?" He is wearing a khaki-colored hat with a turkey feather stuck in one of the ventilation holes, Cuban shades, a khaki workshirt over a TUCK FEXAS crimson T-shirt, baggie jeans, and lace-up work boots. "Hell, I'll be the first." He walks up to a sink, unzips his Wrangler's, and pisses splashily on the porcelain. Guess I won't be washing my hands.

We hit the midway. Terribeth is telling me about her adventures in sponsoring cheerleading in Texas. I don't envy her that. Moms hire hit men over cheerleading conflicts in Texas. More Shiner Bock, then it's time to start making our way to our seats, pushing Bill ahead of us. We swing around the south end of the Cotton Bowl just in time to get caught in the throng waiting for the team buses to arrive.

We maneuver Bill through the crowd slowly, Terribeth whipping out her hand to make the Sooner hand sign at about every sixth step. We get jammed at the road leading to the locker rooms. The buses are here, along with a cadre of Dallas cops on horses. Thousands of people in burnt orange and in crimson T-shirts are screaming violently at each other and shouting hosannahs for their teams. There's honking from the buses, and the cops are blowing whistles. The first two buses squeeze through the crowd slowly. I look up and see a wide-eyed player peering down at the mob from a bus window. Hell, I don't blame him for looking scared. The tension down here on the ground is at such a peak right now that I expect the pitchforks and torches to be broken out at any moment. The buses stop with a loud hissing of air brakes. The yelling is deafening. Terribeth, her mom, and Bill start across the road before the other buses pull in. I start to follow them, but suddenly I'm smashed in the shoulder by the haunch of a horse that looks big enough to be a Clydesdale. The blow knocks me a step backward. "Move it back," a Dallas cop shouts at me from the saddle.

"I'm with that guy in the wheelchair," I say, worried the beast will crush my foot with one of its massive hooves.

The cop looks over at Bill, then back at me. "You better hurry then."

I dart around the horse and catch up with the Seays.

Some people dressed in traditional Japanese attire are playing drums near our gate into the Cotton Bowl. A swarm of Texas cuties moves past, all of them looking good enough to be models, all of them wearing either tight burnt orange leather bell-bottoms or tight burnt orange leather short skirts. Where do these women come from? Bill and his wife head into the stadium to get him situated before the game. Terribeth offers to buy my a beer with some of her tickets for helping out with her dad. We down the beer, then head into a building to find rest rooms. The lines are short here, thank goodness. I leave the rest room and nearly run smack-dab into a young woman in a formal wearing a sash that says Miss Texas Honey. She is standing before a display of an association of Texas honey producers. The image of Miss Texas Honey will be burned into my mind for the rest of the afternoon.

Terribeth and I agree to meet after the game and to share a cab back to the hotel. We then head into the Cotton Bowl to the accompaniment of Japanese drums.

★   ★   ★

The Cotton Bowl is a handsome structure with art deco stylings. To step into it is to feel like you're walking into the very embodiment of football tradition. So many great teams, so many great players, so many great coaches. For decades, the New Year's Day bowl game that shares its name with the stadium ranked with the Rose, Orange, and

Sugar bowls as the major contests of postseason play. Then there are several decades worth of OU games. And, for their first decade of existence, the Dallas Cowboys played here. Here's to you, Don Meredith. When I was a little kid, I used to actually care about the Cowboys and root for them alongside my stepfather in front of the television in our house in Oklahoma. That was such a long time ago. This season, I can't even tell you the names of the starting wide receivers.

Though a chance encounter and some good fortune, I find myself on the Oklahoma sidelines for the game. When you're down low in the Cotton Bowl, you're overwhelmed by how close everything is. Bevo and the Longhorn band are at one end of the field. The Sooner Schooner and the OU band are at the other. OU's RUF/NEKS are a hyperactive spirit group that's been around since 1915 and have been the model for similar groups at other universities. They run around firing off twelve-gauge shotguns and frantically swinging red and white paddles. At the other end, the Texas Cowboys fire off Smokey the Cannon, with its load of two blank ten-gauge shotgun shells. Your ears ring from the blasts. The Sooner band plays "Boomer Sooner" so often (it seems like they play it ten times for every one time that the Showband plays "Texas Fight") that it kind of bores into your brain and you hear it resonating against the back of your skull for hours after you've left the game. Also from the playing field you get a real sense of just how neutral the Cotton Bowl is for the site of this game. Everything north of the 50-yard line is burnt orange. Everything south, crimson and cream. When Texas's fortunes are good, you hear a jet engine howl from the north. When things are reversed, the howl comes from the south. Nearly every important business leader and politician from each state is up there in the stands. And there'll always be a few celebrities. But right now it's just an orange mass on one end, a crimson mass on the other. The tension is unlike anything else I've ever experienced. The OU fans in particular seem agitated, swarming around their end of the Cotton Bowl like angry red ants. When Darrell Royal was the Longhorn coach, he could hear the 30,000 or so Sooners in the Cotton Bowl shout "Sorry bastard!" in unison when he walked on to the field. Back in 1947, the game did come completely unhinged, with a riot ensuing. The referees had to leave Fair Park with a police escort.

★　　★　　★

The day had started out a little cool, and at the two-thirty kickoff, the temperature stood at 61 degrees. But the sky was clear and the sun shone unimpeded into the faces of the people on the east side of the stadium; woe to anyone who forgot sunscreen. There was a steady breeze out of the northeast, which may have led to the dearth of offense.

Things started off well enough for Texas. After Tim Duncan's kickoff rocketed into the end zone, the Longhorns began on their own 20. Chris Simms fired a quick 6-yard pass to Roy Williams, who was quickly smothered by Oklahoma's two outstanding All-Americans, linebacker Rocky Calmus and their own Roy Williams, who played safety. Next, Ivan Williams carried the ball for 3 yards, followed by a 2-yard sneak by Simms. Texas had a first down. It looked like the Horns might be able to move the ball successfully against the vaunted Sooner defense. But then the Texas fortunes took a turn for the worse when Simms threw a pass to B. J. Johnson for a 3-yard loss. A false start penalty two plays later put the Horns farther back into a hole. Then a slant pass from Simms to Roy Williams gained only 7 yards, and it was fourth and 9. Texas had to punt. And even this early in the game, you sensed it was going to be an afternoon of frustration for the burnt orange.

With Nate Hybl directing the OU offense, the Sooners moved the ball from their own 41-yard line to the Texas 43. But their drive stalled there, and they had to punt. After Jeff Ferguson's punt went into the Texas end zone for a touchback, Texas again started on its 20. This time Texas put together a drive that moved all the way to the Texas 45 before Simms threw an interception, which Oklahoma's Andre Woolfolk returned to the Texas 23. Texas was in trouble, but Hybl and the Sooners could not take advantage of the gift from Simms. Tim Duncan's field goal attempt was wide left, and Texas had the ball again. The Longhorns started moving the ball upfield as the first quarter ended. And it was clear what kind of game this was going to be. Texas was going to come out with its regular game plan, perhaps toned down a little for the wind, perhaps a little more conservative than usual because of the vigorous OU defense the Horns faced. Bob Stoops and his staff had devised a game plan that included a conservative offensive approach, with an emphasis on error-free ball. But the keystone was the defensive plan. The Sooners were going to be willing to give up a lot of yardage in the middle of the field, but they would make sure that none of Texas's outstanding corps of receivers ever broke free. Then, when Texas approached the red zone, the defense would tighten up and hold against any scoring surges. Based on how the first quarter went, it looked like the Sooner plan was going to be effective. All OU had to do is figure out a way to put enough points on the scoreboard to win the game.

The game continued to move along in those terms. An injury early in the drive forced Hybl to the sidelines for the rest of the afternoon. Jason White—he of the young-Elvis sideburns—took his place. The game turned even more to OU's favor as White led the Sooners steadily down the field. White proved to be a quarterback out of the Steve Young mold, as adept at running as passing. He carried the ball around the left end for eleven yards to set up OU's first touchdown. With just under six minutes left in the half, the Sooners were on top by seven.

Texas responded by moving the ball from its own 20 to the OU 10, where Simms threw two incomplete passes and Victor Ike gathered only two yards on a rush. Texas had to settle for a field goal with only fourteen seconds remaining in the quarter. The two teams went to the locker room with the score 7–3 in favor of the defending national champions. The OU band already had played "Boomer Sooner" about as many times as Simms had thrown passes.

The Sooner defense continued to stymie the Longhorns. And it was becoming more and more apparent that the gold of Chris Simms was going to fail to shine in another big game. A typical Texas drive went like this: Simms passes to the left sideline to B. J. Johnson for four yards. Ivan Williams rushes over the left guard for no gain. Chris Simms throws for five yards to Sloan Thomas, but Texas is short of the first down. Brian Bradford comes in to punt. Meanwhile White and the Sooner offense began to pile up some first downs if not points, which kept the ball out of the hands of Texas. In the fourth quarter, Texas had its moments. Simms and company took the ball at their 20 and drove to the Oklahoma 34. Then Simms threw a pass that Oklahoma defender intercepted for a touchback. The boos began for Number 1 and the calls for Number 11 grew louder from the Texas side of the Cotton Bowl.

The Sooners ate up nearly half the fourth quarter with their next drive but were forced to punt when they reached Texas's 27. OU stuck Nathan Vasher, who caught the punt, at the Texas 3. With two minutes left in the game, Simms now had the chance to prove himself a hero. He needed to pull a John Elway, run the two-minute drill to perfection, stick the ball into the Sooner end zone, and send the Longhorns back to Austin with a 10–7 victory and the fast track to Pasadena. Simms took the hike, dropped back, and was smashed in the arm by Oklahoma's Roy Williams, undoubtedly the best player in college football, who came flying in on Simms like some sort of superhero. (A photo of Williams's airborne assault on Simms would make the cover of the next week's *Sports Illustrated*.) Simms let the pass go anyway and Oklahoma's Teddy Lehman intercepted and trotted into the end zone.

"I thought that I was going to get a strong side blitz coming off of the edge," Simms said afterward. "They had done it a few times and I was expecting it. We had Roy [Texas's Roy Williams] on Roy [Oklahoma's Roy Williams] matched up and I just didn't throw the ball high enough. I thought they had another safety over the top. I tried to drive the ball in there and didn't get it in."

The victory put OU in control of the Big 12 South title race, leaving Texas with only the slimmest chance of making it to the national championship game in Pasadena. It seemed like it was time for Texas's Roy Williams to reprogram his cell phone so that it no longer read ROSE BOWL.

★　　★　　★

I stand by a tree, waiting for the Seays. The Sooners are delirious leaving the Cotton Bowl. The Longhorns are stiff-jawed, staring straight ahead, ignoring the taunts from the guys in the TUCK FEXAS T-shirts. Finally, the Seays emerge from the stadium, and we set off to find a cab in the gloaming. As we exit the Fair Park gate, I hear Big Tex one last time: "Howdy, folks!"

★　　★　　★

I didn't stay over that night in Dallas. I climbed into my SUV and headed south for the long drive to Austin. I had a bad sunburn. My eyes felt as if they'd been worked over with sandpaper. I had a headache. For a while I listened to a static-filled broadcast out of

Lubbock about Kansas upsetting Texas Tech. Kansas! How embarrassing for the Red Raiders! But then I decided I'd had enough of college football for a day, and I slid a Miles Davis CD into the player and let my mind follow his trumpet to Spain.

With brother Miles and castanets soothing my battered psyche, I thought about my grandmother and her grave in the harsh red soil of Oklahoma. And the tears of relatives I hadn't seen in a decade or more. I thought about Bill Seay coming to Dallas for the last time to see his beloved Sooners play the Longhorns. I hadn't given a flip about Oklahoma football in a very long time. But I can't say I was sorry on this particular Saturday that OU won the game.

CHAPTER EIGHT

Varsity's Horns

WHEN SUNDAY MORNING BROKE, A&M sat with Oklahoma at the top of the Big 12 South. Who would have thought it? But it was a dubious achievement. If Oklahoma got there by an impressive win over one of the best teams in the nation, A&M got there by barely beating one of the worst teams in the Big 12. A&M led by the narrow margin of 16–10 when Baylor got the ball with thirty-four seconds at its own 30-yard line. Quick completions thrown by quarterback Greg Cicero moved the Bears down to the Aggie 40-yard line, with ten seconds showing on the clock. Cicero fired one game-tying Hail Mary only to see it dance off the fingers of a Baylor receiver. With two seconds left, he tried it again, and A&M safety Dawon Gentry came up with the ball. Game over. Bullet avoided. A&M at 5-0 and perfect in conference play. And standing one game above Texas in the Big 12 standings. "By the grace of God," said linebacker Brian Gamble, "we survived." Indeed. To give you an idea of how badly Baylor had fallen since the days of Grant Teaff, consider this: It was the eleventh consecutive victory for the Ags over the Bears. And it was Baylor's twenty-third consecutive loss in the Big 12. That raised a question among a lot of fans: What is Baylor even doing in this league? Wouldn't we have been better off keeping, say, TCU after the dissolution of the

Southwest Conference and the creation of the Big 12 rather than these woeful Bears?

If everyone in Aggieland was impressed with the way the Fightin' Farmers plowed under the Fighting Irish the week before, everyone now was feeling damned skittish about what loomed ahead—a road trip to Boulder to face Colorado.

Meanwhile Austin had become a seething cauldron of bile as the Longhorn fans agonized over the loss to the dreaded Sooners. *Where was Major? Where was Cedric? Yes, Oklahoma has a great defense, but— damn!* You heard the same conversations every place you went to get a sandwich or to buy a beer. *I don't know what Mack is thinking!* Talking to a friend outside a Thundercloud's sub shop in North Austin, I said I thought Brown was just making decisions designed to ensure that the Longhorns would win the game. But my friend, a diehard Orangeblood, was having none of it. He was convinced something else was going on. It was beyond me what that ulterior motive could have been. Basically, coaches live and breathe to do just one thing: win football games. You didn't last very long otherwise. Did that mean I understood why decisions not to play Cedric Benson or Major Applewhite were the best ones to win the OU game? No, I didn't understand. But Mack Brown got paid a hell of a lot of money to make those decisions, and the reason he did was because he was one of the smartest men in all of college football. I thought any rational fan would have looked at it that way, but I didn't hear many rational foot-ball conversations in Austin during the week after the OU game.

Next up for Texas was a road trip to Stillwater to play Oklahoma State. Scott Wilson called to ask if I wanted to ride up with him in the burnt orange Caddy with the longhorns on the front. Looking back, I think it might have been a fun trip to make. But at the time another trip to Oklahoma didn't seem very appealing. I wished him well. And I stayed home.

★   ★   ★

Home.

A couple of miles from where my house sits, the Chisholm Trail cut across Brushy Creek in the days when thousands of longhorns were driven north to satisfy the burgeoning demands for beef and leather from the East Coast. When the drovers hit the creek, they looked for a distinctive round rock that marked a shallow crossing. There they could safely drive the huge herds of longhorn cattle across the water and continue on their way to the railheads in Kansas. A community developed around the round rock and took its name from the stone. Round Rock was sure-enough part of the Wild West for a time. Sam Bass, one of the best-known outlaws of those days, met his end in a shootout on the town streets. Upstream from the round rock, Brushy Creek comes within a half mile of my house. I've read about at least one skirmish between early Anglo settlers and Comanches on the creek's banks. Cowboys, outlaws, longhorns, Comanches, Texas Rangers—all were right here. Probably only a fraction of the passengers in the tens of thousands of cars and trucks that roar up and down Ranch Road 620, the main means of access to the houses and businesses in this area, have a clue about what was here 130 years ago. Now it is suburbia. Housing developments, strip malls, apartment complexes, and chain restaurants. The land of ten thousand minivans, it is predominantly white and predominantly conservative, and it is held in the utmost disdain by people who live in the trendier sections of Austin.

But there was that time when the call of "head 'em up and move 'em out" was a lot more likely to be heard around here than the roar of lawn mowers, although it was just a brief time. The trail lasted only seventeen years, beginning in 1867. Nevertheless, the sale of longhorns pumped money into Texas at a time when, following the Civil

War, cash was a scarce commodity. Moreover, it created a mythology—that of the cowboy—that still dominates the mind-set of the state, for better or worse.

In the booming '90s, high-tech companies in Austin that recruited engineers and computer science majors nationwide had to come up with anti-Texas campaigns in order to whet the interests of college students they were romancing on the coasts. The reason? They found that a lot of students associated Texas with that very mythology—cowboys and cattle—and thought that Austin, being in the middle of the state, probably had a rodeo every other weekend, and pointy-toed boots were required manly footwear. And these students weren't exactly interested in living in Wrangler country. So these companies wanted to communicate to their prospective hires that Austin had as many coffee shops as Seattle (well, almost) and that angst could be cultivated here as well as anywhere—you didn't have to do the John Wayne thing. They created videos that showed jet skiing on Lake Travis, partying on Sixth Street, grungy looking bands playing in smoky clubs, the Ice Bats on their hockey rink—anything remotely cool that wasn't associated with the Old West. You'd guess from watching these videos that there wasn't a cowboy to be seen in Austin. And that's just about true, unless you stray south of Ben White Boulevard. Or unless you show up for a UT football game.

★　　★　　★

There were still fresh longhorn hoofprints in the soft soil south of Brushy Creek when the University of Texas formally debuted on September 15, 1883. It had taken Texas only forty-four years to get its university open. The Congress of the Republic of Texas ordered land set aside for a university in 1839. Later that year, the congress set aside a quarter of a million acres of public land (fifty leagues) to be used as an endowment for the university and another public college. That done, Texas took no further steps toward establishing a university for two decades. By 1858, Texas had become a state, and the legislature took up the matter of a university one more time. To the original acreage set aside by the old Congress of the Republic the legislature added additional land and $100,000 in bonds. An organization to govern the institution also was created. But the Civil War came along before the state government could make further progress on creating the university. The Constitution of 1866 ordered rapid establishment of the university. Just what "rapid" meant to the framers of that constitution is anybody's guess. The legislature did pass a bill to create Texas A&M College in 1871, but action on the state's university was further delayed. In 1876, yet another constitution ordered the legislature to establish, organize, and provide for a "university of the first class." A vote of the people would determine its location. The constitution also set aside a million acres of land in desolate West Texas to add to the university's endowment. And, in a jab that would still rankle Aggies more than a hundred years later, the constitution ordered that A&M become a branch of the university that still did not exist. Though A&M got its independence many years ago, every fraternity man at UT knows that A&M was legally once subordinate to UT.

Voters selected Austin as the site of the state's flagship higher educational institution, and the first buildings started going up on forty acres that had been set aside for just such a purpose on College Hill, north of the present Capitol. The land set aside as endowment—the fifty leagues originally set aside in 1839, plus the million acres in West Texas—became the foundation of the fabulous Permanent University Fund (PUF). Fabulous, that is, after May 28, 1923, when the Santa Rita oil well came in on university property in Reagan County. Land that way back in the 1880s seemed like it would never be good for anything more than goat grazing suddenly became some of the most valuable in the state for the petroleum reserves that lay under it. Fattened by oil money, the PUF started growing until by 1950 it was worth around $300 million—at a time, as they say, when a million dollars was still a million dollars. Legislation passed that allowed a third of the revenue to go to A&M, but it was incumbent on several generations of politicians associated with UT to jealously guard the remaining two-thirds and make sure it went to Texas and Texas alone.

★　　★　　★

So you could still smell a lot of new paint around the Forty Acres when the first Texas football team boarded the train for Dallas in 1893. Football has been wed to the university for virtually all its history. Ever since that first team went undefeated, Texas has demanded excellence on the gridiron. Particularly if Oklahoma or A&M was the opponent.

In those early days, the Texas team was known simply as Varsity— hence the song the Aggies sing about sawing Varsity's horns off. In 1905, a writer for *The Daily Texan* (the student newspaper) tabbed Varsity as the Longhorns, thus embracing the heritage of the fairly recently decommissioned Chisholm Trail that once ran so close to the campus. The name caught on. Five years earlier, the university adopted orange and white as its official colors, replacing the gold and white that fans waved at the first game in Dallas in 1893. The original orange was brighter than what you see on the uniforms now, although at one point the school did flirt with burnt orange before returning to the brighter orange. Once, the orange dye used for the uniforms faded to yellow during washing, and the Longhorns endured being called "yellow-bellies" by their opponents. Darrell Royal took the orange back to burnt orange shortly after being named head coach in the late 1950s. The burnt orange Longhorn emblem became UT's official trademark in 1958. Since then, it arguably has become the most distinctive logo in all of college football. Certainly no mascot in sports is more readily identified with a team than is the living, breathing longhorn who shows up at UT home games and important away games (A&M, Oklahoma, bowl games, conference championship games).

The first official mascot at UT was a dog named Pig Bellmont, brought to UT as a pup in 1914 by Theo Bellmont, the school's first athletic director. Pig had the run of the campus for the next nine years, until he was struck by a car at 24th and Guadalupe and died a few days later. A campus funeral was held that rivaled any funeral A&M ever had for one of its Reveilles, and Pig was buried by the old Main Building.

Two years after Pig arrived, the first actual longhorn steer mascot was forced, snorting and pawing at the earth, onto the field when UT hosted A&M on Thanksgiving Day. The creature was terrified by the then-record 15,000 spectators who had showed up to watch the Longhorns win, 21–7. This first longhorn was dubbed "the most recalcitrant freshman who was ever bulldozed into higher education." I don't envy the short life of this steer. A few months later, some Aggie broke into his stall and branded him with the shutout score A&M had achieved against Texas in 1915: 13–0. (That score was significant because it marked the outcome of the first time the two teams had met in four years, the series having been canceled after the 1911 contest because it had grown too violent.) This was no small brand, by the way. If you look at the photo of him taken afterward, you see the brand taking up a whole side of the poor beast. UT students addressed the situation by rebranding him in such a way that "13–0" was transformed to read BEVO. At the time, Bevo was the brand name of a nonalcoholic beverage marketed by Budweiser that was popular among the students. (Anheuser-Busch says the name Bevo came about as a derivation on the Czech term for beer, *pivo*.) But the worst was not over for this steer born under a bad sign. After serving on the field through the 1920 season, he was slaughtered and barbecued and served up as the main course at a dinner for a hundred Texas lettermen, the team coaches, and even some invited guests from A&M. UT gave the branded half of Bevo's hide to A&M, where some reports say it hung in one of the buildings for a number of years. Currently, no one is quite sure where the hide ended up—nor does anyone know just where the UT half of the hide is. The legend that all Bevos meet the same fate as Bevo 1 is just that, legend. Subsequent steers to serve as Bevo have had a fairly cushy life. I mean, the traditional life of a longhorn consisted of trying to find enough forage to survive on on often inhospitable Texas rangeland, being herded by cowboys, then driven up a harsh bovine trail of tears to a Kansas railhead, loaded onto crowded cattle cars, and shipped to someplace like Chicago to meet the slaughterhouse sledgehammer. Riding in a custom-made trailer a few times a year to stand vigil beyond the south end zone of Royal-Texas Memorial Stadium is not such a tough way to go through life, all things considered. The current Bevo, Bevo 13, has been doing this since 1988 and doesn't seem much the worse for wear.

But 2001 found People for the Ethical Treatment of Animals, or PETA, getting onto UT for its treatment of Bevo. Not so much for his use at UT football games, but for his participation in George W. Bush's presidential inauguration.

Bevo showed up in Washington, D.C., with his handlers, the Silver Spurs—a UT men's service group that dresses in Western garb at Longhorn games. The Spurs took him to Rock Creek National Park in D.C., where they planned to put him up in the park's stables. The problem here was that Rock Creek wasn't expecting him. "We did not know where we had the capacity to handle an animal that size," said Adrienne Coleman, the park superintendent. "We were surprised to see him." Bevo, weighing in at 1,900 pounds and carting around a horn-span of five and a half feet, is not like your typical urban pony looking for a place to rest. After obtaining a signed waiver guaranteeing Bevo's safety and the safety of the horses in the stables, Rock Creek finally let him stay.

Like the president-elect, Bevo had to have a security contingent. Because of rumors of threats from PETA to cause a row at the stables, the D.C. police had to dispatch officers to watch over Bevo. "We've taken the measures necessary to protect Bevo," Park Service concession specialist Steve LeBel said at the time. "The poor animal had been on his feet for a few days, so we wanted to make sure he was comfortable."

Bevo got his rest. PETA demonstrators didn't show. But PETA representative Jenny Woods said, "We think Bevo would be much happier to be on a ranch with other steers rather than at inauguration festivities surrounded by loud music and rowdy partygoers. Subjecting animals to excessive handling and temperature extremes, as well as a night of picture taking with attendees riding their backs, is cruel and unnecessary. We like the idea of bringing the taste of the Old West to Washington, but we prefer not to mess with Texas Longhorns. It's no place for Texas Longhorns. They'd rather be home on the range."

Interestingly enough, an Aggie stepped up to defend Bevo's appearance in Washington. John McNill, associate department head of Animal Science at A&M, said as long as Bevo was fed properly, he could tolerate any conditions he might encounter in D.C. "It would have to be pretty extreme to cause a problem, especially with the age of Bevo. A longhorn can tolerate that kind of exposure, particularly one like him who's docile or been tamed," McNill told *The Daily Texan*.

Hmmm . . . *docile or tamed?* I'm not sure how many Longhorns prefer to think of their beloved Bevo as being emblematic of the docile and tamed. Maybe in defending Bevo, Dr. McNill got a jab in at the Longhorns. He probably said it with a perfectly straight face.

★　★　★

Varsity's horns extend beyond just Bevo. Texas football games are first-rate spectacles. The cheerleaders and pom-pom squad are as good as you'll see anywhere in the country. Big Bertha, the world's largest bass drum, rolls out onto the field. The Silver Spurs and Bevo are ensconced beyond the south goalpost. Another group outfitted in Western attire, the Cowboys, mans Smokey the Cannon III beyond the north end zone. (Smokey I ended up in the muck of Town Lake in downtown Austin after some playful scamps from A&M liberated it and tossed it into the drink.) The world's largest Texas flag—a gift from Governor Ross Barnett of Mississippi presented to UT prior to a bowl game between the Longhorns and Ole Miss—is unfurled over a huge portion of the gridiron. The Showband of the Southwest is one of the most impressive in the nation, with its white Stetsons and cowbells. Sadly, some traditions are no longer present. The distinctive voice of PA announcer Wally Pryor no longer booms from the speakers; he was replaced with a more generic-sounding announcer. For years, Pryor brought applause from the fans by updating them with the latest score from Slippery Rock University in Slippery Rock, Pennsylvania. That kind of levity seems to be judged as unprofessional by the athletic department these days, and you don't hear Slippery Rock scores anymore. Now you can see a slick animated video on the JumboTron as the Longhorns are jumping up and down in the tunnel leading to the locker rooms prior to the game. The animation portrays a herd of longhorns trampling around familiar sights on the Forty Acres, then turning into strange-looking longhorn minotaurs in football uniforms before stampeding in Royal-Texas Memorial

Stadium. When they do, the real-life Longhorns rush onto the field in a spray of steam generated by machines in the tunnel. The crowd goes nuts. The video looks pretty stupid to me, to be honest about it. But I know I'm not in the demographic group the athletic department is reaching out to these days. I'd much rather hear Wally Pryor update the Slippery Rock score than watch a silly video.

★   ★   ★

What a difference a week can make. A week and a whole lot of difference in the level of talent of your opponent.

In Stillwater the next Saturday, the Longhorns defeated the Oklahoma State Cowboys 45–17, with Chris Simms, the goat of the Oklahoma game, returning to his golden form. He threw five touchdown passes, and the sizeable gathering of Longhorn fans present in Stillwater gave him a standing ovation as he left the field. Simms had 235 yards passing, completing 18 of his 30 attempts. Cedric Benson rushed for more than 130 yards in the rout. Reverting to its standard 4-3 scheme, the Texas defense held OSU to just 65 yards of rushing.

An impressive showing—even if it was against a woeful OSU team destined to be among the Big 12 crypt dwellers.

★   ★   ★

In Boulder, the Ags saw their short stay at the top of the Big 12 South come to an end. A&M played well against the Buffaloes, who were still something of an enigma in the college football world. Colorado had been trounced by Fresno State in its opening game of the season, but the Buffaloes had won their next five games in a row, including Kansas State in Manhattan. A&M, ranked twenty-fifth in the nation when the game began, was the second tough opponent in a row Colorado faced. A&M was in the game until the last fifty-eight seconds, which was the point at which Buff linebacker Kory Mossoni smashed into Mark Farris from behind, forcing Farris to fumble. Joey Johnson, another Colorado linebacker, scooped up the ball and thundered through the thin Colorado air into the end zone, making the score 31–21 (after the successful point-after attempt) and putting a smile on Ralphie the Buffalo's face. At least it looked like a smile. Sort of.

The next week Colorado traveled to Austin. Colorado Coach Gary Barnett had ached for the Texas job when it opened following the firing of John Mackovic. Barnett, an absolute miracle worker of a coach who had actually made Northwestern into a football power, had been the top choice for the UT job going into the interview process. After the interviews, Barnett was out and Mack Brown had the job. So you sort of figured that Barnett had plenty of incentive to encourage his team to play especially hard against the Longhorns. From Texas's perspective, Colorado was the last tough opponent it had until the season finale with A&M. The Colorado ticket got pretty hot around Austin.

CHAPTER NINE

A Porch Like a Hereford Bull

I LIKED THE DRIVES I was making between Austin and College Station. My favorite route was taking U.S. 79—a little less traffic, maybe, and the images you saw of small-town life in Texas were a little more revealing. Maybe. After you got past Taylor, you were in Aggieland—no question about it. Signs on the highway indicated to you in bold maroon letters businesses that were "Aggie Owned and Operated," just as you used to see signs outside motels advising they were "American Owned and Operated." These small towns—Thrall, Thorndale, Rockdale—epitomized the bedrock upon which Aggie culture was built. Agrarian, conservative. If I was in need of a quick lunch, I'd stop in Rockdale at an Aggie-owned business that combined Texas Burger and Subway franchises in one shop. Sometimes my SUV would be the only vehicle other than a truck in the parking lot. Inside, you'd find men in the uniforms of these small Texas towns: Wrangler's and feed-store caps and boots crusted with the yellowish mud you find in this part of Texas. You'd hear talk about grain and cattle prices and high school football. Sometimes as I was leaving a town like Rockdale, I'd see someone sitting on a front porch, and in my mind, I'd hear the words of a Robert Earl Keen song and wonder if that front porch was really a big old red and white Hereford bull.

★　　★　　★

If you put a soundtrack to the UT-A&M rivalry, it would be the kind of music first unveiled by Jerry Jeff Walker on his *Viva Terlingua* album back in the early '70s: essentially country music, with some elements of rock and folk thrown in, and featuring a lot of audience participation whenever performed live. Several artists have perfected what Walker introduced back then. One time I was at an ATM in Fredericksburg talking with three young Aggies who had come over from College Station to see one of the most popular purveyors of the art form, Pat Green. "Shit," said one, "I don't mind one goddamned bit driving two hundred miles to hear Pat Green." Jack Ingram is another singer who has fans with a similar kind of dedication, as do brothers Bruce and Charlie Robison. These guys are major stars in Texas, although I wonder if their names register at all east of the Mississippi. And they have huge followings at A&M and within some segments—fraternity guys—of the student population at UT.

No one has traded up on this whole thing as much as Robert Earl Keen. Keen has never quite attained the national following that his old A&M compadre Lyle Lovett has, but that's done nothing to diminish his popularity in Texas. Lovett hung out at Keen's house on Church Street in College Station, and they would sit on the front porch in their underwear, surrounded by four or five hundred beer cans, serenading the Presbyterians leaving their church late on a Sunday morning: "Give 'em something to talk about on their way to Luby's," as Keen recalled. Luby's is a chain of cafeterias in Texas seldom patronized by anyone under, oh, sixty-five years old. It must have been a sight: the skinny, rooster-topped Lovett in his underwear next to his buddy Keen, both grinning and playing bluegrass songs on banjoes.

After college, the two went their separate ways. Lovett hooked up with a big-name label, recorded in Nashville, appeared in movies, and was married to a movie star for a while. Keen, meanwhile, worked the dance halls and frat parties in Texas, honed his songwriting skills until they were razor sharp, and developed an intense cult following. His best-known song became "The Road Goes On Forever," a narrative about a girl who's been around who hooks up with a pot-dealing bad boy. They get into trouble and hit the road—where even more trouble waits for them. The bad boy takes a fall for the girl— he goes to the chair, she hears the news while she's driving a new Mercedes. Each verse is followed by a refrain of "The road goes on forever and the party never ends." It's the kind of song that will appeal to a certain aspect of the Texas mind-set: yearning to be wild and free, even if it means becoming an outlaw. My stepdaughter's high school class used the refrain as its class slogan for graduation. There's probably a little irony in well-heeled suburban kids hooking up to an outlaw song like that. Probably even more irony in its popularity with UT fraternity men: "Hell, it's about everything they're not," a friend of mine who formerly was part of the Austin music scene tells me. Maybe that's exactly the appeal. Whatever, the gigs kept coming for Robert Earl Keen.

If he made some money off fraternities in Austin, he became a superstar among the Aggies. Keen concerts were and are major events. In a hall full of Aggies, Keen can find himself competing with the crowd, who seem to know every word to every song and shout them at the top of their lungs. There's one piece that Keen has to perform in any Aggie-dominated venue. It's simply called "The Front Porch Song," and as you might guess, it's a number he and Lovett wrote about those days back on Church Street in College Station. The front porch is a fantasy place in the song, becoming for a time a big red and white Hereford bull, then a plate of greasy enchiladas, the Palace Walk-in, and even Keen's old landlord. The high point comes during a spoken narrative in which Keen tells the story of his and Lovett's living in the house (*we was Aggies*), the landlord, the Presbyterians, the Luby's—all of that. It's become an Aggie anthem. A friend of mine, a woman who went to A&M, told me about a concert she attended in Houston once with an overwhelmingly Aggie crowd. Impatient for Keen to perform "The Front Porch Song," the crowd started singing it in thunderous unison.

★   ★   ★

A front porch might be a bull or a plate of enchiladas or Agua Dulce, Texas, but I'm not sure it can ever be Manhattan, Kansas. I'm not sure why anyone would even want it to be Manhattan, Kansas, although the Flint Hills are supposed to have their charm. The Little Apple has undergone a rather remarkable transformation over the last ten or fifteen years, however. Once the laughingstock of the Big 8 Conference in football—in fact, there was a time when K State's teams were cited as being the worst in the entire nation when it came to big-time college football—now it was a genuine powerhouse under the coaching of Bill Snyder. Go figure. Powerhouse or not, for the Aggies, Manhattan, Kansas, became a dandy front porch.

But I have to say, it still seemed odd to me that A&M would be up in the Little Apple to play K State in the third week of October, just as odd as Texas hosting Colorado that same day. I still hadn't completely gotten used to the dissolution of the Southwest Conference. Where was TCU? SMU? Rice?

The conference had its beginnings in 1914, the brainchild of Texas athletic director Theo Bellmont and others in the Southwest who wanted to raise academic and ethical standards for the member schools. You have to understand the times. America was obsessed with gambling and boozing in the early years of the twentieth century. Or at least American men were, and even more so than now. The temperance movement was in some ways one of the earliest feminist movements in the United States. In general, women were tired of their husbands going out and betting away the month's house payment on sporting events, many of which were fixed in those days. In the days when sports wagering was governed by odds rather than by the spread, professional gamblers had a hell of a lot of incentive to spend some money to get games, boxing matches, and horse races thrown. This culminated with the rigging of the 1919 World Series, which just about everyone knows about. But given the times, it wasn't an entirely surprising turn of events. You don't have to wade far into the literature about those times—take a look at Al Stump's great biography of Ty Cobb, for instance—to see just how widespread fixing was.

In those days, football games were often fixed by using ringers in place of legitimate players. Of course, not all use of ringers was directly related to gambling. Sometimes it just involved an overwhelming desire to win. David Chapman, archivist at A&M, says that in the days before the formation of the Southwest Conference, you might have gone to watch the Farmers play and seen a team enriched by talent that didn't spend much time sleeping in the Corps dorms. Instead, players with backgrounds at the Haskell Indian Institute in Lawrence, Kansas, as well as at other schools, would take the field wearing A&M uniforms—and, of course, they got some kind of reward for their trouble. That's pretty much how it worked at a lot of schools in the wild and woolly Southwest—and truth be known, the rest of America as well.

Formation of the Southwest Conference helped bring that kind of cheating to an end.

"The eligibility jungle he found in the state appalled Theo Bellmont [UT's new athletic director]," Lou Maysel wrote. "He consulted with Dr. W. T. Mather, chairman of the Athletic Council, and then took action. Letters were written to all of the larger institutions of the Southwest asking if they were interested in forming a new league that would defoliate the jungle.

"The response was encouraging and representatives of eight schools answered the call to a May 6, 1914, meeting at Dallas' old Oriental Hotel. There the Southwest Intercollegiate Athletic Conference, later to be popularly known as the Southwest Conference, was tentatively formed. Such major rules as limiting all athletes to three varsity seasons after a year of residence and a strict amateur code were adopted. Then on December 8, 1914, the SWC was formally organized at a Houston meeting at the Rice Hotel."

Among the positive things to come out of the formation of the conference was the renewal of the rivalry between Texas and A&M.

The two teams first met in 1894, but the series didn't begin until '98 and ran through the 1911 season. The game that year was played in Houston, and tempers were high going in. The Fightin' Farmers from A&M had won the last three matches, including two games in 1909, much to Texas's chagrin. The Farmers' coach was Charley Moran, who was beloved in Aggieland but who had the reputation as a dirty coach among his opponents. (Once an A&M faculty member suggested to Moran that he teach his players to be gracious in defeat. "Hell, I didn't come here to lose," Moran responded. No wonder the Farmers loved him.) In the second game of the 1909 season, Texas fans taunted A&M for having an "all-pro team." In 1910, Texas was heavily favored to win, but the Aggies upset them, 14–8. The odds had shifted back to A&M's favor in 1911 when the two teams met in Houston, but Texas won the game 6–0. And students from Texas were singing:

To hell, to hell with Charley Moran,
And all his dirty crew.
If you don't like the words to this song,
To hell, to hell with you.

Farmer fans were incensed by the loss. Texas fans were head over heels about the victory all right, but they were angry enough to spit over the injury to guard Marion Harold, who had to leave the game with a broken leg. UT fans believed the Farmers broke Harold's leg intentionally. Maysel wrote: "That night it was unsafe in downtown Houston for anyone wearing Texas colors as bands of A&M students roamed the streeets. The situation was judged to be so explosive that Texas fans decided against the nightshirt victory parade [in which students, wearing nightshirts or pajamas, conduct an informal march around the darkened city streets to celebrate the team's victory] there in favor of a triumphant march the next day in Austin."

UT responded to the unrest in Houston by notifying A&M it would not enter into "athletic relations" with the Farmers in 1912. The official statement was brief and gave no reasons for the decision. But Steve Pinckney, the manager of the Longhorn football team, was not shy about sounding off on the situation to the *Austin Statesman:* "The actions of the Agricultural and Mechanical College players during the game last Monday were so unsportsmanlike and unmanly that there was no alternative for the Athletic Council [to cancel the series]. Charles Moran, head coach of Agricultural and Mechanical College, must go. Since he has been coaching the Farmer squad, he has imbued them with the idea that the only way to win a game is to slug and maim the star players of the opposing team and get them out of the game. Instead of an aggregation of real sportsmanlike players, he has a squad of trained thugs."

This prompted the Athletic Council to rebuke Pinckney's statements to a certain extent and say the end of the A&M series had come about because "based on the belief that in view of the heated state of opinion among students and alumni of both institutions, it was the wisest course to pursue."

After the formation of the conference had been cemented in late 1914, the framework was in place for the UT-A&M series to resume. No sooner had the representatives of the schools spit their last tobacco shots into the cuspidors at the Rice Hotel than A&M announced Charley Moran would not be back as coach. It was widely believed that his firing was the price for A&M to pay to resume the series. Everyone, of course, denied it. Joe Utay, A&M athletic director, said, "We felt it was time for the two schools to get back together. We agreed the question of what happened to Moran was something strictly for [A&M] to decide. One of the things that we demanded was that the games be played home and home." Until then, the Longhorns had never set foot in College Station.

Still, it sure seemed as if a deal had been struck. A&M got its home and home series; UT saw Charley Moran take a fast train out of College Station. The Longhorns showed up in College Station for the first time for the 1915 game. Jigger Harlan was directing the Farmers from the A&M sidelines. What a bizarre game it was, too. A&M, fired up by players who wanted to win one for the ousted Moran, downed the Longhorns 13–0—the score the Aggies would covertly brand onto the first Bevo. However, the Longhorns had 215 yards of offense to only 76 for A&M. The Farmers accomplished only 19 yards rushing for the entire game, yet shut out their opponents. Of course, Texas did lose twelve fumbles, and that was the big contributing factor to A&M's victory.

But the important thing to come out of the 1915 game was that it was the start of the unbroken string of meetings in the series that has continued nearly ninety years.

Oh yeah—as for Charley Moran, he would turn up again. "Uncle Charley" surfaced as coach at Carlisle, the Native American school in

Pennsylvania made famous by the world's greatest athlete, Jim Thorpe. Then Moran went to Centre College in Kentucky and molded it into the power that upset mighty Harvard. In 1922, as D. X. Bible was birthing the 12th Man legend on the A&M sidelines in the Dixie Classic, Moran was across the field, guiding the Praying Colonels of Centre. I would guess that A&M had pretty much given up the love for Uncle Charley within a year or two of Bible's stepping onto the campus.

★   ★   ★

Football was terrific in the SWC from the time the membership stabilized in the mid 1920s: Texas, A&M, Baylor, Rice, TCU, SMU, and Arkansas. Texas Tech and Houston eventually joined as well. Because all the teams were in located in Texas except for Arkansas, the intraconference rivalries were intense. No one liked Arkansas because it seemed like a interloper. The game with Texas was big for all the schools because—well, Texas was Texas. TCU and SMU were rivals because they were close to each other, located in the rival cities of Fort Worth and Dallas. Texas and Arkansas was a great rivalry when Darrell Royal and Frank Broyles were at the peak of their coaching careers. And so on. Five Heisman Trophy winners came from the Southwest Conference schools. Between the conference members, they claimed eight national football championships, according to the tally run by *The Handbook of Texas*, as well as many titles in other sports. But alas, it was not to last.

Two things brought the venerable old SWC down. First, the schools were much too slow to integrate. As late as 1969, Texas could claim a national championship with an all-white team. By comparison, Bud Wilkinson had integrated OU's football program more than a decade earlier. While the conference's latter days saw outstanding

African American athletes from Earl Campbell to Eric Dickerson to Andre Ware become stars of national repute, the damage had been done. Too many terrific black athletes left Texas to play for schools out of state. The quality of talent playing in the SWC from top to bottom began to fade when compared to other major football leagues from the 1970s onward.

Second, the very thing that gave the conference much of its character and fire—almost all of its schools being located in Texas—started to work against it as college football increasingly became dominated by television contracts. Texas was a big state both in area and in population, yet a conference centered in the state couldn't pull the kind of demographics that a major football conference needed. The death knell rang when Arkansas fled to the cash-rich Southeastern Conference.

So the conference had devolved to Texas, A&M, and the six lesser sisters. No one thought it could last much longer. One scenario had Texas breaking away to join the Pac 10 Conference and A&M joining Arkansas in the Western Division of the Southeastern Conference. In the end, the conference imploded when Texas, A&M, Baylor, and Tech left to hook up with the Big 8 to form the Big 12 Conference.

As it turns out, the creation of the Big 12 has been a good thing—at least from the standpoint of the business of college sports. But I'm still not sure how much sense it makes for the Aggies to be traveling to Manhattan, Kansas, while ignoring an age-old rival like TCU.

★　　★　　★

I'm guessing the Aggies weren't fretting about it as much as I was. They went up to the Little Apple, turned in mediocre offensive numbers (only 189 yards of total offense), let K State hold the ball for more than half of the game, and wound up beating the Wildcats—last year's Big 12 North titlists—by the score of 31–24. It was the third straight time (over a four-year period) that the Ags had beaten Kansas State.

But maybe the biggest story to come out of Manhattan was the injury report.

Starting tight end Michael de la Torre was giving up football altogether because of a second herniated disk in his back. "He's finished," Slocum said. "He hasn't formally said that, but I visited with him, and after what the doctors told him, it's obvious he's through."

It was a startling injury report. De la Torre became the *fourth* tight end A&M lost to injuries. Lonnie Madison, Fred Spiller, and Joey Perot were already out for the season. A&M now had only a converted defensive lineman, Thomas Carriger, on the roster as a tight end. Free safety Jay Brooks, tackle Andre Brooks, safety Dawon Gentry, receiver Richard Whitaker, and linebacker Jesse Hunnicutt also failed to play the game because of injuries. Another tackle, Michael Mahan, saw limited action because of a heart problem.

At this rate, you had to wonder if Slocum would be forced to bring in players off the women's volleyball team in order to have a full squad by the time the Texas game rolled around.

★　　★　　★

Texas did its part to hold up the honor of the old SWC conference as well. The UT-Colorado game was the only one in the nation that weekend to feature two teams rated in the AP's top twenty-five (Texas rated ninth; Colorado, fourteenth), so all eyes in the college football world were on Austin.

The Longhorns absolutely dominated the Buffs. Chris Simms had Heisman Trophy candidate numbers: 17 of 28 for 234 yards and three touchdown passes. Cedric Benson rushed for 100 yards and two touchdowns on twenty-three carries. He also ran two shovel passes for 59 yards—his first experience running the shovel pass. "That was fun," he said. When time mercifully ran out, the scoreboard read Texas 41, Colorado 7. And the Oklahoma game seemed like it was two years ago rather than two weeks ago. Colorado coach Gary Barnett padded along the sideline during the game, looking as if he'd swallowed something evil.

★　　★　　★

I watched the game from the comfort of the upper deck on the west side of Royal-Texas Memorial Stadium, sipping on a bottle of water I'd bought from a man wearing a "Ministry of Challenge" T-shirt that depicted the image of David slaying Goliath. It was a beautiful day for the game, with a gentle breeze blowing up from the Gulf. And it was easy enough for me to imagine I was sitting up there on the world's longest, highest gallery porch, taking in the action on the lawn down below. At the start of the fourth quarter, when the game had turned into a rout, I decided to get a jump on the crowd and took off.

Before I left, I stopped at the uppermost landing of the ramps leading down to terra firma and looked over at the tower and realized that the view I had from up here must have been about the same as the one that Charles Whitman had on that day when blood flowed beneath the August sun in 1966. A mock Greek temple sits on top of the thirty-one stories of the tower, epitomizing the highest achievements of the human mind. For the first time, I appreciated the irony of Whitman's wreaking slaughter in the shadow of that temple.

The statistics for Whitman's butchery for years stood at sixteen dead and thirty-one injured. But that changed this fall when fifty-eight-year-old David Gunby died in Fort Worth of a wound he'd received thirty-five years earlier during Whitman's rampage. The

Tarrant County medical examiner officially ruled his death as a homicide. One of Whitman's bullets pierced Gunby's kidney as he strolled down the South Mall. He'd been on dialysis for three decades, but the week before he died, he told members of his family that his body had been through enough and he stopped treatments. Thus he became victim number seventeen.

In 1994, Gunby told *The Dallas Morning News* that the tower would always be a sinister symbol for him. "August 1 is nothing you commemorate or celebrate," he said. "I will never see the tower without thinking about what went on there. It used to be the symbol of the University of Texas, and it probably still is. But for some of us, it has another meaning."

CHAPTER TEN

St. Darrell, Uranus, and Pluto

IN A PREVIOUS LIFE, I had a job for the state of Oklahoma that required me to visit most of the county seats in the state. Hell, maybe I went to all of them. I can't remember. It's been too long, and besides, those small towns kind of run together in your memory. One time I rolled my state car into Hollis, the county seat of Harmon County, in the dusty southwest corner of Oklahoma. Hollis had a population of maybe 2,000 people. It was not, as the old saw goes, the end of the world, but you could see it from there. In the other direction, across the Red River, was Texas.

I guess I was in town for a couple of hours, doing my work, before it struck me: Darrell Royal came from here. It was an unimposing place, to say the least, to have produced one of the half dozen or so most important figures in the history of college football.

In the 1960s, Darrell K. Royal—the middle initial is just that, an initial; it doesn't stand for anything—was potentially the most dangerous man in the state of Texas. Two things mattered in Texas then as now, power and money. (Only the nuances change.) To achieve either one involved either obeisance to the "establishment"—as illustrated in James Conaway's book, *The Texans*—or one hell of a birthright. Royal, pardon the football metaphor, did an end run on all that and became the best known (with the only exception being the president, Lyndon B. Johnson) and most popular Texan of his time because, in his prime, his teams could beat the hell out of anyone else's teams on the football field—including Bear Bryant's. By the hundreds of thousands, Texans regarded him as a hero, from bright-eyed schoolboys to adults who should have outgrown hero worship many years before. Had he aspired to such things, he could have spun off his enormous popularity into immediate success in either politics or business at the highest levels in Texas. If, for instance, he'd entered the governor's race, he would have been the immediate front-runner. No doubt to the relief of many Texas powerbrokers, Royal's fires didn't burn in those directions. He seemed content winning football games, playing golf, and listening to country music.

That a man could go as far as Royal did was an amazing thing, given his humble beginnings in a humble place like Hollis.

★　　★　　★

"His boyhood," wrote his longtime friend Gary Cartwright, "was right out of *The Grapes of Wrath:* He can still remember the stigma of being called an Okie and what it means to wear government-issue overalls. Whatever DKR was and is, he is a man with the ability to grow."

And it's true: Royal did have it rough from the get-go, yet he grew. Shortly after his birth, his mother died of cancer, but because people in places like Hollis, Oklahoma, considered cancer as something dirty and shameful in those days, Royal grew up believing his mother died giving birth to him. (He didn't learn the truth until he was an adult.) That's a tough load of guilt to put on a kid, but Royal dealt with it. "The main thing I remember about my early years," Royal told biographer Jimmy Banks, "before I became interested in athletics, was the fact that I didn't have a mother. I guess any kid that doesn't have a mother goes through the same thing. I wanted a mother very much. I used to daydream a lot about what it would be like to have a mother. I had a lot of relatives in my hometown. I got all the love and attention that a child could ask for. But I guess no one can replace a mother, regardless of how much they love you and care for you and look after you."

Not only did he grow up without a mother, his two sisters died during his childhood, one from food poisoning, the other from a heart malady.

The family fortunes were limited at best. He and his brothers loved to play football, but for a long time there was no money for something frivolous like an actual ball. Instead, they used a tin can as a substitute—"a Clabber Girl Baking Powder can, because that was the only one we could find that was the right size." He earned money as a boy with a paper route—which he did on foot, no money being available for a bicycle. He also worked in the drought-stunted cotton fields, probably the most miserable labor in the world this side of mining coal.

Eventually the family made the nearly mythic Okie migration to California in search of work and better times. "I hadn't thought much about being an Okie," he told Banks, "until we hit that highway. . . . When we finally got to California, we got in the fruit harvest like everybody else. But we were living in an old shack. And pretty soon, I started noticing that I talked a lot different from the kids who'd been raised in California. I had that Southwest twang. It was a little bit of show of weakness on my part but I started working hard to keep from talking like an Okie—because they could spot you at the snap of a finger. And it wasn't one of those things you could be proud of because Okie then was really a dirty word. I guess it wouldn't be nearly as cutting as calling a black a nigger, but there is some comparison there, because they sure didn't mean it to be complimentary. I tried as fast as I could to start talking like a person from California, but I soon found that I didn't want any of that. I didn't want to live in California—not under those conditions."

Three months were enough of West Coast living for him. The high school coach back in Hollis offered to find Royal a part-time job to cover his living expenses if he'd come back and play football. Royal packed his few belongings into a gutted Victrola case, paid ten dollars for a ride to Oklahoma, and went home. He lived with his grandmother and pretty well devoted his life to football. "I grew up listening to Oklahoma football on the radio," Royal told Cartwright. "We'd put the radio on my grandmother's porch and play football in the yard and listen to 'Boomer Sooner.' " It was easy enough for him to imagine the band was playing "Boomer Sooner" for him in recognition of his lawn heroics. Sometimes he traveled to Norman with his high school coach to watch Indian Jack Jacobs and Gilford "Cactus Face" Duggan and others on the Sooner squads of the 1930s. He especially liked to watch the great Indian Jack punt and tried to emulate him back home in Hollis.

Royal served in the Army Air Corps during World War II. It must have been an interesting experience for him, since he never gave a whit about shooting anything. When he'd go skeet shooting with buddies, he couldn't wait until his shells were gone so he could stop shooting; and in later years, he'd go out to deer camps in that other great Texas rite of autumn, but he never once shot a deer. Nevertheless, he was trained as a tail-gunner. However, the military soon evaluated Royal's true skills and put him where he should have been: the Third Air Force football team. He was so successful at military football that, once the war was over and he was discharged, Florida, Alabama, USC, Texas Tech, Georgia, South Carolina, Tennessee, and Auburn all tried to recruit him to play his upcoming collegiate eligibility with them. But Royal headed to Norman and OU with hopes that "Boomer Sooner" might indeed be played for him and his name might be remembered with the kind of reverence given to Cactus Face Duggan.

Actually, Royal's timing for going to OU could not have been better. Political and business heavy hitters in Oklahoma had been trying to come up with ways to counter the image the state and its residents had gotten during the Great Depression. In particular, they wanted something that might get people's minds off John Steinbeck's epic *The Grapes of Wrath* and John Ford's equally epic film version of the novel. As George Lynn Cross plainly illustrates in his memoir, *Presidents Can't Punt*, these powers determined that having a championship-caliber football team was the most effective way to accomplish that. Thus Oklahoma became a national power in college football, certainly the only one to be inspired to greatness by a Pulitzer Prize–winning novel written by a Nobel laureate. The military could provide dozens of top-rate athletes who still had their college eligibility, and that's where Oklahoma turned to find instant success. To make sure the skids were fully lubricated, influential OU alumni got out their checkbooks. Royal had the standard scholarship and some money from the GI Bill. And he also had an OU alumnus willing to cover his rent, doctor bills, and the tab at the grocery store.

OU settled on a option-based offense run out of the Split-T formation, which OU coaches Jim Tatum and Bud Wilkinson had learned while airmen at Iowa Preflight School during the war. It's hard to imagine a better match of offensive philosophy and athletic skills—Royal and the option seemed bred for each other. Wilkinson was an offensive mastermind who fully understood the potential of the Split-T and set about refining it into dangerous weapon once Tatum departed OU after one season to coach at Maryland. Wilkinson was an apt tutor for Royal, who seemed to soak up offensive strategy about as quickly as Bud could teach it to him.

Oklahoma has had no small number of terrific players over the past sixty years, but it's hard to imagine any greater than Royal. Had he never coached a down after he left OU, Royal would have been a college football legend just for what he accomplished wearing cleats. In those days, players were required to go both ways, playing both offense and defense. Coaching from the sidelines was a rules infraction, so a quarterback had to call his own offensive plays. Royal proved he could call a good game as a Split-T quarterback. He also could run the daylights out of the ball. He may have been the best punter OU ever had, even better than Indian Jack Jacobs. He also was a dangerous return specialist. And, when playing defensive back, he'd knock the hell out of you.

But Royal, showing the modesty Oklahoma culture of the time ingrained in its people, told Banks, "I really wasn't much of a football player. I contributed and I could do *some* things. The one thing I could do that was exceptional, and I felt all along that I could do all four years, was punt. But I worked like a dog on that. I could punt and play defense, and then, my senior year, I think I quarterbacked the team well. But my other three years, I made practically no contribution offensively."

Amazingly understated—all he did was litter the OU record book with records that stood for years. The records stand for his versatility: He held the record for the most interceptions by a defensive back over four seasons. He held the record for the longest punt (81 yards). He held the record for the longest punt return (95 yards). "I wasn't much of a passer," he once said, "because my hand wasn't big enough." Yet he once threw 76 consecutive passes before he gave up an interception. He had a completion average of 54 percent during his OU years.

After graduating, he set out on a coaching exodus that gave him experience at a variety of levels of football play. Even though he was still a young man with little coaching experience, his knowledge of option football was already highly respected. When Bear Bryant was coaching at A&M, he beckoned Royal, then coach at Mississippi State, to College Station to teach his players how to run the Split-T.

Royal coached the Washington Huskies to a break-even season when word spread that Ed Price was out at UT following the worst season (1-9) the Longhorns had ever had. Royal said later he'd daydreamed about the Texas job, but his getting the job looked like a long shot. The university flirted with some of the biggest names in college coaching: Bobby Dodd at Georgia Tech, Duffy Daugherty at Michigan State. Dodd and Daugherty both bowed out, but in doing so, they recommended that the university take a close look at Royal. But a week before the new coach was announced, Texas's list of prospects proportedly contained more than a hundred names—with Royal's not even on it.

Then, one night, after Royal had gone to bed, the phone rang. The voice on the other end said, "Coach Royal, this is D. X. Bible of the University of Texas."

★   ★   ★

Royal had to grow everything at UT, from the quality of the players to the quality of the facilities. According to Banks, when he arrived, Royal found that his own office was a small cubicle with a chair held together with tape. The practice field was a sticker patch that had to be plowed under and resodded with good grass imported from A&M. No matter the building process required, he turned Texas into a winner immediately, finishing with a 6-4-1, second place in the Southwest Conference, and winning an invitation to play Mississippi in the Sugar Bowl. He lost to Wilkinson and Oklahoma (whose great run was starting to run down) that first season, but his Longhorns squeaked past Bear Bryant's Aggies 9–7. It would be ten years before a Gene Stallings–led A&M team finally beat Royal. (And he went eight straight seasons beating Oklahoma, beginning in 1958). After Bryant left for Alabama, Royal acquired two of his most potent tools at A&M,

assistant coach Willie Zapalac and sports information director Jones Ramsey. They took root in Austin just like the grass that Royal had imported from College Station earlier.

Royal's winning ways immediately made him beloved in Austin. His delivery in 1963 of the first national championship in the school's history was grounds for his beatification. (The college of cardinals wore burnt orange blazers.) He was the best coach in America in the 1960s, better than Woody Hayes, better than John McKay, better than Joe Paterno, better even than Bear Bryant. He lost to A&M just three times in twenty years; to Oklahoma just seven times. He won two consensus national championships, a third disputed national championship, eleven SWC titles, and took his team to sixteen bowl games. Tradition was cemented in Memorial Stadium to the sounds of the recently composed "Texas Fight," punctuated with the recently invented Hook 'Em, Horns hand sign, and colored with the recently resurrected burnt orange of the jerseys. The burnt orange Longhorn emblem on the side of a white helmet became as feared in the ranks of college football as a Comanche war lance had been among frontier settlers a hundred years earlier. Expectations for Texas football were always high among the Orangebloods, but during the 1960s, they extended to the further reaches of the solar system.

And, in the last five years of his career at Texas, you could hear rumblings on Uranus or Pluto when Royal wasn't able to deliver.

★　　★　　★

In many ways, he was the most unlikely of Texas folk heroes—after all, he was from the hated Oklahoma. Davy Crockett might have been the last nonnative to be embraced in the way Royal was. He certainly wasn't a boots and cowboy hat kind of guy. In fact, he was an obsessive neat freak who compulsively washed his hands twenty times a day. He liked dogs well enough, but he didn't like to touch them. His shoes always sported a perfect shine. Even on the golf course, he was natty. But he was, as Kris Kristofferson sings, a walking contradiction. He might have had the grooming habits of the primmest corporate lawyers, but when he spoke, out came the most astonishing flow of folksy aphorisms heard this side of his fellow Oklahoman, the legendary basketball coach Abe Lemons (whom, by the way, Royal in his role of UT athletic director hired to bring respect to the Texas program). Cartwright calls it Royal's "marvelous gift for the shit-kicker metaphor." Some of these probably could be traced back to Will Rogers, just as some of Rogers's quips could be traced to other sources. Some were probably witticisms you could pick up outside a grain store in Dust Bowl Oklahoma. Others he turned himself. Around Austin, they became known as Royalisms. The best known is "We're gonna dance with who brung us." When Royal was at his peak of popularity, you couldn't turn a corner without running into one:

"Ol' ugly is better than ol' nothing."

"The sun don't shine on the same dog's ass every day."

"He's as quick as a hiccup."

"He could run like small-town gossip, although his compass sometimes went batty."

"He's a rolling ball of butcher knives."

"He looks like he needs worming."

"It's down to the necks and gizzards."

"Football is meat on meat, flesh on flesh, stink on stink."

He never did say, "Every coach likes those old trained pigs who'll grin and jump in the slop for him," however, even though it's one of the best known quotes attributed to him. Royal insisted he said *slot*, not *slop*—and blamed Dan Jenkins for misquoting him. He bristled over the substitution of the *p* for the *t*. How were you supposed to recruit talented football players if parents were thinking you were going to train their kids to jump into *slop?*

Young men by the hundreds were ready to do just that, though. Royal's reputation for recruiting outstanding talent was nonpareil. Throughout the '60s, he would snatch up not only the best talent in Texas (then the best breeding ground for football talent in the nation) but also the second- and third-best—the idea being to keep those players from straying over to a school like A&M, where they might cause the Longhorns some trouble. You might have been a stud quarterback back in your hometown who showed up on freshman reporting day to discover ten other sublime athletes who'd also been stud quarterbacks back in their hometowns unpacking their bags. The groundwork was done by an extraordinary corps of assistant coaches Royal had put together. Then a recruit would show up in Austin and be blown away.

Gary Shaw, an 1960s-era high school star from Denton, Texas, arrived one weekend for his campus visit with about thirty other recruits. They lost no time learning how big a deal football was at Texas. They gathered at a lounge at the top of Memorial Stadium, these pimply-faced high school boys, and found the most beautiful coeds on campus there ready to fawn over them, including the university sweetheart. And if sophisticated college women weren't enticement enough, the recruits also were blown away by all the trophies on display, the pictures of the Longhorn greats, the beautiful burnt orange carpet, the long bar, and the color TV—at a time when relatively few homes could boast of color television. In his controversial football memoir, *Meat on the Hoof*, Shaw described himself as shuffling from foot to foot and laughing nervously, while at the same time feeling like the king of the world. What eighteen-year-old boy wouldn't?

Especially as those honey-eyed women in their twenties told you just how much they personally wanted you to don the burnt orange.

Shaw's parents had accompanied him on his UT visit, and they had checked into the late, lamented Villa Capri Motel, *the* place to stay in Austin through the 1960s and '70s if you were in town for anything related to Texas sports or politics or the arts. The Shaws were eating in the motel restaurant—the restaurant that featured a photo of Willie Nelson while few people outside Central Texas had any idea who he was—when Shaw saw Royal for the first time. Royal flashed his charming smile and seemed completely at ease. Meanwhile Shaw and his parents were as nervous as if they had an audience with the pope. In his folksy voice, Royal said, "I'm looking forward to having Gary come down and play some football for us. He's a fine player." Royal offered up suggestions about what the Shaws might do and see with their free time while in Austin and offered to do anything he could to help them out. "He gave us the feeling that what he was doing was a favor, but a favor done graciously," Shaw wrote.

Four years later, Shaw's parents ran into Royal again. He immediately recognized them and called them by name. Three years after *that*, Royal saw them at the Denton Country Club and called them by their first names. An amazing feat for a coach who had recruited dozens of players with God knows how many parents during that seven-year period.

★　　★　　★

After the national championships, all those conference titles, all those appearances in the Cotton Bowl, all those All-America caliber players, the 1970s should have been a time for Royal to have been glorified as one of the greatest men ever to have coached college football—just as Bear Bryant rode out the '70s on a wave of hosannas in Tuscaloosa. But as the '70s moved forward, the decade became the winter of Royal's discontent.

Because his great Texas teams had been virtually all white through the '60s, Royal now became the target of reformers attempting to weed out racism in college sports. An example: In 1970, the Associated Press quoted Royal as telling a meeting of black coaches in Washington, D.C.: "You have not been publicized by your public relations people and the black coach has not reached the point where his coaching is as scientific as it is in the major colleges." The problem was, Royal wasn't at the meeting.

Then, in 1972, came the somewhat notorious (although Cartwright called it "noticeably mild") five-part Associated Press series about racism in UT football. One of the writers, Robert Heard (a survivor of the Whitman shootings, by the way), got the idea for the series after UT failed to recruit any African American players during the 1972 recruiting season. The series focused on the six black players then on the team, and in interviews, those players said they felt there was prejudice at the university—"There's gonna be prejudice wherever you go to school," the great running back Roosevelt Leaks was quoted as saying—and among the coaches. Later the players recanted some of what they said, but that was after the series received national distribution over the AP wire.

In fact, there was racism at UT. How much blame should go to Darrell Royal? Probably not much. As Cartwright wrote, "[Heard and fellow AP reporter Jack Keever] didn't write about the Orange Coats, that splendid assortment of dentists and bankers and contractors and regents who hired Royal in the first place, then attached themselves to the UT football program like ticks on a bird dog. Those were and still are your racists, your true orange-blood bigots. It seems almost unbelievable, but until 1963 the UT Regents explicitly *forbade* black athletes at 'The University.' Even after the Regents rescinded this rule (without a murmur that it was now time to break with tradition), the Orange Coats made it clear that the first black Longhorn had better be two steps faster than Jesus and able to run through a brick wall. It took a Roosevelt Leaks to integrate the Orange Coats with the twentieth century."

Exactly.

Before he came to Texas, Royal coached African American athletes in the Canadian Football League and at the University of Washington. I believe that had it not been for the unofficial power structure surrounding UT—the Orange Coats—Royal would have integrated the Longhorns earlier than he did. After all, coaches want to win games. Black athletes would have helped him win even more games.

★   ★   ★

Then there was the matter of Gary Shaw.

Shaw was never a star at UT. The young man who had been a terrific high school linebacker from Denton became a reserve lineman and special teams player at UT, another face lost in the blur of burnt orange. Six years after he left UT football, however, Shaw became a national celebrity with the publication of *Meat on the Hoof.* More than 350,000 copies of the book were sold, making it one of the best-selling sports books of its time. There had been nothing quite like it, a full-fledged attack on big-time college football and one its most successful programs written by someone who had been there, experienced it firsthand. Shaw was a good writer. His story was compelling. The pages turned quickly. But there was always something a little troubling about his book. Was it credible? How could such a hellhole like the UT football program he described exist and there not be whistleblowers other than Gary Shaw stepping forward? Where were his corroborators? Was he fudging on details for effect?

Shaw portrayed a Longhorn program in which coaches were sadists and players (except for the starters) were chattel. He included horrific descriptions of conditioning drills that really were more like torture sessions under Royal's trainer Frank Medina, whom Shaw described as a "squatty, bowlegged, five-foot-tall Cherokee Indian . . . considered one of the best trainers in the country." Shaw wrote that the drills took place in two locker rooms heated by steam to 120 degrees. Players wore one or two sweat suits, wrist weights, ankle weights, a twenty- to thirty-pound vest, and in each hand carried a thirty-pound dumbbell. In the sweltering nightmare of the locker rooms, Medina had players go through calisthenics, then exercises with the dumbbells. If someone faltered during the drill, Medina would start the whole thing over, while lecturing the players about the need to be in church on Sunday because being a good football player went hand in hand with being a good Christian. Afterward came more torture: jump rope races, sessions with a heavy bag. By the end, players were puking and bleeding.

These sessions took place in January. The upcoming spring training he described would be even worse.

It was the severity of the trainers and coaches in their treatment of the players that caught the most media attention when the book came out. College football in the 1960s was a tough place to be, no mistake about it. Other accounts from that time verify it. But nothing reached the extremes that Shaw described as happening at Texas. At the time the book appeared in 1972, players who had been at Texas when Shaw was there began to step forward and say they didn't remember things being quite as Shaw portrayed them. Royal himself went on record as saying he couldn't recall the drills that Shaw described. Was it accurate?

Worse than the player abuse outlined in *Meat on the Hoof*, from the standpoint of the Texas that idolized Royal, was Shaw's iconoclastic view of the coach he called Daddy D. He suggested that Royal was a duplicitous man, not quite like the beloved folk hero Texans had made of him: "Royal seemed to have the uncanny ability to turn his charm on and off at will. I'll never forget the difference in how Royal and the coaches acted toward me before I signed and after I arrived at Texas. Once we were in hand, the charm suddenly stopped. When we were being recruited there were plenty of smiles and conversation, but once there, it was a 'you're going to have to show me' atmosphere. I knew many freshman who were surprised and bitter at this discrepancy. They naively thought that Coach Royal, or the assistant coach who recruited them, had some kind of personal interest in them. Upon arriving at Texas they felt deceived and abandoned. . . . Because of this contradiction, many of us thought of [Royal] as two-faced."

At the time, you didn't hear many voices of other former players joining in to corroborate Shaw's observations. If anything, just the opposite occurred. And yet Shaw's writing had such an authentic ring to it. It sure *sounded* as if he were telling the truth. Years later, legendary quarterback James Street told Kirk Bohls and John Maher of the *Austin American-Statesman:* "In all the time we played there, he had an open-door policy. But nobody dared to go into his open door. If you heard Coach Royal's side of the story, he'd say, 'God dang, guys, I was here to listen to your problems or anything else.' He's a good guy, but he's hard guy to get close to. It's hard to know Coach Royal." If he seemed distant to a luminary like Street, the distance between Royal and a reserve like Shaw could have been measured in light-years.

Bill Little, longtime sports information director at UT, probably made as good of an assessment of *Meat on the Hoof* as anybody when he said in 1999 that Shaw was "way off base in some of the things he said" but that he also "probably described athletics as they existed everywhere at the time." Little also characterized the book as being unfair to the university.

As for Shaw, despite his moment of celebrity and his bestselling book, life took a rough turn. When freelance writer Rebecca Sherman profiled him in 1990, he was a street person in Dallas, eating out of garbage cans, diagnosed with schizophrenia. His sister, Cindy Yarbrough, told *The Dallas Morning News:* "My perception is that my brother was tormented throughout his life, always hearing the voices," she said. She even heard him telling the voices, "Leave me alone." So the question arose: Did those voices color *Meat on the Hoof*?

Shaw never accepted he was mentally ill and in need of medication. He drifted through the years, a vagrant unable to hold down jobs. He died in 1999 back home in Denton after being rescued from the streets and put up in an apartment a few years earlier. He was only fifty-three.

★　　★　　★

It's easy to understand why Royal might have decided he'd had enough by the mid 1970s after dealing with racism charges and Shaw's book and the surrounding hubbub. Recruiting was growing more difficult. Also, he was in the midst of a long string of losses to OU, and perhaps the ultimate indignity, in 1974, Baylor won the Southwest Conference. Baylor hadn't won the SWC since the days of Calvin Coolidge. Plus the job itself, even in the best of times, is overwhelming. It was then—and remains now—the highest profile job in Texas.

Also, former governor Allan Shivers became a member of the Board of Regents. Shivers was a very conservative man. In his term as governor, he had decided Dixiecrat leanings. He was pro-McCarthy, anti–*Brown v. Board of Education*. He was wealthy, calling the magnificent Pease Mansion his Austin home. And he took a dim view of longhaired, dope-smoking guitar pickers. He questioned whether it was appropriate for the head football coach of the University of Texas to hang out with that sort of person—read: Willie Nelson. When Royal decided to give up his coaching post in 1976, Regent Shivers was glad to accept his resignation.

Though Royal remained as athletic director, he was not allowed to decide whom his successor would be. Shivers's view was that the university didn't become a great institution by letting men choose their own successors. Had it been Royal's choice, the job most likely would have gone to his longtime assistant Mike Campbell. Campbell got an interview, but he never was in the running, not really. Under the presidency of Lorene Lane Rogers, the university seemed intent on changing the image of the school's most visible representative, the head football coach. That meant breaking with the past.

But the legacy of Darrell Royal hung over the heads of all who followed him. They were expected to deliver Uranus and Pluto. Or else.

In 1977, UT hired Fred Akers as Royal's replacement; Akers had brought respectability to the Wyoming program prior to being tabbed for the Texas job. Akers had been an assistant at UT before taking the Wyoming job, but when he came back to Austin, he cleaned house and installed a new staff of assistants. Royal had accumulated national championship caliber players during his last few years of recruiting, and Akers made good use of them. He had Earl Campbell lose twenty-five pounds, then refashioned the offense to take full advantage of Campbell's improved speed by switching to the I formation. As a result, the Horns got within spitting distance of Pluto when they went 11-0 in the regular season (although they lost to Notre Dame in the Cotton Bowl, which cost the Horns the national championship) and Campbell became Texas's first Heisman Trophy winner. Akers was again in the national championship hunt in 1983, once more finishing the regular season 11-0. He saw the national title slip away by one point (10–9) in an upset loss to Georgia in the Cotton Bowl. After that, things went south for Akers in a hurry.

After a 5-6 showing in 1986, Akers was gone. Even though Akers ended up with the second-most victories of any Longhorn coach in history, you sensed most Longhorn fans were glad to see him go, mostly because he wasn't Darrell.

Next came David McWilliams in 1987. McWilliams had been a popular player under Royal in the early 1960s and had been one of the captains of the 1963 national championship team. During his time at UT as a player, McWilliams had been involved with only two losses on the field. Moreover, he was one of Darrell's boys—someone who embraced the legacy of his former coach instead of shunning it. He'd also been a successful assistant under Akers, serving as defensive coordinator for four years before having a successful year as head coach at Texas Tech. McWilliams's first three years were rocky, including going 4-7 in 1988 and 5-6 in 1989. In 1990, everything seemed to turn around for McWilliams as the Longhorns went on the so-called Shock the Nation tour and finished the regular season at 10-1, with the only loss coming at the hands of eventual national champion Colorado. The Longhorns went into the Cotton Bowl ranked third in the nation, where they met number four Miami. In what was perhaps a harbinger of a season to come, the Hurricanes destroyed the Horns, 46–3. At the beginning of 1991, there was talk of Texas competing for the national championship, but the Horns finished the year at 5-6 and McWilliams was through.

In 1992 Texas turned to Illinois head coach and athletic director John Mackovic, who also had been head coach of the NFL's Kansas City Chiefs and had served on Tom Landry's Dallas Cowboys staff. A pass-happy offensive mastermind, Mackovic saw his teams carve up the record books at Texas. The Mackovic years were a combination of giddy highs and leaden lows. He peaked in 1995, winning ten regular season games against one loss and claiming the last-ever Southwest Conference football title. The next year started sluggishly, but the

Horns went on to qualify for the inaugural Big 12 championship game at the TWA Dome in St. Louis. In it, Texas beat third-ranked Nebraska 37–27 in one of the biggest college football upsets of the '90s, thus clinching the first-ever Big 12 title. The year after that, Mackovic's team fell to 4-7, matching the worst record for the Longhorns since 1956—when Ed Price was hanged in effigy. That season included an absolutely horrendous home loss to UCLA, with the Bruins coming out on top 66-3. It was maddening watching Mackovic's teams. When the offense was on the field, you knew you were seeing some of the best football players in the country; he recruited future Heisman Trophy winner Ricky Williams and Major Applewhite. But when it was the defense's turn, the quality fell to mediocre in a hurry. Aloof and cerebral, Mackovic was in many ways the anti-Darrell, and Longhorn fans never really cottoned to him, even during his winning seasons. The university might have loved the clean-cut, cultured image he portrayed, but it didn't really play well in the small rural towns in Texas that the Longhorns still depended on for much of their talent. Mackovic appeared to be the kind of guy who'd rather go to a good wine tasting than to a golf outing sponsored by an affluent Texas ex out in the middle of West Texas somewhere. That, and he talked like a Yankee. Neither trait was guaranteed to win him much loyalty in the land of burnt orange.

What Texas needed was a coach who cleaned up good, as they say, when the occasion merited it, who wouldn't be an embarrassment to Texas. But at the same time, he needed to be able to dress down to jeans and boots and to converse with coaches in places like Nocona or Palacios. He needed to be able to get top recruiting class after top recruiting class, for to the Orangebloods, winning the wars to sign the most highly rated high school talent in the nation was something of a sport unto itself. And he needed to do so in a way that would uphold Texas's reputation for having one of the cleanest programs in the country. He needed to be able to maintain friendly relations with big money donors who believe their dollars should bring them influence on how the team is run. And he had to win, and win a lot, at what's been called the land's brassiest and sassiest football program. A national championship was fully expected—and sooner rather than later.

In short, he had to deliver Uranus and Pluto.

Texas turned to Mack Brown.

CHAPTER ELEVEN

Joking Around . . .
Honest, Just Joking

MEL STEKOLL CAN MAKE A SINGULAR CLAIM: He told me the worst joke I've ever heard. That's no small accomplishment. I've heard some so bad that they would drive away flies. And telemarketers, too—maybe.

I was outside Royal-Texas Memorial Stadium, standing near Stekoll's 1931 Chevy, which, of course, had been painted orange and white. People were stopping by to have their pictures taken with the old car, which for years had been known as the "cheerleader's car" because UT cheerleaders would borrow it and drive it to the stadium on game day. Eventually, Stekoll himself started to drive the car into the stadium while the cheerleaders rode on top of it. Then Stekoll's son took over driving it so Mel could ride in the rumble seat and wave, along with the cheerleaders on the roof, to the crowd as the old Chevy entered the stadium. All that came to an end when UT removed the track that used to run around the field, so there was nothing to drive a car on anymore.

Anyway, Steckoll was holding a burnt orange stick with a giant hand on the end that was making the Hook 'Em, Horns sign. It sort of looked like a jester's wand. And that fit in, because Stekoll was something of a court jester during UT home games, out to make people laugh. The primary weapon in his jester's arsenal was the Aggie joke.

So Mel was saying to me, "Say, did you hear about the Aggie who went to the optometrist to get his eyes examined?"

"No," I said, ever the gullible straight man.

"Well, the optometrist takes a look at the Aggie, then steps back and asks, 'Have your eyes ever been checked before?' "

"The Aggie says, 'No, they've always been brown.' "

Ouch.

Stekoll is one of the more interesting examples of the Longhorn fan taken to extremes. Before his recent move to the small town of Lockhart an hour or so away from Austin, he lived off 32nd Street in East Austin. His house was painted white with burnt orange trim and also sported a Longhorn doormat and mailbox and porch umbrellas, chairs, and flags. "Originally," Stekoll once told *The Daily Texan*, "I painted my whole house all orange and just the trim white, but my wife didn't like it." On game day, he shows up at the tailgate parties wearing a Longhorn cap, square glasses striped with orange and white (which gives him sort of an odd insect look), and Longhorn shirt and pants—the pants bearing a patch on the butt that said "Hook 'Em." But more than anything else, he is a walking compendium of Aggie jokes. There's no telling how many hundreds of them he has at easy recall, most of them achingly bad. John Kelso warned me about the jokes before I ever met Stekoll—I guess so I could prepare myself for them.

Aggie jokes are legion. Sometimes they're reworked into Auburn jokes (and no doubt a few Auburn jokes have been reworked into Aggie jokes). Up in Oklahoma, people will borrow Texas Aggie jokes and retool them into Oklahoma State jokes. I guess that something similar probably occurs everywhere there is a university that fancies itself as representing the elite and a competing cow college. But without question, the hotbed of this kind of humor is in Texas, for better or worse.

★　　★　　★

Okay, Darrell Royal buys a new pickup. He decides to take it on the road to give it a good breaking in. He shows up in College Station, so he decides he'll go by Emory Bellard's house to show him the truck. Bellard by this time has become the Aggie coach. Bellard is impressed with the new pickup. Royal asks him if he wants to go for a ride with him. Bellard says sure. So they head out into the country. Royal says, "Say, Emory, I haven't had a chance to check everything out on this new truck to make sure it works. You want to help me out?" "Sure," says Bellard. Royal brings the pickup to a stop. "Let's start with the brake lights, okay?" "Not a problem," Bellard says, climbing out of the truck. He walks around to the back while Royal rolls down his window. Royal applies the brakes. "Are they working, Emory?" "Sure thing, Darrell." "Great, let's try the left turn indicator. Are you ready?" "Yep." Royal hits the left turn handle. "Is it working, Emory?" Silence. Royal says again, "Is it working?" Bellard says, "Well—yes, uh, no, yes, no, uh, yes, no, yes, no, uh . . ."

★　　★　　★

And how do you tell an affluent flamingo? He's the one with the ceramic Aggies in his front yard.

★　　★　　★

And just how many Aggies does it take to make popcorn? Four—one to hold the pan, three to shake the stove.

★   ★   ★

You get the idea.

Sometimes the jokes are turned around in the Aggies' favor. One of my favorites goes like this: An Aggie goes to graduate school at Harvard. He's walking across Harvard Yard when he encounters four Harvard men. "Howdy, boys," the Aggie says. "Can you tell me where the library's at?" The Harvard men look at each other in disgust and adjust their neckties. "Excuse me, sir," one of them says. "You are now at Hawvawd, and at Hawvawd, we do not end our sentences with prepositions." The Aggie thinks for a moment, then says, "Okay, can you tell me where the library's at, asshole?"

Or this:

Two little boys were playing football in a park in College Station, and one was suddenly under attack by a rabid rottweiler. Thinking quickly, the other boy ripped off a board from a nearby fence, wedged it down the dog's collar and twisted it, breaking the dog's neck.

A reporter for the Bryan-College Station *Eagle* who was strolling by saw the incident and rushed over to interview the boy. FUTURE AGGIE SAVES FRIEND FROM VICIOUS ANIMAL, he started writing in his notebook.

"But I'm not going to be an Aggie," the little boy told him.

"Sorry, since we're in College Station, I just assumed you were," said the reporter. He started again, YOUNG AGGIE FOOTBALL FAN RES-CUES FRIEND FROM HORRIFIC ATTACK . . .

"I'm not an Aggie football fan either," said the boy.

"Well, gosh," said the reporter, "I thought everyone in the College Station area pulled for Texas A&M. Just who do you root for?"

"I'm a Longhorn fan," said the boy with pride.

The reporter started a new sheet in his notebook: LITTLE HIPPIE FREAK-BOY MURDERS BELOVED FAMILY PET.

★   ★   ★

I once tried to run down the history of the Aggie joke, and as far as I can tell, the first one was told about the same time that Noah was busy unloading livestock from his boat. Aggie jokes fit into a line of American humor in which the established segment of society ridicules newcomers or the less fortunate. Usually they take on an ethnic flavor—Polish or Italian jokes, for instance. And in its absolute ugliest form, the Rastus and 'Liza jokes aimed at African Americans. It's been at least twenty-five years since I heard one of those, thank God.

Most of the Longhorns I know view Aggie jokes as good-natured razzing. Most of the Aggies I know will shake their head pitifully when they hear them and maybe give a little smile. But I always get the sense they're sick of the whole thing. Sometimes it ain't easy being an Aggie. In a different context, Bear Bryant once said, "Being at A&M is double rough because . . . everybody is against you, thinking you deserve to be on the bottom, being an Aggie." When you hang around this rivalry long enough, you can't help but sense there are indeed underlying feelings in Aggieland that they are the underdogs out to battle the world.

One manifestation of this is the Great Teasip Media Conspiracy, whose subscribers believe that virtually all Texas newspapers, radio stations, and TV stations are under the control of Texas exes with a mission to do whatever they can to make A&M look bad. You can find Aggies who will discuss at length what they perceive to be the hidden nuances in a headline—as if an editor at the newspaper took great pains to word a headline in just such a way as to disparage the Ags. As an old newspaper guy, I always found this kind of speculation laughable. Under newspaper deadlines, you don't have time to give much thought to nuances, especially if you're the one writing headlines. You're busy enough trying to come up with something, *anything*, that will fill the space before some surly bastard from production is in your face wanting to know where the fuck his goddamned page is. But Aggies who subscribe to the teasip media conspiracy will have none of that. They're sure whole blocks of time in the newsroom are given over to discussion of just how a headline or a lead paragraph can be written to get in a dig at A&M. If you don't believe me, just check out some Internet chatroom postings some time.

★   ★   ★

A&M may have once been legally subordinate to UT, but it is, in fact, the oldest public institution of higher education in Texas. Though A&M sometimes get the rap of being a redneck school with little appreciation for political correctness, some of its roots lie in the Reconstruction period in Texas history when African Americans played significant roles in state government—with the backing of federal troops. For the last few years, some people at A&M have been trying to get the university to make some kind of recognition of Matthew Gaines for his role in the events that led to the founding of the college. Gaines, a former slave born on a plantation in Lousiana, was elected to the Texas Senate, and while there, became a staunch supporter of public education—Gaines himself had learned to read by candlelight using books a young white boy who lived on the plantation smuggled to him. He ended up in Texas after being sold by his Louisiana master, escaping once, only to be captured by the Texas Rangers. (He'd escaped another time before coming to Texas.) Once in the Senate, he backed the legislation that allowed Texas to benefit from the federal Morrill Land-Grant College Act, which provided for the establishment of state colleges "where the leading object shall be, without excluding other scientific and classical studies and including military tactics, to teach such branches of learning as are related to agriculture and the mechanic arts."

Bryan was selected as the site of the new college after residents donated 2,416 acres of land outside of town for it—the future College Station. On October 4, 1876, the Agricultural and Mechanical College of Texas opened its doors with with 106 students and a faculty of six, who ignored the agricultural mandate for the school and taught courses in classical studies, languages, literature, and applied mathematics. Irate farmer groups demanded—and got—the heads of the faculty and the president in 1879, and a new administration was installed. It pledged it would see to it that military and agricultural affairs would rule the day. Enrollment at the college, which had hit the 500 mark, rapidly declined to around 80 students, and there was talk of closing the school. Then Sul Ross became president of A&M in 1891 and was able to get the college back on firmer footing—and he cemented its commitment to agriculture and military training. Meanwhile, the University of Texas had opened in Austin and had grown larger than the older A&M. In 1931, the two-thirds to one-third split of the revenue from the Permanent University Fund was negotiated, with the bigger portion going to UT.

And someone somewhere must have told an Aggie joke or two on the day that agreement was signed.

Stuck out in the woods with only men on the campus—well, with the exception of the occasional "Maggie" or two, a Maggie being the daughter of someone employed by the college or a woman who otherwise would have reason to hang around campus—and getting only half the PUF money that Texas received, it's easy to understand how the Aggies felt they were getting a raw deal. And just to remind them of that fact, they were "entertained" with an endless series of Aggie jokes.

★   ★   ★

The next three games on Texas's 2001 schedule turned out to be jokes—though, of course, the Texas coaches would probably say no game is ever a laughing matter. Visiting the Missouri Tigers, Texas ran up 421 yards of offense with Chris Simms going 24 of 30 for for 229 yards of passing. And the Longhorns won, 35–16. Meanwhile, Oklahoma lost to Nebraska, so Texas found itself tied with its nemesis for first place in the Big 12 South standings. But since Oklahoma had the victory over Texas in the Cotton Bowl, it would get to play in the conference championship game if both teams won the remainder of their games.

The next week, Texas traveled up Interstate 35 to visit Jerusalem on the Brazos (Waco) to take on Baylor. The Bears were 2-5 on the season and 0-5 in conference play, so it seemed likely that the hard seats in Floyd Casey Stadium would be pretty uncomfortable by the time the game ended. Kevin Steele, the Baylor coach, decided to defend Texas's outstanding receiving corps—maybe the best in the country—with man-to-man coverage. Not a good move, Coach Steele. Simms threw for 271 yards, although his completion percentage was not particularly great, and Texas won, 49–10.

The Longhorns' last home game, against Kansas, was such a ho-hum affair in the making that an Austin ticket broker called me to ask if I knew anyone who needed tickets to the game. "We're gonna get stuck with a lot of them," she said. "So I can make somebody some pretty good deals." Well, yeah. Like a lot of people would want to queue up for the car-train wreck in the making set for Royal-Texas Memorial Stadium, I was thinking. But 83,000 did show up for the game, which *Dallas Morning News* writer Rana L. Cash described as being "kind of like stepping over a crack in the sidewalk." Cedric Benson ran for 213 yards, a freshman single-game rushing record, while Chris Simms threw for 284 yards and 2 touchdowns, which brought his season total of passing touchdowns to 22, beating the record previously held by Major Applewhite. Kansas had only 67 total yards of offense. The Longhorns were up 59–0 when time mercifully ran out.

★   ★   ★

Things turned out to be not so sunny over in Aggieland, although the last week of October was bright enough.

The Aggies, coming off a quality win against Kansas State, hosted another good team, Iowa State, and more than 85,000 showed up to watch A&M pull off a 24–21 victory, thanks to a 65-yard touchdown run by Derek Farmer. Still, the game had its troubling aspects: The Cyclones had 26 first downs to only 14 for the Ags. Iowa State also had 445 yards of offense to 322 for A&M. And the Cyclones dominated the clock. Mark Farris was limited to just 17 yards of passing in the first half—and finished the game with a mediocre 132 yards. Still, the win put A&M back into the Big 12 South title picture. It was now tied for the lead with Oklahoma and Texas.

★   ★   ★

Next, A&M had to travel to Lubbock to play Texas Tech. And that cranked up the collective blood pressure readings up on the Cap Rock by about 60 percent. Tech was established in 1923 as sort of the West Texas answer to A&M, minus the cadets in boots. Naturally enough, the Red Raiders began looking at the older, better-known ag school 420 miles to the east as a rival. "No one likes Texas because Texas is Texas," a friend of mine who graduated from Tech told me. "But I absolutely *hate* A&M!" A&M hatred is well woven into Tech culture.

A statue of Will Rogers on horseback sits on the Tech campus, and lore has it that the statue was purposefully situated so that the horse's ass was aimed directly toward College Station. (A woman Red Raider told me, "The rest of the legend of the statue goes that when a virgin graduates from Tech, Will Rogers will dismount his horse and walk around the campus. It hasn't happened yet.")

The rivalry is curiously one-sided. A&M is so directed in its disaffection for UT that it doesn't really have the energy to churn up much in the way of hatred toward Tech or anyone else. Among Aggies, it has been good bull for years to just ignore the Red Raiders—which makes the Tech partisans even more irate. When Aggie fans go to Lubbock, it's not unusual for them to be greeted with hurled projectiles of different sorts, spit, and vile language. Cars with A&M stickers have been vandalized. Once in the stadium, fans and players alike routinely have been pelted with tortillas to the maddening clatter of thousands of cowbells. It's enough to make OU fans seem civilized. "I cannot name one other place we play," an Aggie wrote in a letter to the editor of a Texas newspaper, "including Austin, where we are treated with such hostility and disrespect. Lest you think it is only a few intoxicated students, take a good look the next time A&M plays in Lubbock and see some of the older people hurling insults and profanities at Aggies."

Well, Lubbock is in West Texas, after all. There's no place where football is taken any more seriously, which basically means West Texas is the white-hot center of football passion in the universe.

According to A&M Athletic Director Wally Groff, things were quieter than usual before the game in Lubbock. "There were no fans heckling and throwing objects at the players as they exited the bus, as there have been in years past," he said, adding the Tech administration did a good job keeping the dreaded tortilla throwing under wraps. So far, so good. Then the game started.

You had to wonder where the defenses were. A&M put up 372 yards of offense; the New Braunfels wizard, Tech quarterback Kliff Kingsbury, had 355 yards passing against the Wrecking Crew. A&M got into the red zone a couple of times, only to turn the ball over. Meanwhile, Tech slowly etched 12 points on the scoreboard. When time ran out on the Aggies (by the way, Aggies never admit to losing a game; a loss is described as "time running out"), A&M had nothing to show for all those 372 yards. The game ended with Tech on top, 12–0. It was the fourth straight time the Red Raiders had beaten the Ags in Lubbock.

And all hell broke loose.

About a thousand Tech fans roared out onto the field and started tearing down the goalposts, just as they'd done two years earlier when their team beat A&M. They were perhaps inspired to do so because some A&M players had been quoted as saying they'd been disgusted by the goalpost destruction the last time it happened. Meanwhile, the Aggie fans were congregated in the visitors' seats, singing the "War Hymn" and going through other Aggie postgame rituals. When the Tech fans had one of the goalposts down, they carried it down the field and, shouting taunts, started jabbing it like some humongous frog gig into the section of Aggies. In general, I think it's safe to say, Aggies don't like to be on the receiving end of a gigging, since they fancy themselves as the giggers. To no one's great shock, open combat broke out.

I don't know how many cowbells were beaned off how many skulls nor how many corneas were scratched by flung tortillas before the melee concluded, but I do know that one man emerged from the stands bloodied. He was Mike McKinney, father of A&M's standout offensive lineman Seth McKinney and the chief of staff for Texas Governor Rick Perry. McKinney took a fist while trying to prevent the Tech backers from climbing into the stands, which he compared to the siege of the Alamo. It took eight stitches to close the cut he got from being punched in the right eye. When he saw R. C. Slocum, McKinney said, "Welcome to Lubbock."

And that might have been that: a wild-ass Red Raider decks the governor's chief of staff during a goalpost gigging scuffle.

Except that McKinney's attacker wore not the red and black of Texas Tech but the maroon and white of A&M. That's right. It was Aggie vs. Aggie in the main event. The Lubbock *Avalanche-Journal* carried a story the next Monday reporting Tech President David Schmidly's confirmation that the culprit had indeed been an A&M student. The guilty Aggie had fessed up to Tech campus police. (By the way, that same issue of the paper carried a story about the theft of a 300-pound concrete pig named Jocelyn from a lawn on 78th Street in Lubbock. City police had no leads in the case.) McKinney lay low while the state hooted over the incident like, well, the newest Aggie joke. Particularly that Alamo reference. "Hmmm. I don't remember reading in seventh-grade Texas History class about Jim Bowie taking a swing at Davy Crockett," wrote columnist Keith Whitmire.

While a lot of joking went on about the incident in Tech, inside the football world of the Big 12 Conference, the fight caused considerable concern. A longtime official in the UT athletic department told me, "Tech has a real problem out there. If they don't get it fixed, someone is liable to get killed."

★   ★   ★

The Ags didn't have time to stew over the defeat. Or the punch line to the joke. The next week, they went to Norman to meet the defending national champions. Early on, things looked good for A&M as it went out to a 10–0 lead over Oklahoma. But then the Aggies gave up 31 unanswered points, and A&M left Owen Field with its third loss of the season. The sole A&M touchdown in the game was scored by the defense, so it had now been eight consecutive quarters since the offense had punched the ball into the end zone. Al Carter wrote after the game, "If the Aggies don't double-flush their current offensive designs in the off-season, a lot of Corps members may never get another kiss. Then someone's really going to get mad," referring to the male A&M students' practice of kissing their dates each time A&M scores.

The Aggies creaked back into College Station having lost two games in a row. Now that the Aggies had three conference losses, the Big 12 South title was nothing more than something to dream about in 2002. A bowl invitation seemed likely, but how good a bowl depended on how well the Aggies played against Texas in two weeks. A win over the Longhorns could elevate them considerably in bowl status. But screw the bowls—a win over Texas in itself would be sweeter than any bowl game could ever be. And that's no joke.

★　　★　　★

Now the Lone Star State turned its full attention to the annual Thanksgiving blood feud, and the two-week buildup for the game got rolling. The insults began over the hissing fires in deer camps. The newest round of Aggie jokes started circulating through e-mail. Foolhardy bets were wagered. UT may have had the better team in the eyes of the sportswriters and pollsters, but every maroon-blooded Aggie believed in his soul that the Fightin' Farmers would find a way, somehow, to best the Longhorns. Texas loyalists exuded confidence, as if beating the hicks in the woods were a birthright. There were breakfasts attended in equal numbers by Aggies and Longhorns. The alma maters were sung, insults were traded, all with winks and nods. Everything commenced to build toward the big climax to come on the fortnight on Kyle Field. It was one of Texas's greatest traditions. Even though this year one thing was missing.

CHAPTER TWELVE

A Bonfire of the Heart

AGGIE WEDDINGS HAVE THEIR CHARM and their mystery. To the unsuspecting, the sight of all the Aggies in the wedding party linking arms and legs to saw off Varsity's horns—short!—at some point during the reception must seem a bit peculiar. It's especially kind of weird to the outsider seeing the bride in her gown and veil doing it, but, hey, that's the Aggie way. A wedding's not a wedding in Aggieland unless you sing "goodbye to texas university," no matter what Martha Stewart might have to say about it. Personally, I think it's a great custom.

When it comes time to cut the cakes, a lot of attention is aimed at the groom's cake. It's a chocolate affair, of course, but depending on the skill of the cake-maker, it will more or less resemble tiers of logs stacked vertically, each tier diminishing in radius until the last one becomes a pinnacle—but a pinnacle crowned with an outhouse, not a spire. A replica of Bonfire, in other words.

The legacy of Bonfire is everywhere in the world of the Aggies.

When things were normal as far as Bonfire was concerned, the weeks leading up to the Texas game were a kind of high holy season on the A&M campus, building up to "Push"—the final twenty-four-hour-a-day drive to get the massive stack completed and ready for burning. You could sense something was missing on campus this November, just as there had been a year ago. All the "Bonfire 2002" signs and the hope that the great tradition would return next year did little to diminish the emptiness of the season in 2001. And there was lingering fear that when it came down to delivering the decision on Bonfire 2002 after the first of the year, President Ray Bowen would say no. Meanwhile you heard rumors of outlaw bonfires in the works, planned for secret locations outside College Station.

★   ★   ★

The autumn had been a little bumpy on campus.

Going into the football season, A&M had high hopes for the exposure it would receive through an ESPN "reality-based" series called *Sidelines.* Back in the summer, Steve Miller, an assistant media relations director in the A&M athletic department, sent out an e-mail describing the deal: "ESPN and Texas A&M will team up for a 13-week [series] on Aggie football. It will be an all-access deal for ESPN and unbelievable pub for A&M. Plus they are giving us a very sizeable check. . . . Football is the focus, but they will be spending a lot of time in the community looking at how football affects the businesses, restaurants, students, residences, and school as a whole. Should have the release later today . . ." ESPN crews started filming in the summer, with the first episode to air on October 4.

Sidelines came on late at night, which limited its audience from the start. You didn't hear much hoopla when episode one aired. Aggies were a little perplexed by the emphasis on trains in the show. Sure, a railroad track does cut across campus. It butts up against the baseball field, and when a train passes during an Aggie game, the engineer will sound "Hullabaloo, Caneck! Caneck!" on the engine's horn. And, of course, College Station takes its name from the train station. But it's not like Aggies obsessively line up to watch the boxcars go by. So why so much emphasis on trains?

If the verdict was still out after episode one, it came in swiftly after episodes two and three were shown. *Sidelines* was bad bull.

The second episode included a segment on two women who appeared to be shit-faced drunk outside the North Gate bar called the Salty Dog. This outraged Aggies for several reasons. First, they thought it presented A&M as a dreaded "party school." While beer drinking at North Gate bars is an age-old Aggie tradition—hell, drinking beer anywhere is an age-old Aggie tradition—the school much prefers to be showcased as a conservative, wholesome place where getting whacked out of your mind is frowned upon. (Never mind that one cherished Aggie tradition involves dropping your newly acquired class ring into a pitcher of beer at the Dixie Chicken and chugalugging all the beer. You get extra credit if you can do it without puking.) But there were other things about the segment that pissed off the Ags. It turned out that the two women were not even Aggies at all. Rather, they came from the Bryan campus of Blinn College. The way the segment was edited, you could easily make the assumption that the women had been drinking in the Salty Dog. In fact, one of the women, Kristal Sheaves, told the A&M student daily, *The Battalion*, that she and her friend had had all their drinks at a Bennigan's in College Station, but the alcohol didn't kick in until they were outside the Salty Dog in North Gate. "It was very upsetting," Sheaves, an education major, said about seeing herself on *Sidelines*. "I don't know why they decided to show that, except to say that that type of stuff is what attracts people to watch TV." Salty Dog owner Gary Seaback said: "They made it look like it was all Salty Dog. And not that it matters, because we're all Aggies, and we're kind of getting blamed by ESPN for being a party school. They have no idea how much they're hurting the image of this school. But at least if you're going to put out this image of A&M, use A&M students."

Episode three was even worse, to the Aggie mind. It depicted an apparent lesbian relationship between a female basketball player at A&M and a former A&M athlete. My God—that was the kind of thing you expected to go on at that hippie school over in Austin. And it didn't seem to have anything to do with football.

After the second episode, AD Wally Groff was on the phone to ESPN's Mark Shapiro, telling him he thought the show "was an extreme deviation from what we expected."

"Typical Hollywood-type producers look for this kind of thing and try to find the things other people are used to seeing," Groff said. "I told them this school was really conservative, a Bible Belt school, and we do things different here. We discussed this all back in July."

Shapiro offered to send Groff the third episode in advance of its showing, with the warning "I don't think you're going to like it."

No truer words had ever been spoken.

Groff's reaction? "There's a heck of a lot more to A&M than *that*."

Groff said Shapiro promised to get things back on course, at least from A&M's perspective. And Groff threatened to cancel the agreement with ESPN if future shows didn't take a different direction to focus more on football. Bowen also agreed that the contract should be canceled if *Sidelines* didn't change.

The focus of *Sidelines* did shift. But it failed to capture the affection of the Aggies. "It's on too late at night for me to bother with it," a woman who worked in the A&M administration told me. I got the impression not many Ags took the trouble to even bother with it toward the end. Writing in the *12th Man Magazine*, editor Homer Jacobs characterized *Sidelines* as an "often bizarre docu-drama that did not live up to expectations." That could stand as A&M's official pronouncement on the ESPN series.

★   ★   ★

Then there was the issue of Aggie cheerleaders.

What? Aggie *cheerleaders?*

You have to understand, the whole idea of cheerleaders is anathema to the traditional Aggie. A&M has *Yell Leaders.* The hippie liberal school to the west has cheerleaders. The whole concept of cheerleading is considered, well, effete in Aggie environs. Yelling is what's appropriate, and you're led in your yells by closely shorn young men, preferably from the Corps, in clean white outfits. If you let traditional cheerleading get started, what would come next?

Yet the issue of cheerleading reared its head on the A&M campus in 2001, and the affair is interesting because it is indicative of a problem A&M faces. On the one hand, it is a huge, mainstream university that wants to attract the best and the brightest students from all walks of life. On the other hand, it is a tradition-oriented university that turns loose of hallowed rites only with the greatest anguish. Among the kind of students that A&M seeks to recruit are high school graduates—most of them women—who have been heavily involved with cheerleading as an extracurricular activity. In addition to stirring up spirit in the spectators at games, cheerleaders have their own competitions with squads from other schools—basically seeing who's the best at rah-rahing, cartwheeling, dancing, pom-pomming, and pyramid-building. It's a big, big deal in Texas high schools. But if you're into all of this in high school, you have to say adios to it if you go to A&M. At Texas and other colleges and universities, you have opportunities to carry on with your cheerleading career, if you're so inclined.

So it stirred the waters when sophomore journalism major Shannan Johnson and others organized the Fightin' Texas Aggie Competition Cheerleading Squad and received official recognition from A&M. Although it was clear that the intent of the organization was solely to take part in cheerleading competitions, it was immediately seen as a threat to the Yell Leaders. No one thought that Johnson and the others were up to anything nefarious. The squad had no plans to appear at sporting events or anything like that—that clearly was the domain of the Yell Leaders—but it was a nose-of-the-camel kind of thing. Let the camel stick his nose in the flap of the tent and pretty soon you have the whole beast inside. Sam Seidel, the head Yell Leader, said, "The people have good intentions now, but fifteen, twenty, thirty years down the road, the members of the squad will be asking why they are not a part of sporting events." Seidel thought the recognition of the squad could start the "slow degradation of the Yell Leaders." Seidel's fellow Yell Leader Kevin Graham concurred: "This is just a stepping-stone."

To understand the gravity of this, you have to understand the role of the Yell Leaders around the A&M campus. If the Corps of Cadets are sort of the warrior priests of Aggie Spirit, then the Yell Leaders—the overwhelming majority of whom come from the Corps; currently only one "non-reg" (noncadet) was on the squad of five—are the high priests, maybe the cardinals.

No student was more readily recognized around campus than Sam Seidel, a senior animal science major from Brenham. He was a third-generation Aggie—his grandfather was in the Class of '42—so he'd bled maroon from birth, never considered going to another school, never really gave any thought to not joining the Corps. "Whenever we'd come over to the football games, Dad and I'd always go over to the Quad and watch the Corps getting ready for the game." When I talked to him on a rainy cold day in the late fall, he leaned back and gave it some thought and decided it had been at least sixteen years since he'd missed an Aggie-"t.u." game. And how did he decide to become a Yell Leader? "Well, to tell you the truth, I never really thought about it, never had a desire to do it. It wasn't like a dream or a goal for me when I got here. There's a process in the Corps where you go out and you meet people in your class when you're a sopho-more. It's just a two-week time period when you get to know one another. At the end of that, the person who is going to run for Yell Leader from the Corps is kind of 'brought out,' you know what I'm saying? I was just put in that position, and I'm very fortunate. They just kind of saw something in me and the other guy who is a senior Yell Leader from the Corps." Once chosen as a Yell Leader, a student's life becomes "busy," Seidel said. "That's the only way I can describe it." In addition to classes and Corps activities, the Yell Leaders appear at sporting events and a host of other gatherings. And they also attend meetings of A&M Clubs all around Texas during the summer. Seidel said he made eighty appearances in the summer before his senior year began. So the face of Seidel and other Yell Leaders becomes etched upon the memories of both students and Former Students alike. It's a great way to help you get your start in business or whatever it is you decide to do after you finish college. It can help you in politics, too. You could ask the sitting governor, Rick Perry, the former Aggie Yell Leader, about that.

So to have this ancient, male-dominated tradition threatened in the least by a group of mostly female pom-pom wavers was hardly some-thing that could be brooked. And in fact it wasn't. Only weeks after the Fightin' Texas Aggie Competition Cheerleading Squad was formed, A&M's Department of Student Activities pulled the plug on it—at least as an official A&M activity. "It is totally unfair, but A&M does not want people to think we are the major spirit group at A&M," Shannan Johnson said after the decision had been made. "I feel the alumni's threat to not support their alma mater just because of a cheer squad, rather then their love for Texas A&M, is only skin-deep. They do not really bleed maroon. I feel that they need to realize that things do change, and this is for the better of the diversity of the school." Maybe so. But the Former Students in question had told the *Houston*

Chronicle that they would withhold financial contributions to the school if the sanctity of their beloved Yell Leaders was threatened by skirt-wearing cheerleaders.

Whatever controversies A&M faced with *Sidelines* and cheerleaders in 2001, it was nothing compared to the sorrow and agony that gripped the campus two years earlier.

★   ★   ★

Television always seems to bring the really bad news to us. Maybe that's why I like TV less and less as I get older. Turn it on, and there's a good chance you'll find out something really bad is happening. Or maybe you'll be in the middle of a program when the dreaded interruption comes—just like that horrible morning of September 11. I remember sitting in a San Diego hotel cabana watching *Monday Night Football* in December 1980 when Howard Cosell informed me and a huge portion of the rest of America that John Lennon, one of my cultural heroes, had been murdered. Just like that.

It was the same way on a Thursday morning in November 1999. I'd been out for an early morning run. When I got back, I put the coffee on and turned on the TV. There was a live report on the local ABC affiliate about a terrible accident in College Station. A car wreck? I wondered. No, I learned very quickly. The Bonfire stack had collapsed. That in itself was so stunning. It had happened just five years earlier, when the stack went leaning to one side on drenched ground. But this time the unfathomable had occurred. Scores of student workers on the massive construction project had been sent to area hospitals, some with life-threatening wounds. Others weren't as lucky. When the final tally was made, twelve Aggies had died when the tons of green logs came thundering down with a huge plume of dust eight days before A&M was to host the Texas game.

Twelve. A haunting number, given that twelve is the most significant number in all the traditions and lore to come out of Aggieland. The connotation of "12th Man" was changed forever.

It took crews days to clear up the jumbled mess of some 7,000 logs, all held together with wire. And all Texas—Longhorns included—mourned.

★   ★   ★

The first Bonfire occurred off campus in 1909 when cadets gathered up scrap wood, old pallets, basically anything that would burn, and heaped it all together and set a torch to it to celebrate a victory over Texas. By the 1920s, Bonfire had become an event held prior to the Texas game, symbolizing A&M's "burning desire to beat the hell outta t.u." and had moved to campus. At some point, someone added an outhouse on top—the outhouse came to be a tradition itself, seen to be symbolic of a University of Texas fraternity house. For years, not much changed. If you look at the photo of the stack taken in 1928, it appears to be a mound of scrap lumber and pallets and nothing more—no real design to it at all. The early 1940s re-creation of Bonfire for *We've Never Been Licked* looks about like the 1928 photo.

But after World War II, Bonfire became much more sophisticated. A center pole was added some time in the 1940s, and logs were harvested from the nearby forests to use to build the stack—thus "cuts" were introduced into Aggie tradition. A teepee-shaped stack resulted, with the logs positioned on their ends and leaning inward against the center pole. At this time, the Ags were becoming height obsessed as far as Bonfire was concerned. Every year's graduating class wanted its Bonfire to be the tallest on record. But the teepee shape was limited to being no taller than its longest log. To remedy this restriction, the Aggies developed designs using tiers of logs. Bonfire shot upward. In

1969, it reached a dizzying height of 109 feet using an odd design that sort of looked like a rocket perched on two tiers of logs. A&M officials feared the height fetish was getting out of hand and placed a limit of 55 feet on Bonfire, although students didn't always comply with that limit. In the 1970s, the wedding cake design began to evolve, and by the 1980s the look of Bonfire was set: wedding cake structure, 60 to 80 feet tall, six tiers bound with wire, two-part spliced center pole, and four perimeter poles with guy ropes.

There were no formal blueprints and no professional engineers on hand during construction, but Bonfire was no haphazard affair. As many as 5,000 students with a few Former Students thrown in as well would work on it, all under the supervision of around twenty upperclassman, well experienced with Bonfire construction, called "Red Pots" because of the color of their safety helmets. The Red Pots used notebooks crammed with detailed engineering information about the construction, information gathered from previous generations of Bonfire builders. "The whole tradition of building is passed down based on what does work and what does not work," said Rusty Thompson, a faculty adviser for Bonfire. "If a blueprint exists, it's those little notebooks that each Red Pot carries."

The notebooks included instructions on how to raise the spliced-center pole, how to set the perimeter poles with the guy ropes 150 feet away, how to bind it all together using heavy-gauge baling wire. But most important was the information on how to stack the logs precisely. Using surveying equipment borrowed from A&M's civil engineering department, the Red Pots ensured the center pole was set straight and that each tier was the precise height.

Although cuts went on throughout the fall, it usually took around three weeks to get the stack built, with most of the work done in the evening when students were out of class. Push kicked in around ten days or so before Bonfire was set to burn, and that's when the bulk of the construction would be accomplished, with shifts running from six P.M. to midnight and from midnight to six A.M. (The 1999 collapse occurred during a Push second shift.) Workers used pulleys and a crane donated by the H. B. Zachry Company of San Antonio to lift logs into place, where teams of other workers waited to wire them to the ever-growing stack. All the while, the Red Pots walked the tiers, making sure everything was level and secure. "It is a well-orchestrated and intensive effort," said former cadet Eric Bearse, Class of '93, who went on to serve on the staff of his fellow Aggie, Governor Rick Perry.

That may be true, but another former cadet, Dave Morris, writing for the online magazine *Salon* just weeks after the collapse, said, "Up on stack, anything goes."

Morris wrote: "It's an image I'll never forget: My roommate, a six-foot-six good old boy from East Texas, stood forty feet up on the third tier, pissing on the back of one of our chief tormentors during Push. . . . The junior, who was on the second tier and trapped thirty feet off the ground, could do little but endure the steady stream of my roommate's righteous piss and inspired obscenities. . . . Translucent against the Friday-night lights, the urine cascaded ten feet and bounced off the back of the hated junior, forming a perverse golden halo around his hunched body. . . .

"Push required twenty-four-hour participation from the Corps of Cadets for one week every November. I grumbled bitterly for the four Saturdays every fall semester we were required to rise at dawn and head out to local forests and fell the trees that make up the bonfire . . . I wore my 'virgin stripe,' a white piece of athletic tape around the right leg, that all first-year Bonfire participants wear with pride. Along with my buddies, I spent all night 'fucking' 500-pound oak logs—carrying them to the base of the stack where a crane would pick them up—and watched the sun rise around the ramparts of the great stack. . . .

"Bonfire struck me as much more than a strange college ritual. Like the fraternal bond among small infantry units in combat, with their late-night secret sharing and hidden vulnerabilities, Bonfire construction was a chance to push the limits, to hang in a rope swing forty feet in the air, hurling profanities at your best friends and shivering in unison as a blue norther cold front kicked down from Canada. Like the Apollo missions to the moon and the teams that set out to scale Mount Everest, Bonfire is a Promethean pageant, a monument to man's tragic, hubristic rebellion against gravity and Mother Nature."

Rebellion against gravity—with youthful recklessness, a pinch of Copenhagen, and maybe a beer or two thrown in. For years there had been critics of Bonfire, including some members of the A&M faculty, who contended that those elements combined would eventually result in disaster. So what did go wrong?

★ ★ ★

The Special Commission on the 1999 Texas A&M Bonfire issued its final report on May 2, 2000. It dismissed many of the rumored causes: the center pole snapped; the soil was insufficiently stable to support the 2-million-pound structure; the guy ropes failed; the crane damaged the stack; it was somehow related to the weather or to seismic activity.

The actual cause was "the result of structural failure—a loss of containment strength around the first stack. Containment strength typically is called 'hoop strength.' The actual failure resulted from excessive 'hoop stress' that overcame Bonfire's hoop strength." In other words, the first tier was like an old-fashioned wooden barrel whose hoops weren't strong enough to hold the barrel together once it was filled with liquid. The primary factor leading to the excessive hoop stress was the decision made by the builders not to bind the first tier with steel cable, as had been done in years past, but rather binding it solely with baling wire.

Complicating the hoop stress problem was wedging—inserting upper-tier logs into lower-tier gaps during construction. In 1999, the gaps were more pronounced than in earlier years, so there was more wedging. Another factor: Beginning in 1998, the logs were stacked more vertically than in years past, when they had leaned inward more. This further increased the stress on the wires. Also, the stack was "overbuilt" toward the southeast, meaning that the stack wasn't balanced evenly on top of the first tier. Finally, there is a slight ground slope to the southeast on the polo fields, where Bonfire had been held since 1992. This, combined with the overbuilding, contributed to the hoop stress to the southeast—and the subsequent collapse.

One of the investigating teams (Team 2/4) "found considerable evidence of irresponsible behavior in Bonfire. Alcohol use was substantial, although student leaders reportedly prohibited alcohol. Also, evidence of hazing and harassment by student workers and student leaders as well as unnecessary horseplay and fighting was significant, despite university efforts to control it. Team 2/4 documented dozens of examples of these behaviors, some of which have led directly to accidents in which students have been hurt or hospitalized. In the experience of the investigation team, Texas A&M is unique in allowing this level of irresponsible personal behavior in and around a construction project of this magnitude. Clearly, there is the potential for these behaviors to impact worker performance and thus perhaps structural integrity."

The commission determined that these factors did not directly affect the 1999 disaster, but it was a pretty damning finding nonetheless. Equally damning was the team's ruling that injuries related to Bonfire had grown by 80 percent between 1996 and 1998. It also was not overly impressed by the notebooks that the Red Pots carried.

"Lack of a written Bonfire design or construction methodology is in the Commission's view . . . very relevant to the collapse."

Finally the commission determined that A&M had plenty of warning through previous incidents that a Bonfire disaster could be in the making. It faulted A&M with reacting to individual incidents and failing to appreciate a bigger problem existed. For instance, when excessive drinking during cuts and other activities related to Bonfire was reported, the university reacted with a "Don't Shatter the Tradition" campaign to discourage alcohol consumption but didn't see it as falling into the pattern of a much, much larger problem. Ditto when a student was killed in a cut-related pickup accident: A&M reacted by banning passengers in the back of pickups while ignoring the larger crisis brewing.

The report stated: "In the Commission's view, the evidence of ongoing problems with Bonfire is so overwhelming that collectively these problems should have triggered a broader overall re-examination of Bonfire—one that included Bonfire design and construction. Unfortunately, this did not occur."

It is no wonder that Ray Bowen pondered aloud if Bonfire was a tradition whose time had come and gone.

★　★　★

Bowen's sentiment was the kind of things that left a lot of Aggies riled. You'd see T-shirts saying it was either rebuild the tradition or retreat to t.u. If you were a true Aggie, you'd never retreat.

"You don't understand what Bonfire means to A&M," one cadet told me on a quiet Friday afternoon. "It's important to the Corps, sure. But it's a lot more important for the non-regs. It's the one event where they get to play a big part in the tradition, you see?"

I nodded.

He went on: "Cuts were incredibly important. The students from the dorms learned what they were capable of doing, getting up at five o'clock on a Saturday morning to head out to the woods to work. Each dorm had its own traditions. Each *floor* had traditions. You'd start off by hitting a tree with an ax a number of times equal to the years in your graduating class, you know? Things like that. It required discipline and teamwork, but it was a lot of fun, too. And it was the only way a lot of them could get involved. That was the biggest, most important thing about Bonfire. You'd see Bonfire and know that part of you went into it. They have to bring Bonfire back, sir. They have to."

★　　★　　★

Without question, the 1999 game became the most important in the series.

It was an enormously difficult time for everyone. Mack Brown told me he heard the news while driving to work. He pulled off the road and wept. He later helped organize a blood drive for the injured. The Texas exes canceled the upcoming Hex Rally, held annually below the lights of the Tower. In its place, a Unity Gathering took place—and all funds collected previously from sales of Hex Rally T-shirts were donated to a memorial fund at A&M. The tower was symbolically darkened that evening. Twenty busloads of Aggies arrived from College Station to join with the Longhorns on the South Mall to remember the dead and injured. Some 5,000 people held white candles in the darkness. Rick Perry, the former Aggie Yell Leader, told the crowd, "I honestly can't tell you what the score on the game on Friday will be, but what I can tell you is all of us, maroon and orange, can walk off that field as one team, one community."

A&M's student body president, Will Hurd, ended his speech with "Hook 'Em, Horns." A&M dropped its "Beat the hell outta t.u." cheer for the game.

Meanwhile, back in College Station, work continued to clear the jumble of logs, and university administrators dealt with the crush of media representatives that had descended on College Station by the hundreds. Cindy Lawson, then newly installed as director of university relations, was running on adrenaline, trying to keep up with the press demands. One day, she was rushing from her office to the polo fields, her mind glued to the latest media requests, when her secretary said, "Will you just stop and look around you!"

Lawson did stop and look. What she saw moved her in a way nothing else ever had. A&M students by the thousand were on their knees in an act of simultaneous prayer. "You know that sign they put up at Fish Camp, *From the Outside Looking in, You Can't Understand It. From the Inside Looking Out, You Can't Explain It?* I knew I was inside at that moment because I understood," Lawson, a University of Michigan alumnus, told me.

★   ★   ★

In recent years, Bonfire took place on the Wednesday before Thanksgiving, if the game was in Austin, or on Thanksgiving evening, if the game was in College Station. The '99 game occurred at Kyle Field, and on Thanksgiving evening, in place of Bonfire, Aggies and others by the thousands gathered at the polo fields for a vigil. Usually, between 40,000 and 50,000 people showed up for Bonfire, and the Yell Practice conducted before the torches touched the wood was the most spirited of the year. But on this night, maybe 100,000 people walked past the site where Bonfire should have been burning, and everything was silent—achingly silent, as one witness described it. You had to listen hard to hear any sounds at all: a whispered prayer, sorrowful sighs, weeping. Some of the mourners left tokens of their sorrow: re-creations of the Bonfire stack made of sticks and twigs, sympathy cards, Bibles, letters, drawings, ribbons, stuffed animals, photographs, Aggie T-shirts and hats, a banner from a kindergarten class at Southwood Valley Elementary School with a message from a student named Cole: "The Bonfire fell. We don't know why. I hope you all feel better soon. Aggies are good people." Even some toy tractors were left behind to honor the Fightin' Farmers who had fallen. "It's going to affect everything forever," said Tess Casbeer, a member of the Class of '93 who came up from Houston and brought an armful of flowers to the polo fields. "It's something you can't ever explain." After quietly paying tribute at the polo fields, the crowd moved on to Kyle Field for an abbreviated Yell Practice, which included a moment of silence—maybe a first for a Yell Practice. Many wore memorial buttons made up for the day reading *They Live On.*

Texans who had little interest in football followed the game's every play the next day. More than 86,000 spectators—at the time, a record crowd to see a football game in Texas—were on hand at Kyle Field, former President George Bush, then-Governor George W. Bush, and then-Texas First Lady Laura Bush among them. Texas fans driving over for the game were greeted with signs thanking them for their support, including one large one on Stotzer Parkway. During pregame ceremonies, four F-16 fighter jets flew overhead, delivering a mighty thunderclap to the stadium. One of the jets abruptly veered upward in the traditional representation of the "missing man." All the jets were flown by former members of the Corps. Hundreds of maroon balloons drifted upward as well. And two A&M students, roommates Lauren Harms of Houston and Shaleah Hester of Nacogdoches, released twelve white doves. "It's still a very, very difficult thing for so many of us," Harms said afterward. "It's very important to us that we remember the victims in some way."

Halftime was nothing like anything ever seen at UT-A&M game. The Showband of the Southwest clutched A&M banners. It played a version of the intermezzo from Bizet's *Carmen*. Then came the most moving moment of the day.

"I'd been talking to Kevin [Sedatole, director of the UT marching band] about what might be appropriate," Aggie band director Ray Toler told me. "At that time, there was a member of the Corps who played bagpipes. He showed up at the polo fields one day after the collapse and he started playing 'Amazing Grace.' It really touched the people who were there. So I told Kevin about that, and he said they had a really good arrangement of 'Amazing Grace.' We agreed it would be a great thing for them to play."

And so the UT band played "Amazing Grace"—and played it in a way that tore at the soul. Only the truly heartless were dry-eyed when the last notes sounded. Then the band doffed its Stetsons to the Aggies and left the field in silence.

Next came the splendid Fightin' Texas Aggie Band, the largest collegiate marching band in the nation. It played its signature march, "The Noble Men of Kyle," then formed the familiar block letter T in silence. After holding the block T for a few moments, the entire band dispersed in silence, the only sound coming from boot spurs and the occasional squeak of a snare harness, leaving Kyle Field vacant.

The game itself pitted a seventh-ranked UT team against a twenty-fourth-ranked A&M team. The Longhorns (9-2) had already claimed the Big 12 South title and were looking down the road at a matchup with Nebraska to determine the conference champions. The Aggies (7-3) were playing with the hope of upgrading their postseason bowl appearance. But all that didn't really matter much. The game was about something else entirely. "We thought about those people every single play," said Chris Valletta, an A&M guard. He had the names of the Bonfire victims written on the shirt he wore beneath his jersey.

Things were hardly less challenging on the Longhorn side of the field. Mack Brown had the toughest week of coaching he'd ever gone through in his long career. "It was such a distraction," he said. "But whenever I started to feel sorry for myself, I thought about the parents and the friends of the victims." Distractions from a game do tend to pale in comparison to parents burying their children.

A&M upset the Longhorns that day 20–16. But even the most hardened Orangecoat couldn't begrudge the Aggies this victory. Throughout Texas, there was a feeling that A&M deserved this win. "I just thought it was right the way it turned out," R. C. Slocum said after the game, reflecting back on everything Aggieland had suffered through over the previous eight days. "I'm so thankful it did."

Aggie quarterback Randy McCown said, "We may not have had Bonfire this year, but there was a Bonfire burning in our hearts today."

CHAPTER THIRTEEN

Kings of the Hill

A S THE FRIDAY BEFORE THE 2001 game grew closer, the two coaches found themselves under the most scrutiny they'd be subjected to at any point during the year. There was a two-week gap between the last game and the day after Thanksgiving matchup, but the demands on their time increased dramatically. They were expected to have their teams fully ready for the big game, but they were also expected to avail themselves to the media, appear at various functions related to the game, and speak to alumni gatherings. To a young coach experiencing his first taste of college football at this level, it all might have seemed overwhelming. In fact, it could have overwhelmed the most battle-hardened coaches. But R.C. Slocum and Mack Brown knew how to handle this kind of pressure. It was all part of the kitchen heat for them. And both of them were able to stand up to it.

For Slocum, it was the twenty-ninth time he'd coached in the game, undoubtedly a record. But it was far from old hat to him. When you talked to him about the game, he lit up—a true Aggie excited by A&M's biggest contest of the year. Brown found the game important, to be sure, and he liked the rivalry, finding the various aspects of it intriguing. But he didn't show quite the excitement that Slocum revealed when you mentioned it to him. Maybe it's because they have different kinds of personalities. Maybe it's because Slocum has been doing this so long that it's become part of his soul.

★ ★ ★

Slocum's office on the second floor of the Koldus Building does look a bit cramped compared to Brown's. It had no grand view and certainly no room for a big couch. The walls are covered with photographs capturing high points in his coaching career. Directly behind his desk is a huge color blowup of a goal-line stand at the 1986 Cotton Bowl. The Aggies had gone to the bowl game as Southwest Conference champs, the first time they'd held the title outright since 1968. There they faced Auburn University and a runner of mythical gifts, the magnificent Bo Jackson. The climax came when Auburn had a first down at the A&M 2-yard line. Four times Jackson carried the ball. And four times the Wrecking Crew stopped him. The photo behind Slocum's desk was snapped when the Aggies tackled Jackson for a 2-yard loss. A&M won the game and finished with a 10-2 season and a top ten ranking for the first time in nearly thirty years.

Slocum lights up when he talks about that play almost as much as he does when you mention the Texas game. It is the kind of football he loves, a smash-mouth, defense-oriented game. When it works—and it has almost always worked during Slocum's tenure as head coach—it is also the kind of football that makes the A&M faithful delirious. It represents the tough values the school cherishes. When it comes up short—well, that's another story.

Slocum comes across as a personable guy, the sort of fellow you wouldn't mind having live next door to you, a guy you'd like to talk to over the fence every now and then. He has a deep voice, but it's not really the kind of growl that Bear Bryant had. It is a true Texas voice: "Can't" ends up sounding like "cain't," the *u*'s and *o*'s in words get stretched out really long. If chicken-fried steak and cream gravy could talk, it would sound like R.C. Slocum. And that's not a bad thing. In terms of personality and bearing, as well as looks and voice, he's the perfect coach for A&M. If he could find a way to liven up the offense and win just a few more big games, it would be nearly impossible to find many detractors in all of Aggieland.

He was born Richard Copeland Slocum in 1944 in Oakdale, Louisiana, but at the age of one he moved with his family to Orange, Texas—his eighty-one-year-old mother still lives in the house that was Slocum's boyhood home. In some sense, his upbringing was like Darrell Royal's. He worked hard as youth, throwing papers and shining shoes before eventually going to work in the petroleum refineries that dominate that part of Texas. His upbringing in the heavily wooded southeastern corner of the state, hard by the Gulf Coast, helped instill Aggie roots in him. "I grew up in this state but had no connection to either school. I followed Texas when Coach Royal was there and they were good, but I always kind of liked the Aggies for some reason. The band was always kind of catchy, you know, with that military style. But I don't know why. Still, if you'd asked me back then, in junior high and high school, which one I really favored, I would have said A&M."

At Stark High School in West Orange, Slocum played on a state semifinalist team under Coach Ted L. Jeffries. Slocum was good enough that he received a football scholarship to McNeese State. He began his collegiate coaching career at Kansas State in 1970. In 1972, he came to A&M as an offensive assistant under Emory Bellard, who was taking over the head coach's job from legendary Aggie player Gene Stallings, who'd suffered through a half dozen years of coaching woes at his alma mater. "Stallings had a tough deal," Slocum says. "He's since proved himself to be an excellent coach. But he was here when A&M was moving away from being a small, all-male military school and the facilities weren't very good. And he was just out-manned." Meaning that Darrell Royal was at his peak at Texas, signing up all the best players in the state.

Hopes were great when Bellard took over. Already a legend in high school coaching annals when he joined Royal's staff at Texas, Bellard gained even greater fame when he virtually invented the Wishbone formation, which revitalized Texas's fortunes and changed the college running game. Bellard brought the Wishbone with him to A&M and initiated programs to make great improvements in the facilities. The third deck was added to Kyle Field; the new press box went up. But Slocum says the most important building that went on under Bellard involved the kind of players he recruited. "He led the charge in recruiting African American players. That had not been done to any extent in this part of the country." Just three years earlier, Texas had staked that dubious claim of being the last team to win a national championship with an all-white team. "The first year he was here, we signed nine African American players who came in and made an impact. And I give him credit for that. It wasn't a popular deal at the time. It wasn't something that was in the vogue to do. But Emory had the courage to go out and do that, and it was the right thing to do."

Bellard brought A&M a string of success that surpassed even Bear Bryant's accomplishments, five consecutive years of winning seasons, bowl appearances in three straight years, and a share of the 1975 SWC title. But then, at the midpoint of the 1978 season when the Aggies had a 4-2 record, Bellard suddenly was out as coach and Tom Wilson stepped in to replace him. It's always been widely assumed that he was fired, although Slocum carefully says, "I don't know that he was fired. But whatever happened, it was one of the biggest disappointments of my career. I thought it was a tragedy for Emory to leave the university when he did."

Slocum, who had moved over to the defensive side of the ball, stayed on as an assistant under Wilson and became defensive coordinator in 1979. He left in 1981 to become defensive coordinator at Southern Cal, but came back the next year as assistant head coach when Jackie Sherrill took over the A&M reins. During the next six years, A&M would gain a national reputation as an outlaw program and wind up on NCAA probation. When Sherrill left following the 1988 season and Slocum became head coach, he knew he had a lot of work to do on the image of the program.

"It's hard changing perception," he says. "It takes time. But we have embraced compliance [to NCAA rules]. It's been a wholesale thing, from the president's office on down, that we were going to change that image we had." And at that, A&M has been remarkably successful. In just a few short years, they've gone from renegade to model performer. A former NCAA staffer is now the program's compliance officer, and the NCAA refers schools that are having trouble to A&M to get pointers on how to clean up their acts. Two events illustrate how far A&M has come. School President Ray Bowen says that A&M probably would not have been admitted to the Association of American Universities if it still had a troubled athletic department. And Slocum points to his own appointment to the board of trustees for the American Football Coaches Association as another illustration. "For me, it was a significant milestone for us in our movement for how we want to be perceived. For the head football coach at A&M to be appointed to the board of trustees was a big thing. We're not trying to circumvent the rules anymore. We're going to be an honest program."

As A&M cleaned up its act, an amazing thing happened. It entered an era of unparalleled success on the football field. That's not supposed to happen when you toughen your recruiting guidelines, but the Aggies pulled it off. "In the 1990s," Slocum says, "we won more games than any team in the history of Texas has ever won in a decade."

Slocum reached one hundred victories as a head coach faster than any other active coach—faster than Bobby Bowden, faster than Joe Paterno, faster than Stever Spurrier. His teams have always been tough at home. They won twenty-nine straight at Kyle Field between 1990 and 1995 and twenty-two straight between 1996 and 2000. Slocum has never lost a nonconference game at Kyle Field. He's also won more than he's lost to Texas. If there's a tarnish on his record, it's that he hasn't always been very successful in bowl games, winning only two out of ten.

★　　★　　★

The story goes that Woody Hayes refused to speak to Bo Schembechler the whole time that Hayes was coach at Ohio State and Schembechler was coach at Michigan, even though they'd been close before Schembechler took the Michigan job. That's how heated the rivalry was between those two schools. They also say that Hayes refused to buy gas whenever he was recruiting in Michigan for fear that the Wolverines would find a way to sugar his fuel tank.

If you expect anything like that involving R. C. Slocum and Mack Brown, you're dealing with the wrong rivalry. R.C. and Mack are buds. Says Slocum, "His offensive coordinator, Greg Davis, who's been with him all the way back to Tulane, was the high school coach at Port Neches. That was one of the schools I recruited. Greg had played at McNeese State. He was just behind me in school, so I'd known him for a long time. One year, while I was recruiting at Port Neches, I asked him if he'd ever considered coaching in college. We talked about it and I talked him into coming to A&M as a graduate assistant. Subsequently, he got hired full-time. So he got into the col-

lege ranks through A&M. Then he left here and joined Mack at
Tulane. I'd go down to New Orleans to see Greg on vacation, and
that's how I first met Mack.

"Mack and I talk a lot," Slocum continues. "In this state, no one
understands more about what I go through in a given day than Mack
Brown does. And no one understands in a given day what he goes
through more than I do. So there's some common association we
have because we're both at big universities in the same state with the
same problems and demands. We can get some consolation talking
to each other after a big loss. You know, our programs have been
pretty close in winning percentage. There's only four games difference between us since Mack came to Texas. He's still not won a conference championship. I have, but it's been three years ago. Alumni
expectations never go down, so you have to roll with the punches.
Those are the kinds of things that Mack and I can talk about. I'm
never critical of him in coaching because we have enough people who
are after us without us being after each other." But that doesn't mean
he doesn't get up for the Texas game. He likens the relationship to
the one golfing buddies Frank Broyles and Darrell Royal had when
Broyles was the head coach at Arkansas. "Frank Broyles and Darrell
Royal were close friends, but when they played each other, it was the
real deal."

Not that the arrival of Brown has made Slocum's life any easier as
a coach. "Mack has been in the game a long time, in a lot of different
situations. No question he's done a great job of going in at Texas and
unifying their people. He's done a tremendous job of maximizing
what they have over there. He's brought Coach Royal back into the
program, embraced the former players at Texas, and done a great job
of selling their tradition. No doubt that Mack's made my job more difficult recruiting. Mack without a doubt has recruited as well as anyone at Texas ever has—and maybe taken it up to the next level."

★   ★   ★

It's kind of hard to grasp this these days, now that Barry Switzer is regarded as ranking up there with Jesus and Oral Roberts in the pantheon of Oklahoma icons, but Switzer's coaching tenure at OU was controversial from the start, even among Oklahomans. If he was loved in a lot of the Sooner State as the savior of OU football, he was despised in other parts of that Baptist Belt state for being a sort of freewheeling playboy who gave his players too long a leash. Switzer won three national championships for OU, but unlike Darrell Royal in Texas in his prime, Switzer probably couldn't have gotten elected governor. The NCAA probations didn't help Switzer's reputation among Oklahomans.

There was one thing that Barry Switzer did do as Sooner coach that everyone agreed was a good thing: He hired Mack Brown as his offensive coordinator in 1984, a move that helped set OU up to win its last national title under Switzer in 1985. Brown was immediately popular in Oklahoma, working with quarterbacks Danny Bradley and Troy Aikman to bring the OU passing attack to a level it hadn't seen since the days of Bobby "The Worm" Warmack. When he left the Sooners after only a year to take the head coaching job at Tulane, you heard many OU fans grumble about the wrong coach leaving town.

Brown grew up in Tennessee, where he was a three-sport athlete at Putnam County High School, lettering three times in football. These days, Brown will downplay his abilities as a running back—one of Brown's coaches described his running style as "trudging"—but he was good enough to be recruited by Bear Bryant at Alabama. Among Brown's cherished items is the telegram Bryant sent him offering him an athletic scholarship: "Bear wanted him real bad," said Carl Torbush, who played football and baseball against Brown in regional all-star competition. But Mack followed his older brother, Watson, to

Vanderbilt, then after two years transferred to Florida State. Other players saw him as being a stand-up kind of guy, an excellent student, down to earth. He and his FSU roommate, Hodges Mitchell (whose son would play for Brown at Texas), put in time being what writer Mark McDonald termed "virtual tackling dummies" for then-Seminole assistant coach Bill Parcells's linebackers. Brown blew out his knee his junior year, which essentially ended his playing career. Like big brother Watson, Brown chose coaching as a career.

Like many young coaches, he put about as many miles on his car in his first years in the profession as long-haul truck drivers put on their rigs. He coached receivers at Southern Mississippi for four seasons, then spent a year at Memphis State, then spent three years at Iowa State before winding up at LSU for a season. In 1983, he was head coach at Appalachian State, where he guided the Mountaineers to their first winning season in four years. "At Appalachian State, I didn't know what I was getting into," Brown recalls. "I was thirty-one years old and planned on staying a minimum of five years and we had a 6-5 season. But I didn't have an equipment manager. A student helped with the equipment room. I learned how to order helmets and face masks. I didn't have a sports information director, so I had to do the first media guide. My wife, Sally, said it looked like something a man would do. All laid out in blocks. The coaches at Appalachian had to teach school in addition to coaching. We drove state cars. It was a great learning experience for me because I did everything." Although Brown ended up staying only one season, he's proud of the legacy of winning he left. He smiles when telling you that Appalachian consistently finishes in the top ten in its NCAA division.

Next he had that reputation-making season at OU.

After that, he was offered the head coaching job at Tulane. Tulane is a private school that has a heavy emphasis on academics. An original member of the Southeastern Conference, Tulane stood up for regular shellackings at the hands of Alabama, Tennessee, Auburn, LSU, and Ole Miss for some thirty years before the Green Wave decided to take a different, less painful direction. Before joining the conference in the 1930s, Tulane had been something of a football power, going undefeated a couple of seasons in the 1920s and playing in the Rose Bowl as an undefeated team in 1932. After leaving the conference, Tulane had some bright spots in the 1970s. But by the mid 1980s, things on the New Orleans campus were pretty grim as far as football was concerned. Brown had his work cut out for him.

"Things were bad," Brown says. "There were no crowds. You had a pro team in town to compete against. There was no enthusiasm. We had fifty-seven players on scholarship, and forty-one of those were on academic probation."

His first season, he won only one game.

Brown convinced Darrell Royal to consult with Tulane about its football program. "I can remember walking out onto the field with Coach Royal," Brown told Mark McDonald. "We had half a practice field that was dusty, and I asked Coach Royal what he thought. He said, 'Where's your practice field?' Then our team came out, and I asked him what he thought. He said, 'Where's your varsity?' I knew then we were in trouble." But by 1987, the Green Wave had turned into a winner, going 6-5 and playing in the Independence Bowl. Tulane set school records for total offense and points, finishing the year ranked eleventh in the nation in scoring with an average of 32.5 per game.

Brown's success at Tulane further enhanced his reputation in the college football world. The next year, he stepped up considerably in stature when he moved on to North Carolina, a program he described as once being "great, but it had slipped." Here he faced a whole different kind of challenge: Could he succeed at a university where football is viewed basically as a fall diversion until the real sport—basketball—gets under way? Could he build a football team that the basketball team would be proud of? Could he shine in the shadow of Dean Smith? Moreover, North Carolina stood at the top of the list of public universities with high academic achievements; UT President Larry Faulkner told me that UNC's high educational achievements were ones that Texas tried to emulate, along with those of Cal Berkeley, UCLA, Wisconsin, and Michigan. Academic standards would present recruiting challenges. All that, plus he would get the opportunity to play Florida State every year, once the Seminoles joined the ACC.

"We were really bad our first couple of years," Brown says. And they were—back-to-back 1-10 seasons. But then North Carolina started to win and became a national powerhouse. After coaching the Tar Heels to 10-2 and 10-1 records, he was offered the Texas job following the 1997 season.

And what a challenge he faced there. Few programs in the country received more media attention than Texas. No program had more demanding fans than Texas. Never mind that almost thirty years had passed since the last national championship, the business of football was huge at Texas, and it wasn't performing up to expectations. Many daunting tasks lay ahead of Brown in this, arguably the highest profile college coaching job in the land, outside of Notre Dame.

"There's not a day off," Brown says about the grueling schedule. "At Texas, you're the football coach every day. Texas is so big that you are, as Coach Royal says, recruiting four states. You have three of the ten largest cities in America within three hours of you. Sally and I had the media out to the house—just the media that covers Texas football and that's all they cover—and there were forty-seven of them. Charities ask you to get involved. You're signing autographs. In our first year here, we turned down seven hundred invitations for speaking engagements. We did a bunch of them, but we had to turn down seven hundred. We just didn't have time to go to them all.

"Coach Royal said that the best thing about the job is that there are twenty million people who care every day what happens with Texas football. I asked him what was the worst thing about the job, and he said that there are twenty million people who care every day what happens with Texas football. And after being here, I understand there's a lot of truth to that.

"Coach Royal said to be the head coach of Texas, you need to smile, you need to like the state of Texas, you need to like the people, you need to stop and talk to them, you need to sign those autographs—those are important things here. Then he said you need to know what you're doing on the field, you need to recruit really well, and you need to win all your games. Other than that, it's an easy job."

Brown hardly made a misstep when he arrived in Austin. He did two really smart things early on: First, he publicly connected with the legacy of Darrell Royal more so than any of Royal's other successors ever had. Royal and Brown frequently were photographed together, went on trips together. That Royal was added to the name of Texas Memorial Stadium did as much symbolically as anything to show that St. Darrell was back in the Texas camp and in full favor. Second, he convinced Ricky Williams to stay for his senior season at Texas, a season that brought Williams a Heisman Trophy.

When you meet Brown, you sense that he is a high-strung guy and an emotional man not ashamed to be given to tears. When he spoke at the Houston Touchdown Club following the 1999 Bonfire collapse, he broke down thinking about the parents who had lost their children. "Life and death is pretty serious. It's a lot more serious than a football game." Some members of the media who cover Texas football think he's a little overly sensitive to criticism, but if that's true, he doesn't show it much in public. He actually seems to be the perfect man for the Texas job. His Tennessee roots give him enough of a Southern accent to make small-town native Texans feel at ease. But it's not enough to make him sound like a hick on television. He looks good on

TV. He can put on boots and jeans and hit the rural areas of Texas and people there will think he's one of them. He can dress in a suit and tie and appear at sophisticated functions around the university and not embarrass anyone. He seems to have rapport with recruits from the inner city and the tiniest burgs alike. Most important, he has the energy required to keep up with the busy pace the Texas job requires.

Brown has the same high regard for Slocum as the A&M coach has for him: "A&M and Texas will have great recruiting year after year. We seem to get a little more publicity, but they do a great job of recruiting and coaching over there. I'm a little jealous of R.C. because he's been in the same job for so long. I think it's a neat thing. He's done a great job, and he'll be in the Hall of Fame when he's through.

"It's a real healthy rivalry. It's the most healthy I've ever been around. There's a lot of anger in the Texas-Oklahoma rivalry, and I've been on both sides of that one. A&M and Texas people really want to win the game, they really want to beat each other, but when you look at the stands, there's a lot of families mixed between the burnt orange and maroon. R.C. and I have talked about it a lot. A large majority of the players on the field are from Texas and all the fans, basically, are from the state of Texas. A lot of people in this state would like to see the state of Texas be really, really good at football, and R.C. and I have said we'd like to see the conference championship and the national championship come down to A&M and Texas every year. It's been a fun rivalry for me because I admire the A&M crowd—they're a tough crowd over there. But, on the other hand, a lot of the A&M folks have been really nice to Sally and me."

★   ★   ★

Over the next few days, Brown carried out his public role as head of the UT football program admirably. On the Monday before the A&M

game, he hosted the media at his press luncheon on the ninth floor of Belmont Hall, the building that is attached to the west side of Royal-Memorial Stadium, and patiently answered questions before the TV cameras before sitting down with the print journalists.

That night, wearing a UT letter jacket and jeans, he stood in a chilly drizzle on the Main Mall on the Texas campus for the annual Hex Rally. The Hex Rally was inspired by an Austin fortune-teller, Mozelle "Madame Augusta" Hipple, back in 1941. Some UT students went to her for advice on how to break an eighteen-year streak without a win at Kyle Field. She advised them to burn red candles "for courage." Red candles burned around the Forty Acres that night, and UT beat the Aggies on their home field, 23–0. This was the first Hex Rally to be held since Madame Augusta died at age ninety-three the previous April.

Maybe a thousand students and a few other assorted fans braved the weather with Brown for the rally, which featured the Showband of the Southwest, Bevo, a modern-dance troupe, and an appearance by one of Austin's most famous residents: Tour de France champion Lance Armstrong, whom Brown introduced as an American hero. "Play the game like it's the last game of your life, because you never know," said Armstrong, a cancer survivor. Armstrong brought a roar of approval when he addressed the quarterback controversy: "I hope Chris Simms plays on Friday. I hope Major Applewhite plays on Friday. I hope Chance Mock [the third-string quarterback] plays on Friday when the score's 40–0 in the third quarter."

Ahmad Brooks, a senior safety from Abilene, got nearly as big a response when he told the crowd, "It's time for the Longhorns to unleash the hounds. And if anybody knows what a hound does—a hound eats raw meat."

But the liveliest point of the evening came when Jeff "Mad Dog" Madden, the Horns' beloved strength and conditioning guru, got down and funky leading the band and the crowd in the raucous "Where My Horns At?" cheer.

The rally ended with the ceremonial lighting of red candles.

I left the Main Mall and headed toward someplace a little less wet. I noticed a lot of students hanging out around the library and Jester Center, the huge dormitory, instead of going to the gathering on the mall. Later, I told an Aggie friend about the Hex Rally. "Only a thousand?" he said, surprised. "If they'd had something like that on the A&M campus, *everybody* would have been there. I just don't understand those damned teasips. Don't they have any real spirit at all?"

The next day, Scott Wilson and I went to the lunch meeting of the Austin Longhorn Club. We sat at a table with former Austin Mayor Bruce Todd. The crowd here definitely tended more toward the razor-cut gray-hair set, the people with money. After some club business, Brown rose to speak and received an enthusiastic reception. At the Hex Rally the night before, he'd seemed to be in his element wearing jeans and talking to students. He still seemed in his element today, wearing a sports coat and tie and addressing wealthy boosters, most of whom were older than he. "I just wanted to say before we get to the game with A&M that I'm so glad we have George W. as president," he said. "Isn't he doing a wonderful job? It's great to have a Texan in the White House at a time like this." He gave the club an update on the team's readiness for the Aggies, then patiently answered questions from the crowd before leaving.

Except for a joint appearance by Brown and Slocum at the Houston Touchdown Club, the formalities were pretty well over. It was time for the post-Thanksgiving family feud.

CHAPTER FOURTEEN

Exalted Horns

THE LOBBY OF THE COLLEGE STATION HILTON was already crowded when I checked in late in the afternoon of Thanksgiving Day. It looked to me as if half the people were in maroon and white, half in burnt orange and white. There didn't seem to be a lovefest taking place between the two camps, but there also didn't seem to be much animosity either. In fact, from time to time, you could see Aggies and Longhorns *talking* to each other. Glory be.

I hung around the hotel for a while before heading over to campus at "dark-thirty," the traditional starting time for Bonfire. With Bonfire absent, the Aggies held a Yell Practice at Kyle Field. I'd done my part for participatory journalism earlier in the season, so I didn't feel any need to mix with the student section. Tonight I found a place off to one side. It was a large, enthusiastic crowd. R.C. Slocum spoke of an e-mail he received asking if he was intimidated by the mighty Longhorns coming to town. He responded by counting off the significant victories the Aggies had achieved over Texas in recent years—and, no, he was not intimidated at all.

Later I wandered around North Gate, checking out the Dixie Chicken and other establishments. Sure, there were a few people enjoying some beers, but for the most part, things were quiet. Around eleven-thirty or so, I crossed the street to the campus again and started walking. It was a breezy evening, the wind smelling damp. It kicked up leaves, scooted discarded cups across the asphalt. I enjoyed being on campus in the dark once more. It had not lost the appeal it had for me three months earlier when I went to my first Yell Practice. Somewhere in the distance, I heard a car horn play the opening strains of "The Eyes of Texas," followed by a chorus of boos. I suppose that will happen at every UT-A&M game until Gabriel sure enough blows his horn.

I strolled over to the stadium. It seemed to be a bit of an eerie place right now, lit up at this time of night. A few other people were there, looking at the graves of the Reveilles, at the statue of the 12th Man. The wind rattled the cables on the flagpoles, sending chills up and down my back. I didn't stay long. I headed back across campus.

I saw some students on the steps of the old YMCA Building, going through Yell Practice. It was like stepping back in time sixty years—a Yell Practice on the same steps where that whole tradition started. I watched for a while, then decided to pack it in for the evening. Tomorrow's game kicked off at eleven, and I'd promised Scott Wilson I'd meet him and John Kelso at around nine at the tailgate parties.

★   ★   ★

The next morning, I stepped onto an elevator crowded with a half dozen or so Aggies and three Longhorns who'd just finished breakfast. The conversation was cordial between the maroon and the burnt orange as the elevator ascended. Then the Longhorns got off on their floor. All cordiality left the elevator at the same time. As soon as the elevator door closed, the Aggies let out a loud, hissing horse laugh, as if on cue.

"Horse laughs already, huh?" I said, smiling.

"You know it, honey," said one of the women in maroon.

★   ★   ★

Wilson said he and Kelso would be under the familiar tethered orange blimp of Hornfans.com. The most noticeable thing I saw was the peaceful mingling of Longhorns and Aggies at the tailgate parties. The cynic might suggest it was because it was early in the morning and the beer hadn't had time to do its work. But I think for the most part this thing has evolved into a pretty friendly rivalry, especially after the Bonfire disaster of 1999.

There are plenty of stories, of course, about how tense things could get in days gone by. In years past, so the lore went, cadets stuck together on game day because roving bands of Longhorns liked to do nothing better than pick out an upperclassman who had strayed from the crowd, overwhelm him, and steal his boots—mostly likely the stolen boots would find a resting place alongside Old Smokey in the depths of the green water of Town Lake back in Austin. When the game was held in Austin and the Aggies held their Yell Practice at the Capitol, members of the Longhorn band sometimes would crash it. Aggies once broke into Royal-Texas Memorial Stadium and tried to use chemicals to "saw the horns off" the Longhorn emblem on the field. Longhorn fans in light planes sometimes buzzed Bonfire in College Station. Legend has it that once they tried to ignite it prematurely by dropping Molotov cocktails onto the stack, only to have their plane riddled with bullets.

But it was hard to fathom anything like that happening this morning. The atmosphere was just too peaceful, never mind the Longhorn football player effigy hanging from the arm of a crane in a construction zone south of Kyle Field.

★   ★   ★

Were it not for the pressures of TV money, this game already would have been history, having been played on Thanksgiving afternoon as it was for so many years. "It was kind of more special," Dan Jenkins says, "when they always played it on Thanksgiving Day. It went well with the turkey and dressing."

And Jenkins's take on the game as it currently is: "The main thing about the Horns-Aggies is what you've got are two of the greatest fight songs and school songs in existence. 'The Aggie War Hymn' and 'Texas Fight' are almost unbeatable, as are 'The Spirit of Aggieland' and 'The Eyes of Texas.' Put all that in the same stadium along with a big game that means something and it's the ideal college football package. Maybe it seemed more romantic to me when it was just the Corps [Old Army] against the frat boys or teasippers. Now it's fifty million Austin students who have no memory of anything against forty million A&M students, and they happen to be more or less the same people."

Exactly. As my Aggie friend Billy Moran said, "My first impression would be that while the rivalry between the schools is as strong as ever, the cultural differences in many ways are lessening all the time. A&M isn't as isolated or homogeneous as it used to be. Heck, a student at either school can go buy the same exact clothes at Old Navy right near campus, both have large fraternity/sorority populations, and all the same big consulting firms try to woo potential recruits at tailgate parties before the football games."

★   ★   ★

Certainly a whorehouse doesn't figure into the rivalry as it once did.

As anyone who has seen *The Best Little Whorehouse in Texas* knows, the brothel in La Grange known as the Chicken Ranch, also known as the Oldest Continually Operating Non-Floating Whorehouse in the United States, had a special place in the "unofficial culture" of A&M. "It was the first tourist attraction I heard about when I came to Texas," Al Reinert wrote. "But then, I came to Texas to be an Aggie, so that explains that. . . . The pilgrimage to La Grange sits close to the heat of The Aggie Myth, as central to the catechism as standing at football games and building the Bonfire for the Texas game."

Or as an Old Ag told me more succinctly: "Sure, we used to drive over to La Grange for the Aggie Special. It was eight dollars then. You have to remember, we was in the middle of nowhere with no girls around. So it was either go to the Chicken Ranch or drive up to Waco and pick up Baylor girls."

The whorehouse saw its share of Longhorn trade as well, since La Grange sits roughly the same distance from Austin as from College Station. Of course, Austin had its own whorehouse of some repute (or disrepute) in a motel on South Congress Avenue, but it seemed to cater to legislators and businessmen. La Grange was for the legislator and the businessman, too, but also for the common man and the student—and for the adventurous and those with a sense of history and tradition, since the whorehouse probably dated back to the time when Sul Ross was out searching for Cynthia Ann Parker and maybe even went all the way back to Republic days.

"It was as nice a little whorehouse as you ever saw," Larry L. King wrote. In the hit song "La Grange," ZZ Top growls that the Chicken Ranch had some nice girls. Gary Cartwright has written about his days of yearning as an undergrad at UT and satisfying those yearnings at the whorehouse: "I fell in love with a girl named Patsy from Highland Park on my first visit, and with someone else nearly every time I made the trip." Reinert's experience was a little different, though: "We sauntered into the parlor, where we drunkenly introduced ourselves to a half dozen local farmers, a couple of cross-country truck drivers, and a fellow pilgrim who'd journeyed all the way down from Nebraska—and met three young ladies who either worked there or were truck drivers, too, we weren't sure. . . . My friend Richard, who was still trying to decide if they worked there or were just visiting truck drivers, thought he'd break the ice a little by asking one of them if she wanted to dance, which she didn't. 'What's with this dancing stuff, honey?' is what she said. 'Ya wanna do some business here or not?' That's when we decided that she must be one of the UT coeds we'd heard about."

One of the most interesting parts of the lore of the Chicken Ranch is that in those more innocent days, back before the damnable press started sticking its nose into everything, the winning team of the Texas-A&M game could count on spending Thanksgiving evening at the whorehouse, courtesy of wealthy alumni. King wrote, "Think how fiercely a team might fight to win the Pussy Bowl! Yeeeeaaaah, *team!*"

When I go to La Grange—a pleasant county seat situated adjacent to a line of bluffs along the Colorado River—to visit my in-laws, I never hear anyone mention anything at all about the Chicken Ranch. I asked one of my sisters-in-law about it one time, and she isn't even sure where it was located—and she's spent most of her adult life in La Grange after moving over from Austin. After the meddlesome Houston TV reporter Marvin Zindler got the thing closed down in the early 1970s, some part of it was carefully dismantled and moved to Dallas to house a restaurant: When the restaurant folded, no one cared much about preserving the remnants, and it met the bulldozer's blade. As far as the original site, not much remains there. But a group of Aggies decided to try to revive the Chicken Ranch tradition by holding a Y2K celebration on the property on New Year's Eve, 1999.

My understanding is that got nixed when other property owners refused to give the revelers access to the site.

La Grange, with its strong Czech and German heritage, is a good place to buy a *kolache* these days, not a piece of ass. And the big news around town this fall was the continued success of its high school football team, the Leopards, or "Leps," who made it to the state championship game. La Grange is one of those great Texas football communities. When the playoffs come, it becomes a ghost town as businesses shut down early and residents head off by the hundreds to compete for good seats at wherever the playoff game is being held. Football is good bull in La Grange. But the whorehouse? Well, tourists will ask about it as long as someone somewhere is performing *The Best Little Whorehouse in Texas.* But most people in La Grange these days would probably prefer for all that to fade from memory.

A side note: The term "Chicken Ranch" has turned up again in recent years. Now it's the name of a fried chicken restaurant on Interstate 35 just outside Norman, Oklahoma. Its proprietor? Barry Switzer.

★   ★   ★

I found Wilson and Kelso in the crowd below the blimp. Maybe a fourth of the people in that group were wearing maroon. I had my first Milwaukee's Best of the day, and I recalled a great scene in Billie Lee Brammer's novel in which the hero, the LBJ-like Arthur "Goddam" Fenstemaker, extols the pleasures of a nice cold beer first thing in the morning. It does have a way of cutting the phlegm.

Wilson, an Orangeblood if ever there was one, has a lot of Aggie friends. "They see me as a kind of kindred spirit," Wilson said. When the Longhorn baseball team visits College Station, Aggies will give Wilson a boost up on a railing so he can lead the Longhorn fans in the singing of "The Eyes of Texas." Once after a game, Wilson saun-tered into the Dixie Chicken for refreshment. An Aggie looked up from a table, pointed at Wilson, and said to his buddies, "Looky-there. It's the teasips' Yell Leader." So there's a lot of respect for him in the opposing camp. And Wilson, the ultimate Longhorn, respects the Aggies as well. "When I was a kid," Wilson told me, "I was mak-ing fun of the Aggies once, and my old redneck East Texas aunt got onto me about it. 'Now, Scottie,' she said in that East Texas drawl, 'there's a lot of fine young men who gave their lives for this country that come from A&M. You shouldn't make fun of them.' And you know, she was right."

Still, that didn't dissuade Wilson from telling me with amusement about a plot he was privy to designed to disrupt a Longhorn-Aggie baseball game in College Station with the use of some carefully placed graffiti. Some background: The Texas A&M logo involves the block letter T with the initials A and M on each side of it, so it looks sort of like this:

$$\text{A}\,\mathbf{T}\,\text{M}$$

One of the most common Aggie bumper stickers you find features just the logo in maroon. Some Longhorns like to procure these bumper stickers through stealth, then affix them to their cars, trucks, or SUVs with a little alteration. They buy a couple of stick-on letter Es and affix them to either side of the A&M logo, so that it now reads:

$$\text{EA}\,\mathbf{T}\,\text{ME}$$

Now the plot: A group of Longhorn fans, irritated by the train's play-ing of the "Hullabaloo, Caneck! Caneck!" tune whenever it rolled past the baseball stadium, took up funds to pay some brave soul to try to find the train somewhere on a side track up the line from College Station and spray-paint the altered A&M logo on the side of a boxcar. The Aggie fans would be treated to hearing "Hullabaloo, Caneck! Caneck!" then, just seconds later, seeing EATME roll past on the side of a boxcar.

Unfortunately, from the Longhorn perspective, no one stepped up to take the cash and accomplish the graffiti.

★　　★　　★

One of Wilson's Aggie friends was James Taglienti, a member of the Class of '99. We spent some time talking about Bonfire—"They have to bring it back"—and about the 1995 Texas game at College Station. It was the finale for eighty-one seasons of Southwest Conference football, and UT and A&M came into the meeting tied for the SWC lead. Therefore, the winning school would claim the last ever SWC title. And that seemed appropriate, since UT and A&M were the best-known schools to play in that heralded old league. R.C. Slocum said before the game, "It's really fitting that these two old schools and old rivals line up to play for all the SWC bragging rights one last time."

When the game was over, the score stood at 16–6 in favor of the Longhorns. Not only had the Longhorns claimed the final SWC title, they'd also broken a long home-field winning streak for the Aggies. The UT fans rushed the field, and in College Station, that's a pretty major affront to Aggie tradition. When you visit the A&M campus for the first time, you usually get advised to stay off the grass because you never know if the grass you're walking on is a memorial of some kind. Walking on a memorial can bring down the ire of the cadets in a hurry. But what is and isn't a memorial really isn't cut-and-dried. It's widely believed, for instance, that the band's practice field was a memorial, and I asked Colonel Toler about that. He didn't exactly say it was a memorial, but explained that some dearly departed Aggies who had been members of the band had requested that their ashes be spread on the practice field, so Aggies expect that expanse of land to be accorded some respect. Because of that, if you're out walking around on it and you're not a member of the band, you'll probably be asked to get off the grass. The same kind of thing is true about Kyle Field. While a lot of people believe it is a memorial, it is in fact not, according to a piece in the *12th Man Magazine*, written by Homer Jacobs.

Nevertheless, Aggies expect visitors to respect the field, and when the Longhorn fans rushed it, all hell broke loose. The Corps of Cadets took a stand to push back the Longhorn crowd. Fistfights broke out on the turf, which was already littered with sugar cubes the Longhorns had thrown from the stands—the Longhorns hoped to be invited to play in the prestigious Sugar Bowl with the victory. Accounts of the brawl have it that some of the cadets unsheathed their sabers and threatened their brethren from Austin. Some other accounts also have it that it didn't really matter if the cadets pulled their sabers because the blades were dull. Whatever, the Longhorns were able to break through the cadets' line and thus dis the Aggie's hallowed Kyle Field. At least two people ended up being carted away to a hospital in College Station with injuries suffered in the scuffling. Finally, A&M police and the Aggie Yell Leaders managed to break it all up before things got *really* ugly.

"What gets me," Taglienti, who was present for the after-the-game disorder, was saying, "is that it wasn't students out there. It was mostly guys in orange shirts who'd been out of college for years."

Was it? I talked to Ryan Duffin, who was a student at UT at the time and who was among the Longhorn fans who rushed the field. "Naw," he said, "I just saw UT students out there."

Another UT loyalist who was there, Kristine Hale, said, "I watched the Corps members chasing and beating down male and female fans. I saw swords drawn and pointed at UT fans. A friend of mine in the

Corps told me that it is not their job to keep people from other schools off their 'sacred' field, but to escort fans from the field.

"To me this shows their lack of respect for UT. I do not feel that this would have happened on such an extreme level at Memorial Stadium. We do not send a student organization on the field to scramble and get rival fans off our field, let alone by beating other fans."

To which a lot of Ags would respond that it never happened that way. Any hooliganism that went on was the responsibility of the Longhorns. The Corps just acted to keep things under control.

Whatever, it was a hell of a way to say goodbye to the old Southwest Conference. It also leaves you scratching your head whenever you hear people associated with the two schools describe the rivalry as "fun" and "good natured."

★　　　★　　　★

I spent the next few minutes talking to fans, both Longhorn and Aggie, beneath the orange blimp. One of the Longhorns said, "I think I'll head on over to the stadium. I want to see if they sacrifice any chickens or anything before they start their games."

I decided to head toward Kyle Field myself.

Along the way, I saw three young women wearing maroon shirts with a Bible verse printed on them:

> *I will cut off the horns of the wicked.*
> *—Psalm 75:10.*

★　　　★　　　★

I found myself in a huge crush of people, slowed down by the security checks going on at the gates. Security, of course, had been heightened everywhere I went since the September 11 attacks, but this was the first time delays had been significant. Also, 87,555 people were squeezing into the stadium, setting a record for attendance at a football game in Texas. That was helping to stall things as well. Somewhere in that crowd was Governor Rick Perry, wearing an Aggie sweater. Also in that crowd were twenty-three A&M students wearing white T-shirts with letters spelling out BONFIRE 1999. REMEMBER THEM.

I hadn't paid attention to where my seat was until now, and when I climbed the steps and looked down at where I'd be sitting, I knew I was in trouble. Just a few rows up from where the Silver Spurs had Bevo tethered on the Kyle Field sideline. Two rows up from the Longhorn Hellraisers, one row up from the Hellraiser Honeys. And boisterous UT students on each side of me and behind me. Only me and one other geezer, God bless his soul, stuck in this seething mass of, well, youthful exuberance.

For generations, Longhorn fans prided themselves on maintaining a certain decorum. When Scott Wilson started coming to games with his dad back when Darrell Royal was young, a lot of men still wore ties on game day and a lot of women still wore dresses. All kinds of people went to the games. "Back then," Wilson said, "everybody in Austin was a Longhorn fan. The other day, I met a guy and I was wearing a Texas cap. He said, 'Are you a Longhorn fan?' In those days, you didn't even have to ask. And everyone came to the games—businessmen, rednecks, hippies." When they came to the games, they tended to "act like they'd been there before," as Darrell Royal might have said. They certainly wanted to appear more civilized than those hooligans from north of the Red River. But to a generation who thinks loud and rowdy should be de rigueur behavior at games, the Longhorn fans seemed a little stilted. Hence, the Longhorn Hellraisers were born, inspired in the late '80s by two transfer students from LSU and Michigan State. They brought face painting and chest painting into the Longhorn mix and they certainly always seem excitable, to say the least.

The Hellraisers were already cranked up, and they had the students around them pretty well cranked up as well. And the Honeys were galloping along to "Texas Texas Yee Haw." I was standing on the bleacher—no sitting during this game—next to a student I'll call the Ginger Man. He had hair to his shoulders, and he wore a Texas cap, Texas T-shirt, jeans, and boots. And he was skunk drunk by ten o'clock that morning, thanks to a flask of Jim Beam he had taped on his leg below his jeans. He was shouting into a wireless telephone and I had to wonder just how much he could hear or be heard over the din. He was talking to a friend who was supposed to be where we were sitting but the friend was having, *ahem*, difficulties. "This crazy bastard," the Ginger Man explained to me, "he stayed up till some time after three drinking wine. Then, first thing this morning, about seven-fifteen, he wakes up and the first thing he does is reaches for the wine bottle. He's out of his mind." His wireless phone started ringing again, and the Ginger Man was shouting into it while trying to throw the Hook 'Em sign at the right places during the playing of "The Eyes of Texas." He got off the phone.

About this time, a guy wearing an OU football jersey walked down the sidelines in front of the Texas fans. The Texas fans let out their loudest chorus of boos of the day. The A&M fans in the next section over also started booing. The Ginger Man shook his head, then said to me, "You know, I gotta respect somebody who do a thing like that, wearing an damned OU jersey over here for *this* game. That takes some balls, you know?" I wasn't sure about the guy's *cojones*. It seemed like brain damage would have been a more likely explanation for his wearing an OU jersey to a UT-A&M game.

It was a pleasant day, the kind of day that makes autumn in Texas so enjoyable. The temperature stood at seventy-three degrees when

A&M took the opening kickoff at just past eleven A.M. under a partly cloudy sky. The wind continued to blow in from the south, as it had been the night before, with gusts reaching twenty miles per hour. That would cause trouble all day for both teams.

Things started off slowly. The Aggies kept the ball for seven plays but accumulated a net total of only three yards before Cody Scates punted. The Longhorns did no better with their first possession— seven plays, three yards—before being forced to punt the ball away themselves. On their next possession, the Aggies went three and out. But this time, Texas managed to block the punt. Tony Jeffery recovered the ball for Texas and sped 23 yards into the A&M end zone. The Longhorn Band exploded into "Texas Fight," and the Hellraisers and the other students around me celebrated. For a while you sensed the Texas crowd was ready for a rout to start rolling from that point on.

But it was not to be.

The rest of the half consisted of nothing more than punts, missed field goals by each team, and one Texas interception of a Mark Farris pass. The half ended 7–0 in Texas's favor.

When the Fightin' Texas Aggie Band took the field, the Ginger Man and his friends went nuts. "What is this Nazi shit?" they implored of each other as the band marched by. "Oh, man, I'm not even believing this!" Next they watched in disgust as the Aggies formed the familiar Longhorn symbol on the field, then, while playing "Saw Varsity's Horns Off," broke the horns off the head of the steer. The Texas fans booed and hissed while a huge roar of approval went up from the Aggie sections. "I don't fucking believe it," the Ginger Man said. "I just don't fucking believe it." Behind us I heard a guy question whether the Aggies had any idea that it was the twenty-first century. "That's right," the Ginger Man said. "Jesus, this Nazi shit is so lame."

About that time, a guy on the bleacher behind us started to throw up. We spread out the best we could to clear a space for him. Thank

God, he managed to choke all but a mouthful of his vomit back down. I had this horrifying image flash before me of spending the rest of the game with puke dripping off the back of my shirt. I looked up at the luxury boxes that ring the stadium, knowing that former President Bush was watching from Coach Slocum's box and that former Giants quarterback Phil Simms and Denver Broncos Coach Mike Shanahan were in other boxes. I felt pretty sure they and their parties were having a little bit of a different Texas-A&M game experience than I was.

The second half started off a lot like the first half. Texas took the kickoff, picked up eight yards on three plays, then punted. But this time the Aggies returned the punt 37 yards to the Longhorn 27-yard line. Five plays later, Keith Joseph scored from four yards out, and suddenly the game was tied. Until the middle of the third quarter, the Aggies and the Longhorns exchanged punt after punt, with the punters doing their best to manage in the swirling winds. Neither Farris nor Chris Simms had much luck battling the stiff breeze, either, and both teams ran a conservative attack.

Finally, Texas began to wear down the Aggie defense. Cedric Benson, who had been stifled in the first half, began to crack the Wrecking Crew's line. In the fourth quarter alone, he had 67 yards of rushing (he'd finish the game with 79), and with just over seven minutes left in the game, Benson smashed across the Aggie goal line and Texas recaptured the lead. Late in the quarter, Texas intercepted a Farris pass. Two plays later, Benson scored from eleven yards out.

"I don't fucking believe this!" the Ginger Man cried, leaping off the bleacher and flinging his cup of Jim Beam and Coke straight up in the air. A shower of bourbon and soda rained down on everyone around him. With the score at 21–7 in Texas's favor, a maroon stream of fans started to leave the stadium—even though it is bad bull for Aggies to leave the stadium before the final gun sounds. The guy in the OU jersey walked past again to another outpouring of boos from Aggie and Longhorn alike.

As Aggie security lined up at the south goalpost, the Ginger Man turned and shouted up at the Longhorn fans, "I don't know about you guys, but I'm rushing the field!" No one gave him any heed. And why should anyone? It wasn't the kind of victory that would inspire that sort of thing. The final gun sounded, and the Longhorn fans around me started to file out peacefully. I looked around to see if there was any mischief afoot anywhere, but there was none. I turned to say something to the Ginger Man, but he'd disappeared. I never saw him again.

★　　★　　★

I got hung up in the crowd at the flagpole in the south end zone. As the cadets lowered the Old Glory, the sound system blasted what is undoubtedly the worst patriotic song ever written, Lee Greenwood's "God Bless the U.S.A." It sets my teeth on edge every time I hear it. Don't get me wrong. I like patriotic music. I love stirring marches like John Philip Sousa's "Stars and Stripes Forever." I love Irving Berlin's "God Bless America," especially Kate Smith's version. But "God Bless the U.S.A." is bad compared to classic patriotic music in the same way that contemporary Christian is bad compared to righteous gospel. I couldn't wait to get out of there.

At last I was free. I ran into some more young women with the Psalm 75:10 T-shirts. Naturally, they weren't joyous that the horns of the wicked had survived the day, but they also didn't seem very down about it. The Longhorn fans weren't overly celebratory either. Everyone just seemed to want to get to the car and find something to eat.

Near the steps of the Memorial Student Center, I did see one senior Aggie band member standing with his saxophone still strapped to his neck, looking as forlorn as anyone I'd seen all day. His eyes appeared to be a little swollen. Maybe he'd wept a bit because of the loss. Or maybe it was just allergies. A lot of people in College Station have immune system problems when the town is overrun with burnt orange.

Back at the Hilton, I packed my stuff and got ready to drive back to Austin. Before I left, though, I pulled out the copy of the Gideon Bible in the bedside table drawer. I opened it to Psalm 75. And, sure enough, I found the verse, but the Aggies had fudged a little by not including the *whole* thing. In fact, it did proclaim, "All the horns of the wicked also will I cut off." But the Aggies who'd printed up the T-shirts left off an important part of the verse: ". . . *but* the horns of the righteous shall be exalted."

The Longhorns were exalted indeed on this Friday after Thanksgiving.

★　　★　　★

Exalted and seemingly on their way to one of the major bowls, most likely a BCS matchup in the Sugar Bowl. Not the national championship game, but still one of prominence. And the Aggies? Well, everyone assumed they'd head over to San Antonio and make another appearance in the Alamo Bowl.

It didn't play out that way. The 2001 season ended in a flurry of wacky upsets that left the NCAA in a turmoil.

Even as the fans were leaving Kyle Field, the unthinkable was happening in Boulder. Colorado was giving Nebraska a trouncing of historic proportion—62–36, as bad a loss as Nebraska has ever suffered in its distinguished football history. When the shell-shocked Cornhuskers saw the last seconds tick off the clock, they must have assumed that their chances for playing in the Rose Bowl for the national championship were gone. Colorado now was set to play in the Dallas suburb of Irving for the Big 12 title, where its opponent undoubtedly would be Oklahoma. And the Sooners had to be favored in that one. They had the most talent. So all they had to do was mop up the Buffaloes and hope for a little help in some other end-of-season games, and then they could count on a trip to Pasadena with a chance to repeat as national champs.

But that was not to be either. OU still had a game to play in Norman against lowly Oklahoma State, which ranked with Baylor and Kansas among the worst teams in the conference. However, the intrastate rivalry between OU and Oklahoma State is called the Bedlam Series and with good reason. Crazy things happen. And such an event occurred in Norman. What should have been a big-time blowout on the Sooners' home field turned out to be one of the most embarrassing losses in school history: OSU won 16–13.

Now Texas claimed the Big 12 South title outright. Suddenly Texas was looking at a *very* bright vista. All it had to do was repeat its earlier victory over the Buffaloes and the Longhorns could be traveling to Pasadena after all to play Miami for the whole enchilada. Maybe Texas's Roy Williams should have left his cell phone programmed the way he had set back in the late summer.

Mack Brown and the Longhorns should have been extremely confident going to Irving. The Longhorns easily were the better team on both sides of the ball. Irving was supposedly a neutral site for the championship game, but it was hard as hell to not notice that it would be *Texas* playing in *Texas* Stadium. Everything seemed right—except that Wilson and Kelso watched the game ensconced in a Texas Stadium luxury box owned by a scion of the legendarily wealthy Bass family of Fort Worth. That was something, two beer-and-paper-towel kind of guys, committed bleacher rats, up there in the seclusion of the cognac and pressed linen zone of a luxury box. When I talked to them later, I got the impression they *much* preferred their regular posts down among the little people.

What happened on that terrible artificial surface in Texas Stadium was something, too—something most Longhorn fans would just as soon forget.

Colorado seemed to come into the game still percolating on the adrenaline from their defeat of mighty Nebraska. Chris Simms stoked the Buffaloes' adrenaline even more by giving up three interceptions, one of them returned for a touchdown, and turning the ball over a fourth time by fumbling. The Longhorn coaches pulled Simms and put in Major Applewhite, who damned near performed miracles. With thirty-one seconds left in the game, he connected for his second touchdown pass of the night, bringing the Longhorns within two points of Colorado. But it wasn't quite enough. Colorado and Gary Barnett claimed the Big 12 title by winning the game, 39–37. And Texas, which was a sure bet for a BCS bowl game after beating A&M, was now reduced to playing in a second-tier bowl, the Holiday Bowl in San Diego.

The more vocal Texas fans were ready to blame Chris Simms for the loss. Anti-Simms graffiti popped up at a heavily traveled intersection in Austin in less time than it took to make the return trip from Dallas. Brown wasted little time in announcing that Applewhite would start in the Holiday Bowl.

Things were hardly brighter in College Station. When the post-season seedings were announced, the Aggies learned that the Alamo Bowl had passed them by. Instead they would be playing in the Galleryfurniture.com Bowl in the creaky old "house of pain," the Astrodome in Houston. Instead of playing one of college football's elite teams, they would face one of their traditional old Southwest Conference rivals: TCU.

Longhorn and Aggie alike entered the winter feeling pretty depressed.

Epilogue:

Silver Taps

THE FIRST TUESDAY IN FEBRUARY was a drizzly, cold day in College Station. The gray sky and chilly rain made an apt backdrop for the business at hand. Texas A&M was preparing to engage in one of its oldest and most solemn rites, Silver Taps. The ceremony is simple yet elegant—and tremendously moving. It is how the Aggies say goodbye to their dead.

It started more than a century ago when, at the age of fifty-nine, the beloved Sul Ross died unexpectedly at his College Station home on January 3, 1898. To memorialize his passing, A&M held the first Silver Taps in front of Old Main. Thereafter, the Aggies have conducted a Silver Taps ceremony as a tribute for an Aggie who, at the time of his or her death, was enrolled in graduate or undergraduate courses at A&M. If needed, the event occurs on the first Tuesday of the month during the fall and spring semesters to honor any student who has died during the previous month.

Since 1918, the ceremony has taken place in the plaza in front of the Academic Building, near the statue of Sully, which is where fewer than a thousand Aggies gathered this night in the cold rain to make their farewells to three departed A&M students. Paige Taylor Mixon, nineteen, a sophomore economics major from Arlington, Texas, died in a car crash on January 2 while on a ski trip. That same day, Jonathan

Brian Borowiec, forty-one, a doctoral candidate living in College Station, succumbed to esophageal cancer. Three weeks later, Carmela Beatrice Izaguirre, a senior psychology major from Grandview, Texas, died of bone cancer. She was twenty-one.

Earlier in the day, the flag in the plaza was lowered to half staff, and small cards bearing the names, classes, majors, and dates of birth of the dead were placed at the base of the flagpole as notice of the Silver Taps to come. Notices also were posted in the Memorial Student Center and in Evans Library. At around ten o'clock in the evening, lights around campus began to be extinguished until the whole campus was dark. About that same time, hymns started chiming from Albritton Tower. At ten-thirty, the Ross Volunteer Firing Squad marched into plaza to the statue of Sully, where they fired three volleys. Even though the Aggies in attendance knew the shots were coming, the first seemed to make them jump. It was *that* loud. Then came "Silver Taps." The rendition played by Corps buglers was composed in the 1930s by Colonel Richard J. Dunn, the same man who wrote the music for "The Spirit of Aggieland." It has never been captured on paper. Buglers teach it to their replacements. The mournful tune came from the dome of the Academic Building—exact location within the dome and how to get to it are guarded secrets known only to select Corps members. The buglers played "Silver Taps" three times, once to the north, once to the west, and once to the south. As always, they did not play it to the east because the sun never again will rise on the Aggies memorialized tonight.

Once the bugling stopped, the crowd departed in silence.

★　　★　　★

Some of the Aggies who attended Silver Taps that night were disappointed by the attendance. Some blamed the cold temperatures and the rain. But in fact it probably had little to do with the weather. It was probably more related to the current crisis that had emotions reeling on the campus. The day before the Silver Taps ceremony, A&M President Ray Bowen had announced that Bonfire would not return for 2002. So when the bugles blew "Silver Taps" on Tuesday night, they could have been sounding for Bonfire, too. There was a feeling among the Aggies that if Bonfire didn't return for 2002, it might well not return ever.

The demise of Bonfire hit Aggieland hard. A number of students stomped out of the Memorial Student Center Flagroom, where Bowen's announcement to the press was being shown via closed-circuit TV, when it became clear what the decision would be. As word spread across campus, some students got up and walked out of classes. But Bowen seemed to me to be caught in an unfixable jam. As the litigation related to the 1999 accident showed, any future Bonfire would involve a lot of liability. Covering too much liability would translate to a mighty drain on A&M funds. It had been estimated that 2002 Bonfire would have cost $2.5 million. Each year's Bonfire thereafter would cost upward of $1.3 million. "We simply cannot spend this much money to construct a Bonfire," Bowen said.

He went on to say, "In simplest of terms, the conditions I gave in June of 2000 have not been met, in spite of the dedicated work of the Bonfire Taskforce. As I judge the facts today, without an acceptable Safety Plan, the limited role that has been preserved for students, namely implementation, still carries a danger above what we can tolerate. Also, as we struggle to reach our safety goals, the costs grow beyond our reach. Finally, another driver for costs is the management of legal liability.

"This decision, while extremely difficult for me and many others, is going to be very unpopular. Our community wants a Bonfire. I wish I could make it happen. I have a special compassion for the student members of the Bonfire Taskforce. They have vested a major portion of their last years in college in an effort to save a tradition for all future Aggies. I will fully understand if they do not agree with this decision. I am saddened by the reality that students that I dearly care for will now leave the university with the Bonfire decision standing between us.

"I am also emotionally caught up in the idea that the Bonfire is a great tradition. I am sad today that I am compelled to make a difficult decision. I am sad for our students and for our university. . . . Life is full of challenges, and it confronts all of us with circumstances that we would rather avoid. The Bonfire is such a circumstance for me. My heart does not like what my brain is doing today."

The decision seemed perfectly logical, yet it flew directly into the face of the spiritual investment so many Aggies had put into Bonfire over the years. The next day's issue of *The Battalion* ran a photo of two anguished cadets in the Flagroom watching Bowen's press conference. One cradled his head and stared down at the floor; the other rubbed at his eyes. In the background, a young woman was weeping.

★ ★ ★

Emotions did not die down quickly.

Several days later in Austin, I asked a Former Student about the decision. Her answer was succinct. "I can't wait until Bowen is gone," she said. "Then we can hire [U.S. Senator and A&M presidential aspirant] Phil Gramm so he can bring back Bonfire and fire R.C. Slocum."

But in the end, Gramm was not selected to be the new A&M president. Former CIA Director Robert Gates got the nod.

★ ★ ★

I thought the Aggies had a pretty good football season, all things considered. They defeated two bowl-bound teams (Iowa State and Kansas

State) and won their postseason game against the TCU Horned Frogs in the Galleryfurniture.com Bowl. Sure, TCU was TCU instead of a top ten power, but the Aggies came out on the respectable end of a 28–9 walloping. It was a good enough season to satisfy R.C.'s supporters. To his detractors, it fell short by enough games to keep up the pressure on A&M to find a new coach.

★　　★　　★

Mack Brown brought UT its most successful football season since the days of the Reagan presidency, but within a four- or five-week period, that man was jerked from highs to lows to highs at levels no normal soul could withstand. He came through it in good form.

In balmy San Diego, against an 8-3 Washington Husky team, Major Applewhite finished his Texas career by posting a phenomenal 473 yards of passing to lead the Longhorns to a come-from-behind 47–43 victory. Applewhite also gave up three interceptions in the game, one of them leading to a Washington touchdown. But he didn't let the misfires destroy his game. He pulled through adversity, just as he had many times before in big games. And he brought the Longhorns back from a 16-point fourth-quarter deficit. He left the field with his reputation as a Longhorn hero cemented. And Brown won a lot of respect from the Orangebloods for letting Applewhite go out in style. That and he guided the Horns to an eleven-win season. Something no one at Texas had done since the days of St. Darrell.

★　　★　　★

Chris Simms was not the best quarterback in college football at the beginning of the 2001 season, and he was not the best quarterback in college football at the end of the season. That he wasn't the best back in August probably should have been obvious to anyone who had followed his career closely. Yet the magazine covers and the Heisman hype wrought impossibly high expectations—the next Peyton Manning!—for Simms among a lot of very vocal Longhorn fans. When he failed to meet those expectations, the fans got down on him. I saw a photo of him taken after the Big 12 championship game. He had an expression on his face exactly like that of Henry Gibson, the perpetually sad-faced comedian from *Laugh-In*. It was a far cry from the toothy smiles he had on those preseason magazine covers.

The good news for him was that he could enter his final year of eligibility at UT under a lot less pressure than he had the year before. I didn't think he would make anyone's preseason Heisman list in 2002. Cedric Benson, maybe. But not Chris Simms. When it came time to choose jerseys for the 2002 season, Simms gave up the number 1 that he'd worn in 2001. In the Longhorn spring drills, he came out wearing number 2. A symbolic choice, perhaps, although his explanation was that he took number 2 because it had always been his favorite. He hadn't worn it before because it already had been claimed by a more experienced Texas player, Montrell Flowers. The eyes of Texas would be on number 2 in 2002, but probably not with the intensity that they were on number 1 in 2001. That had to be good news for Simms.

As for Benson, the spring turned out to be a less than balmy time. He was arrested in his hometown of Midland after police responded to a loud music complaint at an apartment complex. Benson and a friend were charged with possession of a small amount of marijuana, possession of drug paraphernalia, and being a minor in possession of alcohol. However, Benson passed a drug test within days after the arrest, and a short time later, authorities dropped all charges against him. It was big news for a while in Texas, and more than a few Aggies had fun with the episode on Internet discussion boards.

★　　★　　★

I found a store in Houston specializing in A&M memorabilia that carried a video of *We've Never Been Licked*, the black-and-white World War II propaganda film that had first inspired my interest in A&M lo those many years ago. No question about it: I had to buy it. One cloudy afternoon after Miami had blown out Nebraska to claim the national championship, I took the shrink-wrap off the box and inserted the cassette into the VCR and sat back to relive a bit of my childhood by watching this film that had once been so rousing to me.

It was a pretty embarrassing 105 minutes.

I expected the film's anti-Japanese sentiment to challenge even the loosest bounds of contemporary political correctness. And it does. It is a racist film. But I didn't count on it having the sappiest story line this side of the Lifetime cable channel. Everything about the first two-thirds of the plot is at once forced and cliched. The last third is even worse. Did Hollywood legend Walter Wanger *really* produce this?

It's a pity, because the cast is not bad. Richard Quine, who later went on to become a director of some note, comes off as a kind of poor man's Jimmy Stewart in the lead role of Brad. Robert Mitchum is good in his small role as Panhandle. William Frawley plays the same character he always played—the gravel-voiced Fred Mertz-type. The best casting is Noah Beery, Jr., as Cyanide. A solid character actor, Beery appeared in about a million Westerns in the 1950s and '60s in sidekick roles. Then in the 1970s, he turned up in his finest role, that of Rocky, James Garner's dad on *The Rockford Files*. Beery, a second-generation Hollywood actor born in New York, is entirely convincing as a cadet, beginning early in the film when he recites the standard Fish response of "Sir, not being informed to the highest degree of accuracy, I hesitate to articulate, for fear that I might deviate from the true course of rectitude. In short, sir, I am a very dumb fish, and do not know, sir!" when asked a question by an upperclassman. I didn't time it, but it sounded like he got the whole response out in fewer than four seconds, as Aggie tradition requires.

The best thing about the film is the stuff in the background. Forget about the story. Look at the buildings. Look at the statue of Sully in front of the Academic Building. Look at the original configuration of the Kyle Field stadium. You get to see horse-drawn caissons and other vintage military equipment. You get to see a Yell Practice staged on the steps of the YMCA building. You get to see a re-creation of Bonfire. You get to see the kind of hazing that was standard for Fish. In short, if you watch *We've Never Been Licked*, you'll have a feel for what the Old Army days were like at A&M. But that's about the only reason to watch it.

After viewing the saccharine conclusion to *We've Never Been Licked*, I put the videocassette back in its box, then stored it on a shelf in a closet. I don't plan on getting it out any time soon.

Afterword

After more than three decades of coaching on the Aggie staff (except for a single year), R.C. Slocum faced 2002 as do-or-die season. With the ax poised above his neck, his team committed the unthinkable: The Ags lost four games at Kyle Field, one of them to a woeful Nebraska team. They suffered a painful, at-home single-point loss to the dreaded Texas Tech Red Raiders. I was in College Station that day—the post-game mood of the folks in maroon was miserable. Aggies who had bemoaned the lack of offense by recent Slocum-coached teams saw A&M make improvements in offensive numbers. Shockingly, the vaunted Aggie defense seemed to disappear in key games. This was unthinkable, given the school's defense-minded football tradition. The situation was so dire that even an amazing upset of then-top-ranked Oklahoma could not quell the discontent of the Aggie faithful.

Slocum's only hope to hold onto the coaching job at A&M that he had loved so much over the years was to upset Texas on the Friday after Thanksgiving. But it didn't happen. In fact, the game was a burnt-orange blowout, with Texas winning 50–20. The Horns ended their season at 10–2, 6–2 in Big 12 Conference play. The Ags were 6–6, with a dismal 3–5 conference record. Slocum was dust in the wind.

★   ★   ★

It didn't take A&M long to announce that R.C. Slocum was being "reassigned" after the Longhorn triumph. Slocum handled it all with grace—at least "from the outside looking in." There was a wild rumor or two floating around in the days after Slocum was fired. One had the legendary Jimmy Johnson visiting College Station to be courted for the vacant coach's job. However, it seemed pretty clear even before that final game with Texas that A&M had its sights set on one man: Alabama's Dennis Franchione. On December 6, Franchione's appointment became official—and left a lot of people in Tuscaloosa plenty pissed off. That a coach would leave 'Bama to take the A&M job—or any other college coaching job, for that matter—spoke volumes about how far things had fallen since the days when Bear Bryant lorded over his crimson minions from his tower on the Alabama training field. Beyond that, 'Bama fans and players felt Franchione had betrayed pledges he'd made to them about staying. To make matters worse, an assistant relayed the news of Franchione's acceptance of the A&M job to the Alabama players, instead of the coach himself.

In Coach Fran, A&M nabbed one of the most successful college-football coaches in America. With a record of 155–73–2, he was among the ten winningest active coaches when he arrived in College Station. He'd worked a near-miracle at Alabama, taking a team that had won only three games the year before he started to a 10–3 record his last season there—all this in the face of some of the most severe NCAA sanctions to come around since SMU received the "death penalty." Before taking over as coach of the Crimson Tide, Coach Fran had established sound Texas connections during the three years he led the football program at TCU; his Horned Frogs beat Southern Cal in the 1998 Sun Bowl to boast the first bowl win for TCU since 1957. He also had successful seasons at Southwest Texas and New Mexico. The only real knock I heard about Coach Fran was that he was an energetic self-promoter—but in his line of work, that's probably not such a bad thing. From my perspective, he seemed like a good recruiter, a terrific motivator and game-day coach, and a leader who knew how to deal with under-performing teams. In other words, just what the Ags needed.

But as I write on this blustery day in January 2003, it looks like college football in the Southwest is poised to enjoy somewhat of a golden era, if Coach Fran can follow through for the Ags. With first-rate programs in Austin, College Station, and Norman, plus up-and-coming programs in Lubbock and Stillwater, fans who follow the Big 12 South should be treated to absolutely terrific football.

★   ★   ★

The enthusiasm in Aggieland about the arrival of Coach Fran was almost rivaled by the enthusiasm of the return of the Bonfire. Sort of.

Afterword

On privately-owned property beyond College Station, an unofficial Bonfire took place prior to the 2002 Texas game. It was a small version of the Bonfire to be sure, with a dramatically lower stack. But its construction followed the old traditions and the work of cutting and stacking was carried out by students, just as in the days of yore. As much as anything, this version of the Bonfire kept hopes burning that the Bonfire might return, under new Aggie President Robert Gates, as an officially sanctioned A&M event.

★   ★   ★

Chris Simms did not go gently into that good night of being a former Longhorn. The A&M game should have been the stellar end to a good season for Simms, a game that would right all the wrongs of his four years in Austin. He had a terrific outing. He passed for three touchdowns against the Aggies, going 16-24 for 278 yards and no interceptions. In fact, he'd been putting up great numbers all season. He threw for more than 3,000 yards in 2002, averaging almost 250 yards a game. He had 26 touchdown passes and gave up only 12 interceptions. Fans who had booed him after dramatic big-games losses during his time at UT rewarded him with a standing ovation as he left the field for the last time in Austin. He finished his career as the second-winningest quarterback in UT history, trailing only the legendary Bobby Layne.

That could have been a sweet ending to an otherwise turbulent tenure. But things didn't quite turn out that way. As Simms was preparing to showcase his skills for the pro scouts at the Senior Bowl in Mobile, he gave an interview to ESPN.com-contributor Adrian Wojnarowski, who also is columnist for a newspaper in Simms's home state of New Jersey, which stirred up all the old animosity many Longhorn supporters felt toward their departing quarterback. The ESPN.com piece opened with an unnamed NFL scout viewing Simms as a terrific quarterback, victimized by less-than-inspired coaching by Mack Brown's staff: "Same simplistic schemes, same vertical routes, same fallout for Chris Simms, cursed with the fallout as a big-game failure."

Wojnarowski wrote about Simms's rough 2001 season, in which he nearly left the University of Texas, quoting Simms as saying, "Last year, I was in a bad mood all the time. I was angry at a lot of people. I was angry at this place [UT], the coaches, the people. . . . I was bitter about everything in the world. It almost did get the best of me. I just wanted to leave here and say, 'To hell with this place.'"

Wojnarowski wrote: "Texas fans vandalized his car, flooded his voicemail with vicious and vile messages, scrubbed 'Simms sucks' on cars in Austin and ultimately left him hesitant to ever leave his off-campus apartment," after Texas lost to Colorado in the Big 12 championship match.

Not surprisingly, the ESPN.com piece inspired a great deal of turmoil in the land of the Orange Coats. The UT football program responded by posting a story on its website claiming that Simms was a misunderstood athlete and countered Wojnarowski's quotes with quotes from Simms of its own: "I love everything about The University of Texas, Austin, my coaches, teammates, and all of the fans. Everyone was great to me, and if I had it to do all over, I would definitely pick Texas again."

One guesses the truth lay somewhere in the middle. I suppose it should have been no shock to anyone that Simms would go out with a bang instead of a whimper.

★　　★　　★

Bless the Horns and the Aggies. You gotta love 'em.

W.K.S.
Austin, Texas

Appendix

Date	Site	Texas	A&M
1894	Austin	38	0
1898	Austin	48	0
1899	San Antonio	6	0
1900	San Antonio	5	0
1900	Austin	11	0
1901	San Antonio	17	0
1901	Austin	32	0
1902	San Antonio	0	0
1902	Austin	0	12
1903	Austin	29	6
1904	Austin	34	6
1905	Austin	27	0
1906	Austin	24	0
1907	Dallas	0	0
1907	Austin	11	6
1908	Houston	24	8
1908	Austin	28	12
1909	Houston	0	23
1909	Austin	0	5
1910	Houston	8	14

Appendix

Date	Site	Texas	A&M
1911	Houston	6	0
1915	College Station	0	13
Nov. 30, 1916	Austin	21	7
Nov. 20, 1917	College Station	0	7
Nov. 28, 1918	Austin	7	0
Nov. 27, 1919	College Station	0	7
Nov. 25, 1920	Austin	7	3
Nov. 24, 1921	College Station	0	0
Nov. 30, 1922	Austin	7	14
Nov. 29, 1923	College Station	6	0
Nov. 27, 1924	Austin	7	0
Nov. 26, 1925	College Station	0	28
Nov. 25, 1926	Austin	14	5
Nov. 24, 1927	College Station	7	28
Nov. 29, 1928	Austin	19	0
Nov. 28, 1929	College Station	0	13
Nov. 27, 1930	Austin	26	0
Nov. 26, 1931	College Station	6	7
Nov. 24, 1932	Austin	21	0
Nov. 30, 1933	College Station	10	10
Nov. 29, 1934	Austin	13	0
Nov. 28, 1935	College Station	6	20
Nov. 26, 1936	College Station	7	0
Nov. 25, 1937	College Station	0	7
Nov. 24, 1938	Austin	7	6
Nov. 30, 1939	College Station	0	20
Nov. 28, 1940	Austin	7	0
Nov. 27, 1941	College Station	23	0
Nov. 26, 1942	Austin	12	6
Nov. 25, 1943	College Station	27	13

Appendix

Date	Site	Texas	A&M
Nov. 30, 1944	Austin	6	0
Nov. 29, 1945	College Station	20	10
Nov. 28, 1946	Austin	24	7
Nov. 27, 1947	College Station	32	13
Nov. 25, 1948	Austin	14	14
Nov. 24, 1949	College Station	42	14
Nov. 30, 1950	Austin	17	0
Nov. 29, 1951	College Station	21	22
Nov. 27, 1952	Austin	32	12
Nov. 26, 1953	College Station	21	12
Nov. 25, 1954	Austin	22	13
Nov. 24, 1955	College Station	21	6
Nov. 29, 1956	Austin	21	34
Nov. 28, 1957	College Station	9	7
Nov. 27, 1958	Austin	27	0
Nov. 26, 1959	College Station	20	17
Nov. 24, 1960	Austin	21	14
Nov. 23, 1961	College Station	25	0
Nov. 22, 1962	Austin	13	3
Nov. 28, 1963	College Station	15	13
Nov. 26, 1964	Austin	26	7
Nov. 25, 1965	College Station	21	17
Nov. 24, 1966	Austin	22	14
Nov. 27, 1967	College Station	7	10
Nov. 28, 1968	Austin	35	14
Nov. 27, 1969	College Station	49	12
Nov. 26, 1970	Austin	52	14
Nov. 25, 1971	College Station	34	14
Nov. 23, 1972	Austin	38	3
Nov. 22, 1973	College Station	42	13

Appendix

Date	Site	Texas	A&M
Nov. 29, 1974	Austin	32	3
Nov. 28, 1975	College Station	10	20
Nov. 25, 1976	Austin	3	27
Nov. 26, 1977	College Station	57	28
Dec. 2, 1978	Austin	22	7
Dec. 1, 1979	College Station	7	13
Nov. 29, 1980	Austin	14	24
Nov. 26, 1981	College Station	21	13
Nov. 25, 1982	Austin	53	16
Nov. 26, 1983	College Station	45	13
Dec. 1, 1984	Austin	12	37
Nov. 28, 1985	College Station	10	42
Nov. 27, 1986	Austin	3	16
Nov. 26, 1987	College Station	13	20
Nov. 24, 1988	Austin	24	28
Dec. 2, 1989	College Station	10	21
Dec. 1, 1990	Austin	28	27
Nov. 28, 1991	College Station	14	31
Nov. 26, 1992	Austin	13	34
Nov. 25, 1993	College Station	9	18
Nov. 5, 1994	Austin	10	34
Dec. 2, 1995	College Station	16	6
Nov. 29, 1996	Austin	51	15
Nov. 28, 1997	College Station	16	27
Nov. 27, 1998	Austin	26	24
Nov. 26, 1999	College Station	16	20
Nov. 24, 2000	Austin	43	17
Nov. 23, 2001	College Station	21	7

Texas leads series, 69-34-5

Acknowledgments

A NUMBER OF PEOPLE deserve recognition for helping to make *Backyard Brawl* a reality. First on the list is Jan Reid, without whose support this project would never have taken root. Jan led me to my capable agent, David McCormick. David, in turn, led me to Pete Fornatale, my editor at Crown. Pete patiently guided me through some tough deadlines while sculpting this book to make it a much better work than it otherwise would have been. In the process, he's become a friend as well. Thanks to Dorianne Steele and everyone else at Crown for their help. I interviewed numerous people while doing my research, and I want to thank them for taking time to talk to me, in particular Ray Bowen, former president of Texas A&M, and Larry Faulkner, president of the University of Texas. R. C. Slocum and Mack Brown gave me chunks of time out of their extraordinarily busy schedules, and I'm grateful for that. Thanks go out to the athletic departments of both A&M and UT, with a special thank-you to Bill Little at Texas. At A&M, Cynthia Lawson, Lane Stephenson, and Leanne South opened doors for me. Geoffrey Leavenworth, a good writer in his own right, did the same at UT. Dan Jenkins, the greatest sportswriter of our time and one of the funniest writers ever, was helpful and encouraging early on in the project. Thanks to Dan and to Jim Dent for their kind words about the book. And a special thanks to Peter Gent, a good and generous guy. John Kelso helped get *Backyard Brawl* off the ground. He introduced me to Scott Wilson, to whom I'm deeply indebted. Without Scott's help on a lot of fronts, this book would not have been possible. Thanks also to Jennifer Corvino, and to Richard Lord for sending me her way. For general support, advice on the manuscript, and sanity checks, I want to thank J. M. Roe, Callie Jones, Don Clinchy, Ruth Coleman, Billy Moran, Mark Belanger, Laura Austin, Margaret Dornbusch, and many friends and colleagues at National Instruments, as well as some writers with whom I eat lunch with some frequency: Jan Reid, Jesse Sublett, David Marion Wilkinson, and Christopher Cook.

As for secondary sources, UT and A&M have two of the best university newspapers in the nation, and I found both *The Daily Texan* and *The Battalion* to be essential for my research. I relied on the excellent coverage of the two teams by *The Dallas Morning News*, especially the stories by Al Carter and Rana L. Cash, to give me a sense of the flow of the season. I also made use of coverage from the *Austin American-Statesman*, the *Houston Chronicle*, and the *San Antonio Express-News*. For the past thirty years, *Texas Monthly* has chronicled the Lone Star State in remarkable ways, and I read and re-read numerous articles from its pages to help get a feel for how this book should develop. I also read many books with material related to the rivalry and am particularly beholden to the following authors and their works: Billie Lee Brammer, *The Gay Place*; Gary Cartwright, *Confessions of a Washed Up Sports Writer*, *HeartWiseGuy*; Dan Jenkins, *Saturday's America*, *I'll Tell You One Thing*; Lou Maysel, *Here Come the Longhorns*; Paul Bryant and John Underwood, *Bear*; Mickey Herskowitz, *The Legend of Bear Bryant*; John Maher and Kirk Bohls, *Bleeding Orange*; Richard Lieberman, *Personal Foul*; Jim Dent,

Acknowledgments

The Junction Boys; Larry L. King, *Of Outlaws, Con Men, Whores, Politicians, and Other Artists, The Whorehouse Papers*; Gary Shaw, *Meat on the Hoof*; Jimmy Banks, *The Darrell Royal Story*; Duane Thomas and Paul Zimmerman, *Duane Thomas and the Fall of America's Team*; and William Broyles (editor), *The Best of Texas Monthly 1973–78.*

Finally, thanks to my family for allowing me to miss holidays and enduring my long bouts of early-morning and late-night typing, often on a seven-day-a-week schedule. And thanks to Sally for being there.

W.K.S.

MAY 2002

Index

Index

Index

Index

Index